COACHING GIRLS' BASKETBALL SUCCESSFULLY

Jill Prudden

Head Coach
Oak Ridge High School

Human Kinetics

Library of Congress Cataloging-in-Publication Data

Prudden, Jill, 1955-
    Coaching girls' basketball successfully / Jill Prudden.
        p. cm.
    Includes index.
    ISBN 0-7360-5611-4 (soft cover)
    1. Basketball for girls--Coaching. I. Title.
    GV885.3.P75 2005
    796.323'082--dc22   2005010785

ISBN-10: 0-7360-5611-4
ISBN-13: 978-0-7360-5611-3

The Web addresses cited in this text were current as of April 2005 unless otherwise noted.

Acquisitions Editor: Jana Hunter
Developmental Editor: Kase Johnstun
Assistant Editor: Cory Weber
Copyeditor: John Wentworth
Proofreader: Erin Cler
Indexer: Betty Frizzéll
Graphic Designer: Nancy Rasmus
Graphic Artist: Kim McFarland
Photo Manager: Dan Wendt
Cover Designer: Keith Blomberg
Photographer (cover): Tank Johnson/The Oak Ridger
Photographer (interior): Photos on pages 5, 9, 14, 20, 24, 36, 192, 208 courtesy of Tank Johnson/The Oak Ridger; all other photos by Dan Wendt
Art Manager and Illustrator: Kareema McLendon
Printer: United Graphics

We thank Rantoul High School and the Rantoul girls' basketball team in Rantoul, Illinois, for assistance in providing the location and models for the photo shoot for this book.

Human Kinetics books are available at special discounts for bulk purchase. Special editions or book excerpts can also be created to specification. For details, contact the Special Sales Manager at Human Kinetics.

Printed in the United States of America   10 9 8 7 6 5 4 3 2

Human Kinetics
Web site: www.HumanKinetics.com

United States: Human Kinetics
P.O. Box 5076
Champaign, IL 61825-5076
800-747-4457
e-mail: humank@hkusa.com

Canada: Human Kinetics
475 Devonshire Road Unit 100
Windsor, ON N8Y 2L5
800-465-7301 (in Canada only)
e-mail: orders@hkcanada.com

Europe: Human Kinetics
107 Bradford Road
Stanningley
Leeds LS28 6AT, United Kingdom
+44 (0) 113 255 5665

e-mail: hk@hkeurope.com

Australia: Human Kinetics
57A Price Avenue
Lower Mitcham, South Australia 5062
08 8277 1555
e-mail: liaw@hkaustralia.com

New Zealand: Human Kinetics
Division of Sports Distributors NZ Ltd.
P.O. Box 300 226 Albany
North Shore City
Auckland
0064 9 448 1207
e-mail: info@humankinetics.co.nz

I lovingly dedicate this book to the two people I admire most—my parents, Harley and Mary Prudden.

It would be impossible to list all of the things you have done for me. The greatest gift you have given me is the example I see in your daily walk with Jesus Christ, our Lord and Savior. I especially want to thank you for your unconditional love and for the blessings of a wonderful family. Thank you also for providing the opportunities that helped establish a successful path in my life; your continual support has inspired me to pursue my goals. You gave me the wonderful gift of laughter and the ability to share a sense of humor with others. Finally, you have taught me how to live a joyful life by your example of serving others with the fruits of the Spirit: love, patience, kindness, and goodness.

CONTENTS

Part IV   Coaching Defense

Part V   Coaching Games

Part VI   Coaching Evaluation

FOREWORD

Girls' and women's basketball has never enjoyed a larger stage or as many exceptionally skilled players in the history of the game. The excitement surrounding our professional players and teams continues to grow as more and more stars emerge and as players develop a rapport with their teammates and coaches. Women's college basketball sets attendance records year after year in both the regular season and at the Final Four because the level of play has risen dramatically in the past two decades.

At the root of our sport's success are the hundreds of thousands of girls playing basketball in junior high, in high school, and on AAU teams. But just as important as the number of players participating in basketball is the commitment level those players are giving back to the game. Younger players are developing the work habits and fundamentals needed to strengthen the game at the college level, which in turn improves the game at the professional and international levels.

To keep the sport progressing, we need to make sure the quality and commitment of the coaches keeps pace with the quality and commitment of the players. An important part of maintaining the integrity of the game is maintaining integrity in the coaching ranks.

Coaching Girls' Basketball Successfully provides the concepts, guidance, and day-to-day information that will take coaches of girls' basketball to a higher level. Coach Jill Prudden's approach to the game, to her players, and to her program is first-rate not only for basketball instruction but also for working with people. Her top priorities are to provide her players with great experiences in the game and to teach them life lessons that extend beyond basketball. Her book's guidance will show that this approach leads to success on and off the court.

Many coaches can teach the skills of basketball or draw up the Xs and Os that will help teams win games. But few can also teach the off-court and intangible aspects of coaching that help build a successful program year in and year out, as Prudden has done in this book. Her clear guidance on difficult, yet crucial, aspects of the job—such as developing a coaching philosophy, communicating with and motivating players, and organizing administrative tasks—combine with her excellent instruction on playing the game to create a book that any coach of female basketball players can learn from.

Coaching Girls' Basketball Successfully will help our sport continue its rise by helping our coaches continue to grow.

Coach Van Chancellor
Head Coach, WNBA's Houston Comets
Head Coach, 2004 USA Women's Olympic Gold-Medal Team

ACKNOWLEDGMENTS

To my Lord and Savior who has blessed me with such a rich coaching experience and whose ultimate victory far exceeds any earthly victory.

To my family: Dad and Mom, Pam, Miguel, Jacki, Jared, Tom, Kelsey, MacKenzie, Boo, John, Joey, Jesse, and Jackson whose unconditional love and support provides me with a healthy perspective and balance in my life. The love, laughter, caring and sharing that we experience within our family is the model I use in my relationships with others.

To Mr. Helton who gave me the opportunity to begin my coaching career at Oak Ridge High School. Your door was always open and you so willingly shared your time, wisdom, and unwavering support with me as I grew under your leadership. You were my boss and now have become a dearly loved friend.

To my loyal friends who have hung in there with me through the drama that can be created in the world of coaching. Thanks for helping me keep my life in balance and reminding me that people are far more important than wins and losses.

To my friends in coaching: I have so enjoyed the journey of learning from and with each of you. My faith has been enriched by the Christian coaches who have I have seen create such a positive environment for the kids whose lives we touch.

To the players I have coached: Thank you for the hard work, dedication, and sacrifices you made in building the Oak Ridge Lady Wildcat basketball tradition.

To the parents who have entrusted me with the opportunity to coach their daughters: Thank you for allowing me to be their coach and supporting the coaching staff's efforts to help these young ladies be the best they can be on and off the court. A special thanks to those of you who reached out and helped numerous players in our program and who continue to do so to this day.

To the Oak Ridge community: Thank you for the tremendous support of the Lady Wildcat program you have shown throughout the years. You have given of yourselves monetarily, you have filled the stands, and most importantly you have always had a genuine interest in the overall success of the young ladies who comprise our program.

To the Oak Ridge administration and teachers: Your support of the Lady Wildcat basketball program is greatly appreciated. These young ladies are students first and athletes second. Thank you for encouraging and guiding them to be successful students.

Thanks to David Clary of WATO Radio for the numerous hats you have worn in support of Oak Ridge Basketball. I appreciate the many years of dedication you have given to the program, as evidenced by your loyalty, your time commitment, and your quality of work.

Thanks to the *Oak Ridger*, our local newspaper, for the coverage it has provided the Lady Wildcat basketball program. A special thanks goes to Tank Johnson who helped with the photos for the book.

To Carol Callum and USA Basketball: Thank you for the many coaching opportunities you allowed me to have with USA Basketball. I worked with outstanding coaches and players from across the nation and was afforded the opportunity to represent our country in international competition. The memorable experiences and my association with USA Basketball is a coach's once-in-a-lifetime dream.

To Jana Hunter, Kase Johnstun, and Human Kinetics: Your support, direction, guidance, and patience with me throughout the book-writing process were answers to a prayer. You helped make an almost overwhelming process doable. I could never have written this book without your positive feedback, helpful suggestions, and never-ending encouragement. Thank you.

PREFACE

I come by my competitive nature honestly. My childhood family experiences shaped both my love for the game of basketball and a craving for competition. I grew up in a family that loved sports, and I can vividly recall many wonderful memories. In the winter months, as soon as dinner was over, my dad and I would head down to the basement to begin our ping-pong marathons. He hated to lose as much as I did, but we were fairly evenly matched, so we both got our share of humble pie. My mom was and is *the* sport's junkie. During basketball season we kept two TV sets side by side in our living room so she and I could watch two games at the same time. Coaching from the living room couch, my mom has never lost a game. Her love for the game was infectious. I loved both watching and playing. I played one on one with my older brother night after night until it was dark, hoping and believing one night I might actually beat him. Did I ever beat him? Maybe not. But at that time I wasn't drawing up the game plan.

If my family helped get me started in basketball, it has been the relationships I have developed with people over the years that has kept me in the game. I feel fortunate and blessed by the many people whose lives have crossed my own and have positively influenced my basketball journey. I have coached many special young ladies, some who continued their careers in college and beyond and some who themselves are involved in coaching today. I have made some lasting friendships through the coaching profession. My closest friendship today is a result of a basketball opportunity afforded me. So many wonderful people have contributed to my life and guided my basketball journey.

As a former high school and college player, I have enjoyed being on the *other* side, and I still remain quite competitive. But now I express that by trying to positively affect the lives of the young people I coach. I want to help them be winners on the court and in their lives. In writing this book I have had the opportunity to give back to the game that has given so much to me. As a young coach in the profession, I read every coaching book I could get my hands on. I attended every clinic in my area. Even after all these years, I still believe we should be lifelong learners.

Perhaps this book can help novice coaches who need some directions and guidelines as they begin their coaching journeys. For a veteran coach, this book can stimulate new ideas or approaches to a philosophy that's perhaps already well intact. When I read a book or attend a clinic, sometimes I walk away with just a couple of new ideas, yet these often serve as catalysts to get my juices flowing. I hope parts of this book might serve you in the same way. My coaching philosophy has changed considerably over my 25 years of coaching. Much of what's in my coaching package is a compilation of great ideas from coaches I admire and respect.

When I started out as a young coach, my goal was to build a successful basketball team. Now I realize how important it is to build, and also maintain, a successful basketball program. Those "players" in the program include assistants, faculty, the student body, community members, and feeder program coaches. A program is a lot more than just the players on the roster. I hope this book illustrates the important roles of all key players in your program. Successful teams come and go, but successful programs build rich traditions.

Finally, many of the coaches I admire are great teachers of the game of basketball. They teach with attention to the littlest details. This was often reflected in how their teams executed on the floor. I hope that this book provides the insights and details that add to your appreciation of the game and benefits you in the coaching role.

KEY TO DIAGRAMS

→   Path of player

- - - →   Path of ball

〜〜〜→   Dribble

⊢   Screen

◯   Offensive player

◯   Player with ball at start of play

①   Point guard

②   Guard

③   Guard

④   Post

⑤   Post

X   Defensive player

X_1 Player assigned to 1

X_2 Player assigned to 2

X_3 Player assigned to 3

X_4 Player assigned to 4

X_5 Player assigned to 5

ⓒ   Coach

△   Cone

PART I
COACHING FOUNDATION

CHAPTER 1
DEVELOPING A COACHING PHILOSOPHY

I have been fortunate to coach at Oak Ridge High School in Oak Ridge, Tennessee, my entire career—25 years of coaching and teaching. My first year began with one of the most significant changes in the women's game: the changeover from six-on-six basketball to the current five-on-five game. I was fresh out of college, had never played nor even seen a six-on-six game, and was extremely naïve about how difficult the change would be for high school players.

My philosophy those first years and my philosophy today are significantly different. I charged forward as a rookie coach, basing my philosophy on my experiences as a player, student of the game, and fan. My inexperience as a coach in regard to determining tactics and developing a coaching style and my lack of knowledge on how to capitalize on my personality made for a lack of depth in my original coaching philosophy. I gave little thought to the impact the change in rules would have on my team, spent little time understanding the differences and similarities in the two versions of the game, and forgot that my actions and leadership were key factors in how much my players and staff enjoyed their experience.

It's not that my initial philosophy was wrong—it was my best effort and what I knew at the time. But my experiences both on and off the court throughout my coaching career led me to constantly rethink the way I managed my team. Two of the most important aspects of a coaching philosophy are developing one that works for you and continually working to strengthen and adapt that philosophy so you can apply it to every decision and situation you face.

WHAT IS A COACHING PHILOSOPHY?

A philosophy provides direction for the entire program, players and coaches alike. The legendary coach John Wooden has a wonderful definition of coaching philosophy. He compared one's philosophy to "a pair of glasses that filter reality through one's personal experiences, opinions, values, and beliefs." Consequently, our philosophy has a direct influence on how we see and understand the world we live in, what actions we take, and why we choose to behave in the ways we do.

You must consider the *hows* and *whys* for everything you do as a coach. You must analyze your basis or reasons for your approach. As you formulate your philosophy, you might ask yourself the following questions:

- Is my approach educationally sound? (For example, Do my drills serve a purpose?)

- Is my approach appropriate for my players? (For example, Does our offensive scheme match my team's talent level?)
- Is my philosophy ethical? (Remember that you are a role model for your athletes.)
- Can you explain why you use or do something? (To instruct and motivate your athletes, you have to be able to justify what you do.)
- Is your coaching philosophy compatible with your personality?

After analyzing all the factors involved in coaching and developing your own philosophy, you should put your philosophy down in writing. Being able to express your philosophy in words will allow you to share it with administrators, parents, athletes, and other coaches. Keep in mind that coaches are first and foremost role models and teachers. As a coach, ask yourself this question each day: "Is what I'm planning to do today in the best interest of my athletes?"

Foundation of a Philosophy

A coaching philosophy involves many factors, combines countless variables, and calls on a wide range of knowledge and emotion. All of these blend together to form the basis for what you choose to do as a coach. To begin developing your coaching philosophy, ask yourself four questions:

1. What do I value?
2. What are my priorities?
3. What do I want this team to accomplish?
4. What are my priorities regarding the development of athletes as players and people?

Taking the time to arrive at answers to these questions will help you set a solid foundation for your coaching philosophy. The more time you take to examine your ideals and the more specific you are with your answers, the more useful your philosophy will be.

So much of who I am today is based on my years of playing and the players and coaches I encountered along the way. I was fortunate to play college basketball at Michigan State University. During my four years I played for three different coaches—and I mean *different* coaches. Their philosophies, coaching styles, and personalities were each quite different from one another. Much of what I encountered I appreciated, but there was also much I disagreed with, and I made mental notes of how I would do things differently if I were in charge.

When I first entered the coaching ranks, 25 years ago, the many coaches I had played for shaped my early philosophy of coaching. I had my lists of dos and don'ts. I realized later that I was naïve and unrealistic to think I could immediately impart my philosophy to my players and they would buy into it hook, line, and sinker. Perhaps they were doing as I was doing as a player: filtering out the good and the bad. Those early playing years set the tone for my coaching philosophy, but it has evolved through all my years of coaching.

Your philosophy is like a perpetual melting pot. It incorporates life experiences (both basketball and nonbasketball related), reasons for coaching, personality, and coaching style. Those deeply ingrained principles, habits, background, and characteristics all play a significant part in the development of your philosophy, whether you know it or not. The more consciously you apply them to practice, the more successful you will be as a coach. You weed out what you hear and see that doesn't fit your coaching style and beliefs, and you adopt those ideas that you believe do adhere to your beliefs and style.

Every day brings new experiences, new challenges, new thoughts, new processes, and new outcomes, each of which influences you and brings adjustments to your philosophy and ways of doing things. The process is ongoing.

Coaching for the Right Reasons

Why go into the coaching field? Surely, it's not for the money or the short work week. It's important to ask yourself this question because your answer helps shape your coaching philosophy. Some people have had a very positive association with athletics in their early years and want the association to continue. Although this is a valid reason for getting into coaching, be aware that not all good players make good teachers

A good coaching philosophy can be applied to lessons on and off the court.

of the game. We can't relive our glory days by living through our athletes.

Positive experiences in playing a sport can inspire you to want to stay with it and give back to the sport that has given you so much. Coaching does provide an avenue to give back to the game, but remember when you move from player to coach your roles change drastically. In my own experience, I did have a desire to give back to the game. I loved all that basketball had to offer: the friendships I made, the competitive nature of the sport, the trips I was fortunate to take. I truly thrived on the discipline of the sport—the workouts, conditioning, and time management—and this became an integral part of my coaching philosophy.

A desire to teach the game of basketball was my greatest motivation for getting and staying involved in coaching. The best coaches I have encountered are great teachers. If I am the teacher, my players are my students and the gym my classroom for teaching. The more you understand, accept, and embrace the role of teacher, the more positive the experience will be for you and your players.

I wanted to teach young ladies not only the fundamental skills and team concepts of basketball but the off-the-court life lessons as well. I have wanted my players to be the best

they can be on the court, in the classroom, and in the community. I have remained coaching at the high school level because I see these years as so crucial to the growth and development of who we are as people. I believe the game of basketball simulates the game of life. If I can teach young women the game of basketball, they might be able to transfer what they learn and apply it in other areas of life.

The role of the coach has changed dramatically over the last decade. Today, many of the players I coach come from one-parent households. Another big change I see is a much more permissive attitude toward youngsters today. Discipline seems to be a word and behavior of the past, yet I see it as a valuable tool for success in today's world. My job as coach and teacher extends beyond the dimensions of the basketball court. For me, coaching is a calling. I want to guide young ladies to healthy and productive choices.

Personality and Coaching Style

I played my high school and college years for several different coaches. Each coach had his or her own coaching style. Some styles I admired, some were very effective, some I resented as a player, and some seemed to distance players. However effective or ineffective their styles were, their styles did match their personalities. I believe the coaching style I have adapted is a combination of what I respected in those coaches, what I believed was effective then and now, and what matches my personality. I tried to take the best parts of each coach I've been associated with and mold them to fit me. You have to be your own person.

There are probably as many different coaching styles as there are coaches. No one style is necessarily better than another. No one style guarantees success. It is easy to look at successful coaches and want to adapt their style, but you can't be someone or something you're not. Part of what makes a style successful is how well it matches the coach's personality and goals.

Your style is often an extension of your personality. You might flex your style or shift from one style to another to get the most out of your athletes. This shift or flex can be dictated by circumstances. Regardless of any adaptations, coaches who hold certain traits or skills as non-negotiable will lead teams whose on-court play and off-court behavior can be recognized as having developed under their guidance.

You will probably be more successful in coaching if your philosophy and personality are compatible and in sync. Is your approach to coaching in line with your personality? Or does your philosophy go against your basic nature? Here are some things to consider:

- Are you a cautious person or a risk taker?
- Are you a control freak or are you laid back?
- Do you consider yourself patient or impatient?
- Are you a planner or are you impulsive?

Remember—you have to be true to yourself. Players will see through phoniness, even if it's not intentional. I live my life in a very orderly and organized way. That is how I run my basketball program, down to the smallest detail. My coaching style is really an extension of my personality. In addition, players tend to take on the personality of their coach. If you watch me during a game, you see that I'm intense, energized, professional, and extremely tuned into the game. Consequently, my players play with intensity and emotion, but they know the rules and abide by them. They are not clones of me, and I don't want them to be. But, to a degree, their personality takes on my personality. If as a coach you rant and rave and complain about the officiating, don't be surprised to see your players slip into this mode. Yes, you have to be who you are, but remember that you're a role model for your impressionable young athletes. Strive to behave in ways that you want to see your players behave.

Your coaching style will influence your decisions on how to teach skills and strategies, organize your practices, prepare for games, and discipline your athletes. The degree to which you let your assistants and players have a role in decision making is also influenced by your coaching style.

As today's athletes are quite different from those of 10 to 20 years ago, so are coaching styles. When I played basketball in the late 1970s, most coaching styles were authoritarian. The coach was in charge, making all the decisions without feedback or questioning from players or assistant coaches. Today's athletes are encouraged to ask "Why?" They want and are encouraged to seek more ownership in their athletic experience.

To determine the style of coaching that fits you, ask yourself, "What kind of coach do I want to be?" Today's successful coaches seem to have a blend of coaching styles, dictated somewhat by the circumstances. This allows them to be in charge when they need to be but also engages their athletes in some of the decision making. Athletes today want to feel they have a voice in their training and competition, and this is fine, but keep in mind a team needs to be well organized to function effectively and efficiently. As coach, you must provide direction and instruction. When appropriate, allow your athletes to make decisions and assume responsibility.

Being able to adjust your coaching style allows you to help your athlete deal with all the areas that now fall under the "athletic umbrella." This includes helping the athlete cope with pressures, maintaining concentration, adapting to changing situations, keeping winning and losing in perspective, teaching discipline both on and off the court, and helping to build and keep positive self-esteem. As the coach, you must be in control of both your athletes and yourself.

My initial coaching style was autocratic. At 22, I was a young coach and thought I needed to be in charge to gain respect. I decided what was to be done and how it was to be done, and the athletes had little involvement in any decisions. Now my assistants are a vital part of input into my program, and my players provide insights and feedback when appropriate, especially on team and individual goal setting. I realize now that the more involved my assistant coaches and players are in the program, their feeling of ownership increases, and the better our basketball team becomes.

STRENGTHENING YOUR PHILOSOPHY

A coaching philosophy is the solid groundwork on which a program is built, but this doesn't mean the ground shouldn't shift now and then. Shifting, in fact, can strengthen a philosophy.

Constant attention and examination of your priorities and values can lead to positive changes in your philosophy. Four aspects that I've found to recharge my philosophy are to keep learning, be myself, have fun, and build relationships. You need to be able to shift within a program as you grow with the game, work with many different players, and encounter unique situations. Always be prepared for the unexpected so that you can adapt to whatever situation comes along.

Keep Learning

As coaches, we need to be lifelong learners. If we expect our players to grow and develop, we need to expect the same of ourselves. Use as many resources as you can. We all start with our own experiences, those that are most familiar and comfortable to us. Whether they were filled with watching games on TV or playing games in the neighborhood, our early years begin the thought process for a basketball philosophy. Of course, taking advantage of the experiences and lessons of other coaches and leaders will broaden your perspective.

The game is ever changing, as are the players. As coaches, we need to grow with the game. I have always found that as I learn new ideas, my excitement for the game increases. The off-season is a great time to reflect on your basketball system and identify areas you want to explore. Often it's in the off-season when you evaluate your players and your team's potential for the next season. You might decide you want to change many of the things the team did the season before. Next year's team might have completely different strengths and weaknesses than last year's team. There are many ways to increase your knowledge.

Attending clinics is an excellent way to learn from some of the top coaches in the game. You might pick up a new play, an offense or defense, a strategy, or other ways to improve your team or program. Coaches often allow time for a question-and-answer session. Clinics provide an excellent opportunity to learn and grow in the game and continue the development of your philosophy. You have the opportunity to hear a lifetime of learning in a short presentation.

A wealth of coaching information is available in pamphlets, coaching magazines, books, and videos. Full-length books often provide the deepest insights into a successful coach's basketball program and can help you mold your philosophy. Coach Pat Summitt, one of the premier coaches in the game today, has written several books covering the Xs and Os of coaching as well as work ethic, discipline, and goal setting. Her books are excellent road maps for coaches wanting to define or redefine their basketball philosophy.

One of my favorite authors is John Maxwell, who has written several excellent books on teamwork and leadership. I used his book *The 17 Indisputable Laws of Teamwork* as a team-bonding exercise one season. My players applied many of his principles to our team setting. Here are some of the best chapters in the book:

- The Law of the Chain—how the strength of a team is affected by its weakest link
- The Law of the Bad Apple—how rotten attitudes can ruin a team
- The Law of the Price Tag—how teams fail to reach their potential when they fail to pay the price

I would recommend Maxwell's book to any coach looking for insights into team building. Reading it together as a team was a wonderful team-sharing and learning experience. It was also a way for me to share my philosophy with my players.

Along with books, you can use Internet search engines to find virtually any basketball-related information. Keeping abreast of articles and ideas posted by coaches and players from around the country is a great way to continue growing in the game and to fine-tune your coaching philosophy.

The off-season (if there is one) is a good time to set up one-on-one meetings with successful coaches at the high school, college, or even professional level. Visit the coach at his or her school. Have an agenda. Take the opportunity to pick their minds and learn what makes their program or coaching style successful.

Several years ago the boys' staff at our high school started a program called The Coaches Club. Coaches from across the country at various levels were members of this club. The idea of the club was for each coach to share a piece of coaching expertise with other members of the club. The information, including Xs and Os, drills, motivational ideas, and other material, was then distributed through the mail. You mailed your information one time to all coaches, and in return you received mail from each of the other club members. Such a club is a terrific way to form a network of coaches across the nation.

Often, what we get out of something is based on what we put into it. Have an open mind as you seek new information. Be eager to learn and be driven to be the best coach you can be. Our job is to have our players and team come as close as they can to reaching their potential as people and players. We have to work at this. Continue to be a student of the game. The rewards will be great for you and your team.

Reversing Roles

Last year I had the opportunity to meet with Lady Vol assistant coach, Nikki Caldwell, who is a former player of mine. She is a quality person and a terrific high school and collegiate player. I nicknamed her "Pony" in high school because she was literally the horse we rode during her senior season. Nikki came out to my school and first met with our Titans' Club. She challenged young middle school students to be the best they can be, which meant making smart, positive, and safe choices. She asked them to make the most of every day. Academically, Nikki challenged the group to be the best students they could be. Perhaps not everyone can be an A student, but settling for less than their academic best should not be acceptable. It was obvious that Nikki's talk came from her heart, and her audience was quite receptive to her message. Nikki is a terrific example of a former student who made the most of every day, which paid off with success in and out of the classroom. After giving her time to these youngsters, she met with our boys' coach and me for an hour. She was so willing to share ideas, bat around strategies, and answer any questions we had. It was a terrific session of give and take. I learned a lot and was also reminded of the importance of giving back to the game. Nikki is a giver. That day she was my teacher and I was her student.

Be Yourself and Have Fun

Similar to your coaching style, your coaching philosophy has to be *yours*—the personal fit is what makes it work. By accessing all avenues available to you, you can gain a wealth of knowledge about basketball and successful coaches in basketball, but your success comes from being you. Nobody likes or respects a phony. If you value honesty and sincerity in others, then you as the coach need to lead the way. Integrity comes from actions matching words. Players learn to trust what they see as real.

My philosophy might be a compilation of ideas from great coaches I have known, but I am my own person. Pat Summit, women's basketball coach at the University of Tennessee, is a coach I greatly admire. I have read her books, been to her practices and games, and have chatted with her in person. Basing my opinion on Pat's six national championships, I'd say her coaching philosophy and style have been extremely successful for her. I particularly admire the discipline she instills in her players and program. This is something I have learned from her and have incorporated into our program at Oak Ridge. Yet I have added my own approach to working with my players. I do believe there are right ways and wrong ways to do things, with no gray area in the middle. Part of doing things the right way is to be yourself.

A big reason I continue to coach and have stayed at the high school level is that it's fun for me. Coaching, teaching, and learning are enjoyable to me. I am blessed to have Kim Tisdale as my assistant coach. Kim was a former player of mine, played with Nikki Caldwell, and has now been coaching with me for several years. Kim is a very positive and upbeat person. I love to laugh, and Kim and I laugh daily. She's a big part of what makes coaching fun for me. Yes, coaching is my job, but how many people can go to work every day and say they love what they do? How many can say they work with someone they love being around?

Although coaching is fun for me, I know I need to make it fun for my players as well. I call "fun" the "f-word." When I meet with a player who appears to be struggling, 9 times out of 10 they tell me the game is no longer fun. When it's not fun, the game becomes a job to players (and the same is true for coaches). They clock in, do their work, and clock out. Their heart is not in it, and their performance reflects this. I believe one of the coach's greatest challenges is to make and keep the game fun for the players. I have come to realize that every player has a different definition of fun. Some like competitive play, some like less intensity, and some have fun as long as shooting is involved. One of the things I address with my team early on is the idea of basketball being fun. We all agree that we work too hard and put in too many hours, so what we're doing needs to be enjoyable. However, I also put part of the "fun responsibility" on them. I believe that fun comes as a by-product of working hard with people you enjoy. Often it's the product itself that becomes the fun.

Isn't it fun to make a team turn the ball over several times because of outstanding team defense? Isn't it fun to work out daily with some of your best friends? Yes, fun can be a drill they love, or a shortened practice, or a skit, but fun that lasts is often the result of hard work. If you love the game, you'll work at becoming the best you can be. That process needs to be fun and enjoyable for everyone, coaches and players alike.

Make It Fun

When I was in college, one of my three coaches loved to put in a new drill every day. She thought it would be fun for us to learn something new and be challenged daily. Some of my teammates couldn't wait for that segment of practice. The new drill brought excitement and increased our energy level. This same coach also tried many things to bring us together as a team. Two or three times a season we would perform skits for our teammates. She liked the idea of doing something off the court in which we could incorporate our own personalities. Most of the skits were hysterical. We would practice our parts for hours so as not to be outdone by another group's skit. To my coach's credit, she always came up with unique ideas to bring us closer as a team while having fun in the process.

Build Relationships

Some of my fondest memories in coaching are centered on players and coaches. When I recall a season, it's most often not the games

Quality assistant coaches are key to a quality program.

I remember but the people who touched my life and other lives that season. Yes, the world often judges our success based on our win–loss record, but a greater indication of success is the positive influence you have on the people in your program, especially your players. Be the kind of coach you would want to play for. Be the kind of coach you would want your daughter to play for.

Within your coaching philosophy, never lose sight of the fact that you have a tremendous influence on the lives of the players you coach. They might look to you as the ultimate authority figure or as the one with all the answers. Your shoulder might be the one they need to lean on. Always remember that basketball is just one part of their world. They often are trying to juggle sports, family, friends, and academics during one of the most challenging times of their lives. Try to be the constant in their ever-changing world. Be aware that it's often not what you say but what you *don't* say. Players tune into your voice as well as your body language. Remember that you are a teacher both on and off the court. It's your responsibility to be a positive influence in their lives. Teach your players lessons that can help them both on the court and later in life.

One of my greatest rewards as a coach is to watch former players get into the coaching field themselves. Both my assistant coach and freshman coach were former players of mine. Because they had a positive experience when they were players, they now want to stay connected to the game and help younger players enjoy that same positive experience. As players, they experienced the discipline, leadership, teamwork, work ethic, and love of the game, and now they are helping to instill these same qualities in the current players in our program.

ESTABLISHING OBJECTIVES: BUILDING FOR SUCCESS

After establishing your coaching philosophy, you need to establish objectives for your players, your team, and yourself. Objectives for your players and team can be done with input from your players and assistants. I have devised a plan for our team called the Lady Wildcat Success Plan, which is based on Summitt's Definite Dozen. Within this plan, objectives are outlined for how to be successful as a person and player and ultimately as a team. It's also important to set objectives for yourself and your coaching staff. A successful team reflects the sum of its parts. Successful people within a team reflect characteristics such as honesty, loyalty, and unselfishness. Along with the development of quality people comes player development. As coaches, we need to help all players improve their individual basketball skills. The better each player becomes, the better the team can become. Each player builds on the others. This combination of successful people and successful players gives a team the greatest chance of being successful.

If you want a successful team, you need to start with successful players. Part of the process of building successful players is to have successful people. Each builds on the other to form a strong foundation.

To be successful as a person, a person must

- be responsible,
- be respectful,
- be honest, and
- be loyal.

To be successful as a player, a player must

- commit to work hard,
- commit to become a smart player,
- put the team before herself, and
- possess a winning attitude.

To be successful as a team, a team must

- be coachable (coaches and teammates must communicate effectively),
- have great leaders, eager followers, and willing role players,
- influence its opponent, and
- constantly be motivated.

I have my players divide into three groups, each focusing on the characteristics that make a successful person, player, or team. They then teach those traits of the Lady Wildcat Success Plan to their teammates. Players give both positive and negative examples to explain their part.

Additionally, our players are expected to be successful in the three Cs: the court, classroom, and community. Most players understand what's expected of them on the basketball court. They understand that comes with being a team member. Being successful in the classroom includes academic performance, positive classroom interaction with students and teachers, an appropriate attitude, and respectful behavior.

Sometimes we have to explain the three Cs more than once for their significance to sink in. Involvement in the community is not always an easy sell to players. I teach and coach in a small community. Everyone knows me, and everyone knows my players. Our actions are constantly on display for the community to see. This is part of why I tell them they must represent themselves and their team in the best light possible. I want them to be seen as leaders and positive role models for the young people in the community. We hope that success on the court, in the classroom, and in the community transfers to being a successful citizen.

I will also let our players know what's included in my philosophy that will affect them on the court. We will be a well-conditioned team. We will play with intensity on both ends of the floor. We will demonstrate a winning attitude. These are all nonnegotiable expectations. Our program has a great tradition, one that we and our fans expect to be carried on from team to team, year to year.

Once you have identified person, player, and team objectives, it's time to look at yourself and set your coaching objectives. You want your team to have every opportunity to be successful. For that to happen, you want everyone to be well prepared. This process is ongoing and starts with you, the coach. Your players must continue to learn and practice as you continue to study and advance your knowledge of the game. At Oak Ridge, we know our teams are going to be well drilled in the fundamentals, be able to build team concepts, and learn to distinguish when they need to *run* a play and when they need to *make* a play. I am going to scout opponents, read books, watch video, and talk with coaches to constantly seek ways to give my team an edge. Coaches need to be lifelong learners. Stay hungry. Grow with your players. This will keep you inspired as each new season approaches.

SUMMARY

- Your coaching philosophy involves many factors and variables and will call on a broad range of knowledge and emotions.
- Your coaching philosophy has a direct influence on how you see and understand the world you live in and the actions and decisions you make.
- Be a lifelong learner. Be eager to learn from as many resources as possible, including books, tapes, coaching clinics, and talks with coaches one on one.
- Be yourself. Develop a coaching style that fits your personality.
- Find ways to make the game enjoyable for your players. Allow them some ownership in establishing objectives.
- Remember that you're influencing the lives of the young people you coach. Make sure your influence is positive.
- Teach your players to be the best they can be as individuals, players, and team members.
- As a coach, be well prepared so your team has every opportunity to be successful.
- The impact you have on your players is far greater than your win–loss record.
- Evaluate your reasons for coaching— remember that you're first and foremost a role model and a teacher.
- When your philosophy and your personality are compatible, you'll probably be more successful as a coach.
- Never lose sight of the influence you have on the lives of those you coach and those you coach with.
- Build for success by identifying objectives you want to attain as a coach and aligning them with player and team objectives.

CHAPTER 2 COMMUNICATING YOUR APPROACH

Communication seems to be a lost art. Yet, for any relationship to be successful, good communication is essential. Ironically, we live in an age in which avenues of communication are limitless. But our increased resources are not leading to more efficient and productive communication. As a high school coach, you need to be an effective communicator to many people, including players, assistant coaches, school personnel, parents, and other community members.

Personal communication within a basketball family allows a bond of family care and concern to develop. Direct one-on-one communication helps prevent misunderstanding and gives meaning and importance both to the topic and to the individual you're talking to.

TEAM OF COMMUNICATION

Being an effective communicator entails speaking clearly, yes, but it also involves nonverbal cues, written words, and listening skills. Communication is a two-way street; part of your job as a coach is to teach players communication skills and how to use them appropriately.

Early in my coaching career, I assumed players knew how to communicate. It didn't take me long to realize that assumption was wrong. Now I realize the importance of teaching players not only the "hows" of communication but also the "whys." Players need to know that what they have to say is important to their coach; they need to understand that not only the coach communicates. Sometimes they need to be taught how and when to express their thoughts.

I tell players from the start that I might not always agree with them but that I'll always listen to what they have to say, provided they communicate in an appropriate way and under appropriate circumstances. For your team to run smoothly, you want your players to talk to you and express their thoughts. I recommend keeping an open-door policy in which players are encouraged to express themselves at their convenience. They might request a meeting before practice, after practice, in the evenings, or over lunch. Face-to-face discussions, although difficult for some players at first, are usually the most productive.

Sometimes to become a better communicator you need to adjust your coaching style and personality. This was true in my case. I am an intense competitor and very active in practices and games. In addition, my practices are extremely structured. Drills are timed, and we waste little time between drills. My players kid me that I practice at "Yankee speed," which means at a fast pace.

Creating a non-threatening atmosphere is key to opening up communication between coaches and players.

Intense. Highly structured. Inflexible. Fast paced. These terms don't bring to mind a person who is effective at communication. Knowing this, I really try to put myself into another gear when I talk one on one with my players. I consciously try to relax and create a calm and nonthreatening atmosphere. For many players, one-on-one conversations are intimidating. With this in mind, I try to slow down my pace to give players ample time to express themselves. One of the first things I do when I talk with a player is to thank her for taking time to meet with me. I let her know how much I appreciate her willingness to communicate. I want from the start to create a positive atmosphere because this usually leads to the best results.

Direct communication keeps everyone in your program informed and on the same page. Players, assistant coaches, and parents should not have to wonder what you are thinking or where you stand on a particular issue. That type of atmosphere can promote gossip, which is detrimental to your program.

Head Coach's Role

It's a good idea to provide plenty of feedback during both practices and games, both in the preseason and the postseason. I recommend starting each practice and every game with a team meeting to set a positive tone and give your players direction. I encourage players to initiate coach-player conferences with me as I will with them. During the season, try to arrive at practice just before your players so you can greet each one. You don't have to say much, maybe just hello, but try to personally connect with every player. This will help you get a pulse on your players' moods. If a player has had a bad day, she might have little to say, but she will appreciate your concern and attention.

Loyalty is extremely important to a team's success. In terms of communication with players, this is displayed in our confidentiality policy. For instance, I won't talk to a player about another player's playing time. If a player entrusts me with confidential information, she needs to know she can trust me to make the best decision on her behalf. The only breech of this confidentiality is when I believe the player is in danger or is a danger to others.

To Whom Much Is Given, Much Is Expected

If I know a player has potential, and she's not playing up to it, I will challenge her continuously. These challenges might take different forms—I might yell at her to "Turn it up!" or ask, "Is that the best you can do?" Or we may run as a team if a player is loafing. I tell my players it's my job to make them the best basketball players that I can. I "stay on them" because I see the potential they have. I tell them that I'm going to try many different ways to get their attention and push them to reach their potential. When I have exhausted all my strategies and see no improvement in performance, they'll notice that they hear their name called less and less. Less is not better. When KeKe Stewart was a freshman, I could sense she had a very bright and promising future. She had a wealth of talent, but her work habits did not match her talent. To make things even more difficult, she played her freshman season with a veteran squad. That veteran squad worked hard and expected the same from her. I couldn't holler out her name fast enough in practice as we drilled post defense and rebounding post moves. The pace and intensity of practices made her head spin. Often I could sense she was overwhelmed, and the next thing I knew, tears began to flow. KeKe could not understand why I was "always on her." Slowly but surely, as the season progressed, KeKe realized I was only challenging her to be the best she could be and that no one should settle for her being just another "good athlete with lots of potential." Today KeKe denies ever having cried when I got on her. She wonders why the younger players are so fragile when challenged. Just the other day she told me I challenge her in a different voice and urgency than I challenge our new players and it all makes perfect sense to her. KeKe has even shared with me how glad she is that I hold her accountable to be the best she can be. She has grown not only in her basketball skills but in her understanding of the phrase, "to whom much is given, much is expected."

I love coaching. I especially love teaching the game. I hope I communicate this to my players through my enthusiastic approach. I believe in high energy, as a coach and a player. Enthusiasm is contagious. I tell my players I want to coach them, not cheerlead them. I won't coach effort. If players are excited about what they're doing, you'll see it in their results. My goal is for enthusiasm to be a shared experience for coaches and players. I believe it starts with the coaching staff.

Every player should feel good about her contribution to the team. Praise players for the positives they bring to the team and challenge them in their areas of weakness. At Oak Ridge, we're trying a new way of communicating this fall that I hope will help players hear both the "good" and the "bad." I got the idea from Coach Summitt. It seems so often when you talk to a player, she walks away from the conversation remembering only the negative things that were said. To help players hear better, we're going to ask them to respond to a positive comment from a coach with the phrase "two points" and to a criticism with the word "rebound." I think this verbal expression helps players realize that coaches praise them as well as critique areas that need improving.

We are fortunate to have all our games broadcast on radio as well as covered in the local newspaper. As a result, I have many opportunities to share my thoughts and opinions in a public forum. I tell my players I will never embarrass or humiliate them. I also remind them that I don't write the articles. I might praise five players after a game, but the reporter might mention only one or two. I will single a player out for an outstanding performance, on or off the court. However, I will never single out a player for a poor performance, on or off the court. Don't humiliate or embarrass your players. It only destroys their confidence and sense of self-worth. Sometimes you can't build back up what you have torn down. Rarely have I seen a player perform well who has just been berated.

Players' Roles

Our players are taught that they are leaders in the school and community as well as role models. We tell them they will be held to a higher standard by being a member of our team. Our coaching staff helps players learn the right ways and wrong ways to communicate. Players are asked to treat those they talk to with respect, the same way they can expect to be treated. Our players say, Yes ma'am, No ma'am, Yes sir, and No sir. Manners go a long way in opening doors for communication. One year my team gave me the book *Ms. Manners* as a gag gift. It was their way of letting me know they understood the importance of manners in our basketball program.

I try to help players learn to communicate with teammates, coaches, teachers, parents, and members of the community. From day one, I explain to players it is their responsibility to be the communicator of their thoughts, needs, questions, and concerns. They don't send messages via their friends or their parents. This is quite an adjustment for some individuals.

Players are expected to communicate their concerns to the coaching staff. As mentioned earlier, I will try to arrange times to meet with players throughout the season. I realize that face-to-face discussions are difficult for some players. I encourage players to find additional ways to communicate with me. Some express themselves well in writing. I encourage them to write me a letter, drop me a note, or send me an e-mail. We'll usually follow up with a face-to-face discussion. It's a big waste when a player goes through a season upset about something but never shares this information with anyone on the coaching staff. What a sad and frustrating season for that player. If you help players learn how to communicate and then allow them opportunities to do so, this should never happen.

Throughout the season, we share information with players through handouts. If a handout is informational, I encourage players to share it with their parents or guardians. I want players to keep their parents informed. Yes, I do communicate with parents when necessary, but the majority of communication about our program comes from the player to the parent. I hope this helps keep lines of communication open between parent and child.

Players are encouraged to ask for feedback from their teachers, especially on ways to improve their academic performance. Most teachers are impressed by a student who takes the initiative and asks for ways to improve her classroom performance.

Our basketball program is located in Oak Ridge, Tennessee, a wonderful community that's very supportive of their basketball team. We're the only high school in town, so our players are highly visible in the community. Through various programs, our players are actively involved with youths and adults in Oak Ridge. Some players visit the elementary schools during their lunch hour to read with elementary students as part of a reading program. Others work in the youth basketball leagues officiating or keeping score. Many players are asked to speak to the hometown newspaper *The Oak Ridger* or do postgame talks on the radio. We want our basketball players to be positive ambassadors for our program, and one way they can do that is through positive communication with their community.

Assistant Coaches' Roles

I view my coaching staff as a team, just as the players are a team. To get the most out of my coaching staff team, constant communication is invaluable. I don't want my assistants to be "yes" people. They need to be able to voice their opinion, even if it challenges the status quo. Before a season begins, we spend many hours discussing the direction of the upcoming season. We outline our goals and define and discuss our coaching expectations and roles. Throughout the season, meetings, phone calls, e-mails, and coaching retreats promote constant communication within my staff. Communication with assistants is essential to keep all parties working together toward the same goals. I want my assistants to feel that we have a partnership in coaching the team. I want them to feel they have a voice that matters and that they have some ownership in the program.

PROGRAM COMMUNICATION

The world of basketball is much greater than just you, your staff, and your team. In our town, basketball is a community event. The interest and support are wonderful—from parents, to teachers, to fans. We want our product to be the best it can be, and we want to represent ourselves in the best light possible. This means reaching out to many different groups and always putting our best foot forward.

Team Meetings   We all want more time with our players. Because our players are high school students, our time together is limited and somewhat inflexible. Ideally, if time allowed, I would schedule team meetings more often. Meeting together with the team off the court is valuable in many ways. It provides an avenue for coaches and players to share information. It can be a time to address issues or iron out team problems. Often, I allow players to have their own team meeting to address concerns as a family without involvement from the coaching staff. On the court, players recognize who the bigger contributors to the team are. Off the court, basketball skills don't determine status. Some players have lots to offer but are reluctant to speak up on the court—team meetings are their opportunities to share information in a setting they feel more secure in.

On Court   You need a system of communication you can depend on during a ball game. Take into account that gym noise might hinder or even prevent much verbal communication during a game. In our system, we use several modes of communication. First, my point guard acts like a coach on the court. She's expected to be very verbal with her teammates throughout the course of the game. She looks to the bench often to get her offensive and defensive cues. Second, the coaching staff uses hand signals for most of our offenses and defenses, which minimizes the need for verbal communication. On every free throw, our team huddles up, faces our bench, and receives the next set of offensive or defensive cues. Third, we have phrases or words for segments of the game when quick decisions need to be made. For example, when we're behind in a game and I think it's time to foul, our call is "red." This indicates to every player on the court that we must foul immediately.

Of course, there are times on the court when players have to make a decision without my input. But as much as needed, we have a communication system in place so that when I need to influence our game plan, I can communicate instructions quickly and efficiently.

Team Sharing

Each year we set aside Wednesdays for scheduled team meetings. We pick Wednesdays because they work well with our school schedule. Prior to practice on that day, players are scheduled to "share" with their teammates. Their topic, time allowed, and presentation style are open ended. I want players to have a chance to express to their teammates anything they feel will be beneficial in achieving team goals. To break the ice, I present first. I often have a handout or two that I believe applies to the team at that particular time in the season. I have been amazed and pleased at what and how players have shared with their teammates. Players who are quiet on the court have shared wonderful insights about themselves and their teammates during this sharing time. Some have read from a book called *The Edge* (a collection of motivational thoughts), others have written poems, and this year one player showed a video. These meetings have been excellent opportunities for coaches and players to see other sides of one another. This season, one of my players, Mallory Jones, shared a familiar handout titled "It's Only One Possession." As she read aloud, coaches and players laughed together at the number of lines that could have easily been referring to *our* team *and our* season. Some of the lines sounded like actual dialogue between Mallory and me. How could she have found such a perfect handout to share? "And I thought you never heard a word I said," I told her. I was very happy to be wrong!

Officials   Impress on your players the value of winning over the officials. If players were getting their role models from what they see on TV, I'm not sure I could end a ball game with enough eligible players—they'd all be thrown out for poor sportsmanship. First and foremost, I tell our players it's *my* job to discuss calls with an official, not theirs. I expect our players to be polite to officials and to go the extra mile when necessary, such as chasing a loose ball at the end of a play and getting it to the official. Our players are not allowed to show negative body language or facial expressions in response to a call. We handle situations we don't like with class. Class starts with the coach.

I'm fortunate I have time before the start of each game to talk briefly with the officials. We have an administrator's meeting that includes coaches, the head official, security, and the game administrator. During this brief meeting, coaches are reminded of sportsmanship, and officials often reiterate their points of emphasis. This can be a good opportunity for the coach to ask officials about rules that seem to be officiated a bit different from game to game. During the course of the game, a good official will allow a coach to speak with him or her on the sidelines during dead balls. Asking questions and challenging calls are two very different modes of interaction. Constant complaining to an official usually results in the official turning a deaf ear. I'm fortunate to have coached in the same league for 25 years. I know most of the officials and believe we have a good rapport. If you treat officials with respect, they'll usually treat you the same and perhaps give you a little rope. But don't try to take too much. Remember that you're the role model for your players. You might need to challenge an official at times, but berating an official won't help your cause and sets a lousy example for your players.

Parents or Family Members You can share your philosophy and goals with the parents or guardians of your players in a number of ways. Before the start of your season, you might hold a parents meeting. This is not a conference but an opportunity for all parents and guardians to get a closer look at their child's coach and to hear the program's philosophy. This way, all parents and guardians hear the same message at the same time. If some parents or guardians can't attend this meeting, send them a letter detailing what was discussed.

Another way to communicate well with parents and guardians is to have short meetings at the player's house before the season begins. Such meetings are great opportunities for the coach to share information and get some insight into the player's home situation. These meetings show parents and guardians that you're willing to take the time to talk to them and listen to what they have to say. Just one meeting at a player's home can build a season's worth of good faith.

At Oak Ridge our practices have always been open. Any parent or guardian who wants to come watch us practice is more than welcome.

At some point during the season, some parents or guardians become concerned about their child's amount of playing time in games. I tell everyone that playing time is decided primarily in practice and invite them to come watch their child practice. This doesn't always solve all questions, but I want the parent to know the coaches have nothing to hide and that there are no secrets to playing time. I also have an open-door policy for parents and guardians to call me or set up a conference. I have found the best way to hold a parent or guardian conference is to have a third person attend. That person is usually an assistant coach or my athletic director. I don't want any information misinterpreted, and I don't want the meeting to be confrontational. I've found the additional person helps keep the meeting on task and more productive.

Guest Coach

A few years back we started a "guest coaching" program, inviting people from the community, teachers, and initially our administrators to be our special guest coaches at the ball games. For each game we invited three or four coaches. They attended our team pregame meeting, sat on the bench during the game, and then attended part of our postgame team meeting. They were not a part of our half-time talk or the postgame final talk. We wanted our guest coaches to have an inside look at our program but also wanted to protect the privacy of our team. This setup allowed us to do both. It was a wonderfully successful program and a terrific way of communicating to administrators, teachers, and community members. They enjoyed the special attention and a chance to be a part of the game. Did they do any actual coaching? Of course not. But if we won the game you could hear them saying, "I'm undefeated in my coaching career."

Administration and Faculty Our school administration shows great support for our basketball program. It's not unusual for us to play a game in front of our athletic director, principal, assistant superintendent, and director of schools. To keep administrators informed, we send them a schedule and a roster at the beginning of the season. We have a VIP hospitality room open during games at which snacks and drinks are served. I recommend inviting your administrators to your hospitality room during the game as a way of thanking them for supporting your team.

I believe that players and coaches need to reach out to the faculty at their school. At the beginning of the school year, you might ask your players to introduce themselves to their teachers as members of your basketball team. One way to do this is to have them give their teachers a letter from the coaching staff that names the coaches and players and gives the coaches' phone numbers and e-mail addresses, lists games and game times as well as any class time to be missed throughout the season, and includes a statement of academic support from the coaches. If teachers know that the players and coaches value academics, it's easier to build a good player–teacher working relationship.

Student Body Getting the student body involved in supporting the basketball program is always a challenge. For many students, by the time they enter high school, their interests are elsewhere and their schedules full. Many of our high school students work. But players love to have their classmates at the games. We've tried several promotional ideas to solicit student support at our games. The basketball schedule is posted on a scrolling computer screen located in the main hallway. This area is well populated by students and advertises both home and away games. In addition, homeroom teachers read a daily bulletin that reminds students of game nights. At the beginning of the season, each class—freshman, sophomore, junior, and senior—gets a free admission night to a home game. If you can get students to games early in the season, and they have a positive experience, they'll likely return to support the team. We also have a student pep section. We give these students free admission to home games, supply them with a T-shirt, and rope off a section for them to sit in. This group has come out in numbers and provided a rowdy cheering section, especially during tournament time. Our players love it. If you can get a core group of students to start following your games, the numbers are likely to grow. Student body support is truly what excites the players. They want to perform well in front of their peers.

Sixth Player

It was our regional semifinal, and the gym was packed. The winner advanced to the regional final and a substate game, and the loser went home.

We entered the game as the favorite and played that way for three quarters. We got up by as many as 20 points and seemed to answer every run they made. Then it happened—a missed shot here, a quick turnover, some bad decisions. Suddenly, we were losing our confidence and our lead. To make matters worse, our opponent had a tremendous student section. With every mistake we made, their students roared with delight. They were loud and extremely animated. What looked like 50 students sounded like 500 students. They really ignited the comeback of their team. Our crowd tried desperately to get us back into the game, but I think they were as stunned as we were, and their best efforts couldn't dull the roar from the opponent's crowd. Momentum had swung their way. Their cheering section was clearly the sixth player in that game. We ran out of gas emotionally and mentally, while their students gave them a much-needed shot of adrenalin. They beat us and advanced; we packed our bags and went home. I strongly recommend finding a way to get your school's students behind your team. They can be a difference maker.

Community When you're the only high school in town, it's generally easier to get your community's support. To help with this, make sure you have a program they want to be associated with. Make your games visible, affordable, and entertaining. We have a local paper and radio station, so our community knows when the games are and who we're playing. To get community groups to our ball games, we hold special nights and admit groups at no charge. Some of our promotional nights, among many others, are Senior Citizens Night, Girl's Club (and Boy's Club) Night, and Civic Organization Night. We want the community to feel a part of our basketball family. If we invite them to a free game, maybe they'll enjoy what we have to offer and come back to support us regularly.

Along with bringing your community to the games, find ways to take your players into the community. Get them involved with senior citizens, civic organizations, and feeder programs. The more contact a team has with its community, the more community members feel part of the program.

Meet the Wildcats Night is an event we host to introduce our players and support staff to the community. We want this night to be fun, festive, and enjoyable for all who take part. We start the evening with a barbeque for families, players, and coaches. This is a wonderful social time and encourages families to get to know one another. The next part of the program includes players and support staff introductions, which we follow with an intrasquad scrimmage. We want our players to have a chance to play in front of a crowd before our first game. This year we added come competitive player challenges prior to the intrasquad tip-off. The players

Hosting an event to introduce the team to the community will jumpstart support for the program.

really liked the challenges, which included ball handling, passing, and shooting. An event like this is a chance to showcase your team's talents early. We play an intrasquad game so that all players can play a good part of the contest. We want this to be a positive experience for players and fans.

Civic Organizations Throughout the season, speaking to civic organizations is another way to keep the public informed about your team's status. A good way to contact these organizations is to write each club a letter in the fall requesting an opportunity to speak to their group, perhaps at a breakfast or lunch meeting. Our boys' basketball coach, Ricky Norris, and I work closely together on this. We speak to as many civic groups as we can to share what's going on in our programs.

These talks have opened many doors for our program. This past season, the Oak Ridge Breakfast Rotary Club helped our boys' and girls' basketball teams host a Thanksgiving Basketball Hoop Classic at our gym. The club provided us with funds to pay the officials and with manpower to sell tickets, serve as hosts and hostesses, and work the concession stand. Without their help we could have never hosted such an event. Civic groups are always looking for positive community events to support or participate in.

Media In our community, the local paper runs our basketball schedule, prints our roster with a team picture, and covers all our games, home or away. The adjoining community newspaper keeps up with league scores and stats. This keeps all interested parties informed. Most newspapers will also accept special articles on your team or an individual player. You might have to do the work on the front end, but this is one more way to get some nice coverage for your program. Sometimes players or coaches are asked to do a clip on the local news. Although this can be disconcerting, remember that positive press is well received by administrators and community members. I tell our players that talking to the media is an opportunity to say something positive about our program. They're instructed to never criticize an opponent or the officials. I want our players to be polite, well-spoken ambassadors for our team. Handling the media can be challenging.

For example, the media may innocently ask about an opponent, but an answer may not make your opponent look good. Players are again reminded NOT to negatively comment on opponents. you'll want to weigh each decision on whether an interview or news clip is in the best interests of your players and program. Whether we accept an offer or not, we always let the media know that we appreciate their efforts to showcase our program.

Collegiate Recruiters It seems every year I hear more parents make the same two requests: more playing time for their child and a chance for their child to receive a college scholarship. I believe it's part of the high school coach's responsibility to do as much as he or she can to market the team's players and help them make the necessary connections with college recruiters. This can be done in a number of ways. Early in our season, I fax many colleges our basketball roster and schedule. I make sure they're aware of the tournaments we're playing in. Often a college recruiter wants to see a player in a competitive game, which tournaments can provide. I encourage players to fill out college questionnaires to help in their recruiting process. This can become overwhelming for some players, so I assist in the process as much as I'm needed. I inform college recruiters that our games are all videotaped and that the films are available on request. Many of our players play AAU basketball in the off-season. College recruiters are informed about the teams they're playing on and the coach of that team and are given a schedule of games. I want my players to be seen in as many different arenas as possible.

Exposure is the key to being recruited, and getting players exposure is part of the high school coach's job.

SUMMARY

- Communication is essential for a basketball program to be successful.
- Communication is a two-way street. Be a good listener.
- Communicate to players and assistant coaches what they can expect from you as well as what you expect from them.
- Allow players and assistant coaches to communicate in different ways as long as they are respectful.
- Establish a system of communication with players for on-the-court game situations.
- Win the officials over as a coach and teach your players to do the same.
- Keep an open-door policy for parents, guardians, and family members.
- Help players reach out to administrators and faculty members.
- Find ways to get your "sixth player," the student body, involved in supporting your basketball program.
- Get your team connected with community groups.
- Look for opportunities to market your team's success stories.
- Help your players connect with college recruiters.

MOTIVATING PLAYERS

As a coach, you want your team to realize its full potential. For this to happen, you need to find ways to motivate your players and keep them motivated. We have all seen very talented teams play uninspired basketball and produce sub par results. On the other hand, it is not unusual to see a team with average talent overachieve because they were highly motivated. A challenge all coaches face is that there's no magic formula that guarantees player motivation. Different players respond in different ways to different types of motivational strategies. What might have worked one year with a particular player or team might produce quite different results the next season. Thus, a coach needs to be insightful, flexible, and resourceful in seeking ways to motivate each player and the team as a whole.

One way to gain insight for player motivation is to get to know your players one on one. Find out what buttons to push for each player to produce your desired results. Almost all players respond positively to praise, but even giving praise can be tricky. What's positive praise for one player, such as a coach's verbal praise in front of the player's peers, might cause embarrassment for another player. If you get to know your players, you'll get a feel for what they respond to best. I can offer one tip I've learned through experience: Don't try to motivate a player by challenging her when you're upset with her. Sometimes your emotions may overshadow your point and a teaching moment is lost.

One effective strategy I have found in connecting with players and discovering what motivates them is simply to ask them for feedback. During one of our first team meetings, I ask players to respond to a questionnaire. One of the questions is, What is the best way to motivate you to perform at your highest level? Another question is, What can coaches do or say that automatically turns you off and produces negative results? Reading my players' completed questionnaires is often eye opening for me. The information you receive gives you a starting place with your players as you work toward finding ways to motivate them.

PROVIDING VERBAL MOTIVATION

Communication between a player and a coach is essential for a positive working relationship. A coach who is effective at verbal communication expresses expectations to players and motivates them to meet them. The key is to find what works with each player. Some players can be challenged, or motivated, by a coach who raises his or her voice loudly. For this to be effective,

Athletes play a key role in motivating each other on the court.

it's important not to embarrass or humiliate the player. Phrases such as "push yourself" or "you can do better" can be used as quick motivators without demeaning the player. For another player, a very calm speaking voice might get her attention best. Pulling a player off to the side for a quick chat sometimes gets desired results. There are many verbal ways to motivate players without using putdowns. Sometimes just calling a player's name out loud quickly gets her attention—let her know your eyes are on her. Perhaps the phrase "you are better than that" or "we can play better than this" is a way to let individuals know their efforts are not getting the job done. A simple reminder such as "pick it up" might help players recognize a lapse in intensity and that they need to take it up a notch.

As you challenge players, always remind them that it's their behavior that bothers you, not them as individuals. Let them know this at the outset. Often when players get their feelings hurt, they no longer listen as well. Avoid this whenever possible. When players shut down and no longer hear instructions, breakdowns develop on the court. Players tune out coaches and teammates and can become lost offensively or defensively. They might lose their focus and become unreceptive to changes.

PROVIDING NONVERBAL FEEDBACK

Saying nothing at all to players can sometimes send a very loud message. There are subtle ways to get your message across. For instance, when a drill is getting lackluster results, try adding minutes to the drill. Your players quickly realize that you're extending the drill because they weren't giving it their best effort. This should raise their level of intensity. You might catch the eye of one of your captains during a poor segment of practice. It might take only a look for her to understand what you're thinking. A coach's body language can make his or her pleasure or displeasure very clear. Recognize this, and take care not to miscommunicate. The way you look, hold your head, or place your hands all send messages to your players.

There are many positive nonverbal ways to let players know they have performed well. Simple gestures such as a wink, a smile, a pat on the back, or a high five can lift a player's spirits and serve as a quick form of motivation.

MOTIVATING THE INDIVIDUAL

Sometimes a player just needs to be noticed. This seems so easy to do, yet sometimes we become so busy we forget the easy and important little things. Try to find ways to individualize your attention to your players. In a practice session, just calling a player by name or shouting "good job!" might give her the attention she needs. Ask your assistants to help with individual motivation. Encourage and remind them to reach out to players. If you have a couple of assistant coaches, players can receive a lot of individual attention during a practice or a game.

I always try to recognize players who give a great effort in practice. Depending on the player, I use different methods. I may praise them during the practice, at the end of the practice, or at the start of the next practice. Some players might not like being singled out in front of teammates, even when the feedback is positive. I may pull them off to the side or give them a call at home that night. Most players seem to remember negative comments better than positive comments, so you need to find ways to praise your players frequently.

If a player is not performing up to her potential, address this problem as quickly as you can by giving this player individual attention. Sometimes just a few words to show you recognize what's happening are enough to turn the behavior around. Persistent poor performance might require an individual meeting. There might be outside issues affecting the player. Meeting with her one on one gives her the chance to explain.

Some coaches use written notes as individual motivation. If you get your assistant coaches involved, you can divide the team up and ensure that all players receive a note every week or two. Use written notes to offer praise, to let players know you're thinking about them, or to identify areas of improvement.

Setting team and individual goals helps provide direction for players and teams alike. Measurable goals can also help you evaluate a player's or the team's progress throughout the season. Setting individual goals is also an effective way of motivating players. Some players are very goal oriented, so goals might ignite their performance. Players can set goals for practices or games or both; their goals might be long or short term. It's a good idea to meet with each player and offer suggestions to help them attain their goals. Goal setting might be an effective approach for some of your players and not so much for others. All players need to realize the value of goal setting, but all might not be motivated to accomplish the goals they set.

For our 2004 season, my assistant coach helped players set game goals in an attempt to motivate them. Before each game, players turned in an index card listing a couple of goals for the game. The next day, players turned in another card that evaluated their game results and the degree to which they accomplished their goals. If they accomplished all their goals, they added goals for the next game. If they did not meet a particular goal, they discussed the reasons with the coach, planned strategies, and then tried to meet the same goal in the next game. Many players found this extremely motivating.

Holding an individual film session with a player can be an excellent way to correct a problem and help motivate her. You might show a clip from a game or use a practice tape. In our 2004 season, one of my excellent three-point shooters was in a shooting slump. We tried many things to help get her shot back on track. One thing that worked for her was an analysis of her shots during a game. I took a game film and edited the tape to show our offensive series when she shot the ball. We watched the tape together, analyzed her shot selection and technique, and discussed the results. She found it very helpful to see herself on tape. For her, this was a good teaching tool and motivated her to work on her shot. Over the next few games I noticed she made better decisions on when to shoot the ball. She was also able to get back to the gym with some confidence and work on her shooting technique. It wasn't long before her accuracy returned.

Conferences with players, either scheduled or nonscheduled, can have good success for motivation. You might have a set agenda for a conference or it might be wide open. Either way, you're sending a message to your player that you care enough about her to meet with her. This is an excellent opportunity to clear up any miscommunications. A conference also provides a coach and a player a chance to talk about issues outside of basketball. If you know your players well, you can use conference time to tap into their interests or discuss their concerns.

MOTIVATING THE TEAM

Most teams develop their own personality as the season progresses. Once you identify your team's personality, you have an easier time finding ways to motivate them. As I've said, all players are not motivated in the same way. So, how *do* you motivate a team full of different players? You have to try many different things and discover what works best with your team. It might be helpful to identify key players or leaders on your team and zero in on what motivates them. If you can motivate your leaders, others will likely follow.

Game Goals

Setting team goals can be helpful in building team motivation. Instead of telling your players what their goals are, try having them come up with their own goals as a team. Let them come to a consensus about what they want and think they can accomplish together. I usually give my team guidelines to help them in goal setting. I tell them not to make their list of goals so long or so difficult that it's unrealistic they will accomplish their goals. Most important, I ask players not to list a team goal that they are not willing to work for, each and every player. I use the example of a state championship. Almost every player across the state wants to win a state championship. But how many players are willing to do the work it takes to accomplish such a lofty goal? Establishing team goals can be the driving force to help motivate the team through a difficult practice or game.

Setting game goals is another method to motivate your team. Again, you can ask your team for their input, but you and your staff might know best what's realistic for your team to accomplish during a game. Game goals will likely depend on the opponent and time of season. You might need to stress an area of deficiency or challenge your team in an area of strength. Rewarding game goal accomplishments often helps motivate players. Rewards can be tangible or intangible, such as a shortened practice the next day. Goals that are not achieved might be altered, if they seem inappropriate, or players might be highly challenged to meet them the next day in practice.

In our program, we have offensive and defensive game goals. We give individual and team rewards and punishments, depending on the results of our play. Punishments usually include some type of running, but the running is also considered part of conditioning. For every offensive goal not met, players run a 10-second sprint. They run a 30-second sprint for every defensive goal not met. However, outstanding individual performances are also awarded, and players can minimize team runs if they have great individual statistics. Players are rewarded for excellent stats such as double figure rebounds, taking a charge, or double figure assists. In addition, we have challenges in practice in which players can earn themselves out of a sprint. Running, or lack of running, has been an excellent motivator for many of my teams.

Motivational speakers are another way to get your team fired up. If you don't consider yourself a good speaker, ask an assistant or perhaps a fellow teacher or coach. There are also many terrific motivational movies that might boost your team's morale.

Little Complaining and Few Excuses

One of the best motivational videos I've seen was one I watched when I was working with USA Basketball two summers ago. The video was in two parts. The first part included highlights of the Olympic Games held in Sidney, Australia. It gave me chills to watch great athletes achieve phenomenal results. The second part included highlights of the Paralympics. Now we were watching athletes with disabilities perform great feats. There was not a dry eye in the room. What a powerful message those two diverse segments sent! This video really raised the level of practices over the next few days. Players hardly complained and made very few excuses. This video turned out to be a great source of motivation.

Team outings away from the basketball court can bond your team and increase motivation. Outings might include team meals, motivational movies, outdoor adventure settings, or just a gathering at a church or a park. Low levels of motivation are sometimes the result of players feeling they are in a rut. A new experience together might refresh a team that's feeling a little stale.

On-Court Goals

Players need to know your on-court expectations from the moment they step onto the court until the horn sounds. Most of your expectations will involve attitude, effort, and execution. Help your players know there's a right way and a wrong way to practice and to play the game. As you set your expectations, be careful not to fence yourself in with too many rules. Teach your team how to practice and play the game, and let them know you tolerate nothing less than full commitment. As their coach, be their example. If being on time is important, make sure you're not late. If you want them to be respectful to coaches and fellow players, treat them with respect. Try not to make a major deal out of a minor issue. Let your players know the consequences of their mistakes and for a poor attitude or a lazy effort. If their mistake can be addressed quickly, do it and move on. Major infractions typically require tougher penalties. If all expectations, responsibilities, and consequences are spelled out clearly on the front end, unpleasant incidents are minimized.

In my 25 years of coaching, I have tried many ways to deal with a poor performance or a poor attitude. Some ways were effective, and some were not. However, I've found that the two greatest motivators have not changed over the years—sitting and running. The punishment does not have to be extreme to get a player's attention. Most players don't want to lose playing or practice time, nor do they revel at the thought of additional conditioning. When I have asked my players the best way to get their attention the quickest, they most often say, "Run me or sit me down."

Off-Court Goals

Coaches often wear many hats. We can be our players' coach, teacher, mentor, friend, and counselor. As you wear these hats, you find yourself involved in your players' lives both on and off the court. In my program, I address this by explaining to my players the "three Cs." Players are expected to be their best on the court, in the classroom, and in the community. Basketball players are often referred to as "student athletes." Players need to know academics are a high priority. Good grades are necessary to be eligible to play basketball, but, more importantly, they are the ticket to their success after high school.

It might be helpful to assign an assistant coach to monitor your team's academic prog-

ress. Teachers will appreciate your staff's involvement in your players' classroom performance, both in academics and in behavior. Let players know what you expect from them in the classroom. If they need academic assistance, tutoring might be helpful. If you preach the importance of academics, make sure you back it up with your actions. If a player needs to miss part of your practice for academic support, make sure you have a plan to address this situation. Actions and words need to be aligned. At some point, you might need to involve parents or guardians.

If a player misbehaves in the classroom, a school-sanctioned disciplinary action might be issued. If the discipline is up to you as a coach, have a plan for this. Players need to be aware of your discipline steps on the front end. If they can be respectful of you, they can be respectful of other adults, including their teachers.

Players should know what you expect from them while they're not under your supervision but out in the community. Remind them that they are role models. If a player misbehaves in the community, and you feel you need to take action, be sure to match the punishment to the crime. For example, if a player manages her free time poorly, you might place her on a time-management program in which she is accountable to you for each minute of her day. I have used this type of plan with several players and seen positive results.

Some behaviors are nonnegotiable by school and team rules. Players are not allowed to drink alcohol, smoke cigarettes, or take nonprescription drugs. These behaviors can lead to serious school discipline procedures and might result in dismissal from the team. These rules and their consequences need to be explained to your players at the outset of your relationship with them.

When rules are broken, different players require different kinds of discipline. You should treat players fairly, but not necessarily equally. An exception to this might be if a player violates a school rule and a predetermined punishment has been set. But as a coach you might need to flex your discipline procedures if a player has an extenuating circumstance. You need to make a call that suits the situation. One player might love running whereas another hates it. One player might have a terrific support system at home whereas another often fends for herself. In any case, it's most important that players are treated fairly and with respect.

There are many ways to reward players for positive off-court behaviors. Catch players doing the right thing and let them know you're proud of them. Encourage teachers to e-mail you regarding your players. Let them know you want to hear the good and the bad. At Oak Ridge, we have an academic honor roll each nine-week grading period. If a player makes the A-B honor roll, her name is posted in our team room and displayed all season.

Many schools have work programs through which students attend classes part of the day and then work in the community another part of the day. If this is the case for one of your players, try to keep in touch with their employers. Let them know you're there for support and that you appreciate the opportunity they're giving your player. Often, employers will share positive interactions they have with players. Communicate these to your players, perhaps at a team meeting. Let them know you're proud of the example they're setting in the community.

There are many ways in which players might be involved in their community. They might be active in their church or work with local youths. Encourage your players to find a niche and give back to their community. This is terrific PR for your program and often a positive experience for your team. Let your players know you're proud that they're positive ambassadors for your program.

USING REWARDS AND PUNISHMENTS

Why is it players can quote you verbatim when you get on them but rarely remember the positive feedback you express? Whenever possible, use more rewards than punishments because rewards and other forms of positive feedback don't seem to make the impression that negative feedback makes. You'll need to use both rewards and punishments, but try to tip the scales to the side of positive reinforcement.

Rewarding good behavior can be as easy as praising a player in practice to handing out an award at your year-end banquet. Extrinsic rewards, though more time consuming for a coach, are often better remembered by a player. Extrinsic rewards might include letters or notes of praise, newspaper articles highlighting a good deed, or calls home to parents or guardians to express your pleasure with their child.

Direct any punishment toward altering certain behaviors of your players—do not direct it at the players themselves. Remember that you're working with young people who are going to make mistakes. If you teach your system well, the need for discipline can be minimized. Of course, having good people in your program also minimizes problems. Character is important when selecting your team. I have a plaque on my desk that says, "Sport does not build character—it reveals it." Ideally, you want a team of character and talent. But if I had to choose between the two, I would pick quality people of high character over talented athletes with attitude problems or a lack of character.

SUMMARY

- Highly motivated players can achieve great results.
- Not all players are motivated in the same way.
- You can motivate a player by what you say and don't say.
- Your nonverbal communication can shout your approval or disapproval.
- Get to know your players one on one and find out what motivates each of them.
- Learning the personality of your team can help you motivate your team.
- Be flexible and creative in finding ways to motivate players individually and as a team.
- Make sure your players know their on- and off-court expectations and consequences.
- Teach your players how to make good decisions. Be their example.
- Make your punishment fit the crime.
- Catch your players doing the right thing and acknowledge it.
- Be positive with your players; find ways to praise them often.
- Character counts. Select your team wisely.

CHAPTER 4
BUILDING AND MAINTAINING A BASKETBALL PROGRAM

There's a big difference between having a few great basketball seasons and maintaining a successful basketball program. Successful programs are measured more in terms of their long-term productivity than their short-term success. How do you make a successful program? Well, there's no magic formula, but you can probably guess some of the ingredients it takes to produce a quality program that endures.

The concept of "program" is vast, covering your season, off-season, and preseason; all your personnel and all your players, past and present; your feeder programs; your team's community involvement; and more. Sometimes the amount of work involved in sustaining a quality program can be overwhelming. The best pieces of advice I can give a coach are to divide the work load up between yourself and your staff, divide the calendar year into monthly to do lists, and always be enthusiastic and eager about the growth of your program. After 25 years at the same high school, I'm still looking for new ways to make my program better.

If you're a new coach starting out, don't bite off more than you can chew. One of the first things you'll want to do is determine how much help you have. Once you know this, you'll have a better idea how much you can tackle your first season. Find out how much help you can count on from your assistant coaches, if you have any. Find out what their backgrounds are in, what their strengths are; ask them if they have any coaching experience. Then determine how much support you have from your administration and community. If you have no assistant coaches and little administrative support, you as a coach now will have to prioritize your to do list and decide what you alone can and should accomplish. Once you have your priorities, devise your strategies. Remember, don't be too ambitious if you are running the show solo. Prioritize the components of your program and devise a strategy for addressing your priorities. If I were you, I'd try to do just a few things my first year and do them well rather than trying to do just a passable job on everything that needs doing.

DEVELOPING A SYSTEM

I often use the word "system" when speaking to my staff, players, and attendees at a coaching clinic. For me, a system incorporates all the components that you as a coach have in your program. A system is a blueprint for how your team and program will run. Your system might develop over time. Ideally, by the time a player is a senior in your program she'll be able to help incoming freshman learn the system.

As soon as a player enters your program, she will begin to learn the hows and whys of what you do—what's acceptable and what's not. You want to build a rich history for your program, both on and off the court. If you can trickle this sense of history and tradition down to your feeder programs, they'll have a clearer sense of the expectations for them once they become part of your program. Your rich history is really the tradition you will build. You want to define how people view your players, team, and program. You want to set your program apart from others.

Before your season begins it's a good idea to describe your system on paper and include this description in your coaching packet. At Oak Ridge, our coaching packet includes our coaching responsibilities, our offensive and defensive philosophies and goals, and our offensive and defensive schemes to consider for the upcoming season. This packet should be something that's easy to share with your staff and the coaches in your feeder program. For our players, we distribute a handout listing the five basic components of our Lady Wildcat system. These components are physical conditioning, offensive unselfishness, defensive commitment, understanding and playing your role, and TEAM versus me. Much of what I address with my team on the court falls into one of those areas.

Keeping Priorities

In the public school system you can't recruit players. You basically play basketball with the hand you're dealt. That's not to say good players don't move or pay tuition to play in a better program than the one they're zoned for. If your school has good athletics and good academics, your program might be the recipient of such a player. However, in most years you'll coach the players who come up through your feeder programs. Your talent will vary from year to year. Your style of play should match the talent you have. For example, without a dominant player, your offensive system might give several players the green light to shoot the basketball. On the other hand, if you have a dominant post player, your system might require that player to receive several more touches on offense than her teammates receive. With quick athletes you might coach a style of basketball that incorporates running and pressing. In general, you try to match your system to your players, which is

why your system is likely to change at least a little every year.

We've been blessed at Oak Ridge to have a number of talented athletes play in our program. This has allowed us to play a baseline-to-baseline style of basketball most years. In a hallway that leads to our gym, there's a painted sign that reads, "We have more FUN because we PRESS and RUN." Our message is loud and clear to our team and to our opponents. You too will want to emphasize to your team and other teams what your team stands for and how you see the game. Our slogan does that for us. Create a slogan that suits your priorities.

Early in your season, or perhaps in the preseason, sit down with your coaching staff to assess your talent pool and identify your players' strengths and weaknesses. Then you can customize your style of play to match your personnel. I believe that regardless of your players' talent level you can still emphasize your priorities each season. For example, if you believe defense is the key to winning games, you don't have to change this belief because your new group of players has less talent than the last. The type and style of defense your team plays might be affected, but not your priorities. I think this is important to remember.

I'm a defensive-minded coach. I tell my players if they *won't* play defense, they *can't* play in my system. I believe all players can play defense if they work at it. Our 2004 season only reinforced this idea. In most of our games our team hovered around 30-percent shooting, a percentage that makes for some very ugly basketball games. However, we played outstanding defense, night in and night out, and we finished our season with 30 wins and 5 losses. If not for our defensive efforts, we would have been barely .500. Stick to your priorities. Defense has always been a priority for our basketball program. Offense can sometimes take time to gel, but defense can be a weapon right from the start. A great defense keeps you in a game until your offense wakes up.

Although you have strict priorities as a coach, it's important to stay flexible, not only year to year, but within a season. You and your coaching staff might determine early in the season that only two players on the team are high-percentage scorers. Thus, it seems to make sense that you gear your offense around these two players. Keep in mind, though, that illnesses, injury, foul trouble, and discipline issues can quickly take your strategy south. Plus, you hope all of your players improve during the season. As the season progresses, you might have some players really step up for you, and now you need to add them to your offensive mix. If you have stayed flexible and open minded, you'll be prepared to adjust in the way that's best for the team.

Choosing Coaching Staff

It's a great situation if you can pick your own coaching staff, but sometimes this isn't possible. You might inherit a program with coaches already in place. If you get to choose, it's important to decide what you're looking for in filling your staff positions. You'll need people who complement you and your philosophy. You need to decide what qualities and characteristics you value in others. I look for character, work ethic, and loyalty when seeking an ideal assistant coach. Basketball coaching is not a nine to five job, so look for people who will be willing to put in the long hours. Assistant coaches also need to be good teachers. They need to be able to teach the game the way you want it taught.

Quality people build quality programs. I would rather have good people with limited basketball experience than basketball gurus with weak people skills. I can teach the game of basketball to my assistant coach but not the game of life. I think it's also important to look for individuals who are excellent role models, good teachers, and students of the game.

Most important, your staff needs to have people who truly care about your players. These players are going to need role models, coaches, and teachers; they might also need mentoring, counseling, or even "parenting." I'm a big believer that coaching is not about me but about the kids.

I'm fortunate to have an assistant, Kim Tisdale, with all the characteristics I look for. Kim cares about our players, on and off the court. She spends many hours outside of practice time helping players with academic studies and personal issues. Many players spend their lunch hour in Kim's classroom, sometimes studying, sometimes just talking. Kim is always willing to go the extra mile for the girls or for our program. It's not unusual for her to spend virtually every night during the preseason on a scouting trip, at a scrimmage, or attending a team function. Loyal, hard-working assistant coaches like Kim are worth their weight in gold.

Help your assistants find their niche in your program. Give them some ownership. Use their strengths, and help them with their weaknesses. With luck, they'll challenge you to become a better coach. Be flexible and allow them to grow just as you hope your team grows. Take time to reevaluate their roles throughout the season. Help assistants make the best fit in your program.

Choosing Student Assistants

Good student assistants can really help take the work load off a coaching staff. They can be extremely helpful during practice and games. Identify the role you need them to perform. Our student assistants fill water bottles before practice, run the clock during practice, and chart statistics as needed throughout practices. Each student assistant is assigned several duties on game nights. One might be in charge of water bottles and towels; another might be charting stats throughout the game. Duties are divided depending on the number of student assistants and the needs for each game or practice. These are important duties that really help the coaching staff. Let your student assistants know their importance to the success of the team. They put long hours in and usually get little recognition, so do what you can to make them feel a part of the program.

In the spring at Oak Ridge, before our next season begins, we hold a meeting for students interested in becoming Lady Wildcat student assistants. I go over the role of a student assistant and the expectations involved. Interested students then fill out a form to provide the coaching staff with feedback. Information requested includes his or her basketball background, his or her nine-week class schedule and grades, and his or her reasons for wanting to become a student assistant. In addition, these students are asked to bring back a teacher's recommendation. Just as with your players, you want to choose quality individuals as team assistants. You might not be as familiar with these students as you are with upcoming basketball players, so check them out a little before you ask them to join the program.

Once you select quality student assistants, orientate them to your program and their roles. This might be a job for your assistant coach. Make sure your new assistants feel a part of the program. Let them know how much your staff appreciates the role they will play for the team.

IMPLEMENTING THE SYSTEM

Once you have defined your system, it's time to apply it. All members of your coaching staff should be united within the system and share in the responsibility of implementing it. Try to give each assistant coach a voice, whether it's a lead role in practice or in team meetings. Players need to hear a united theme from all coaches. This reinforces the system and also gives your assistant coaches greater credibility with the players.

Implementing Rules and Guidelines

Part of your system needs to include the rules and guidelines for your basketball team. Initially, your school will have guidelines for athletes that your players will have to adhere to in order to stay eligible for your team. At Oak Ridge, there are several forms that players and their parents (or guardians) receive and need to sign before participation in a sport can begin. Once the school's criteria are met, I implement our program's rules and guidelines.

Every basketball player at Oak Ridge fills out a Sports Information and Permission form that includes a parental permission and medical release section, an insurance disclosure form, a field trip expectations agreement (away contests are categorized as field trips), and a medical evaluation form for female athletes. Figure 4.1 shows the section of the medical evaluation form that focuses on the personal history of an athlete. If you are coaching females, it is important that this form include questions specifically

addressing concerns for female athletes. Your school probably has a similar form. In the best interests of the players, parents, and coaches, it's important to include all these areas in one form or another. I keep our completed forms in my office and bring them with us to all our contests on the road.

As a coach, you'll need to devise your own set of additional rules, guidelines, expectations, and consequences for failure to meet them. These rules should be explained to all players and their parents or guardians. Make sure you and your staff are comfortable with the consequences, especially if you have them written down. A good way to check this is to ask yourself these questions: Would I give the same consequence to my star player as I would to the 12th player on my roster? Do I warn first before levying consequences, or is there no warning? Do I give any extra chances to a troubled player?

I've found the importance of treating players fairly a good rule rather than treating all players equally. For example, if a player is late to practice, she immediately runs. After a timed run (depending on the number of minutes late), she lets us know why she was late. If it's a poor reason, she might run some more at the end of practice. If it's a good reason, she probably won't have to run at the end of practice. Some of your rules might be cut and dried, especially if they involve illegal activities. But for other rules, you and your staff might want to allow some room to consider circumstances. Don't fence yourself in with rules and consequences that you and your staff are not comfortable in enforcing.

A couple of years ago all coaches in our athletic program were told to submit our rules and guidelines to the director of schools. He wanted to know not only the rules but also the consequences for failing to follow them. I realized then that I wanted to have some leeway in handling some of our discipline problems. I try to take into account several factors when implementing discipline, the most important of which are the severity of the rule broken, the frequency of the rule broken, and any extenuating circumstances. I want to help my players learn from their mistakes, but I want to adhere to the rules we've put in place. It might also be necessary to keep the best interests of your player and your team in mind when disciplining individual athletes.

TMA / TSSAA Pre-Participation Medical Evaluation Form

To be completed by Student & Parent/Guardian

Personal History

Name	Sex	Age	Date of Birth

Sports	School	Grade

Personal Physician(s)	Address	Phone #

Have you ever had a pre-participation physical before? _____ Yes _____ No   Where:

Please answer questions below. Explain "yes" questions at bottom of page.   YES   NO

1.   Have you ever been hospitalized?   _____   _____
     Have you ever had surgery?   _____   _____
2.   Are you presently taking any medications or pills?   _____   _____
3.   Do you have any allergies? (medicine, bees, or other stinging insects)   _____   _____
4.   Have you ever passed out during exercise?   _____   _____
     Have you ever been dizzy during or after exercise?   _____   _____
     Have you ever had chest pain during or after exercise?   _____   _____
     Do you tire more quickly than your friends during exercise?   _____   _____
     Have you ever had high blood pressure?   _____   _____
     Have you ever been told you have a heart murmur?   _____   _____
     Have you ever had racing or skipped heartbeats?   _____   _____
     Has anyone in your family died or had heart problems before the age of 50?   _____   _____
5.   Do you have any skin problems? (itching, rashes, acne)   _____   _____
6.   Have you ever had a head injury?   _____   _____
     Have you ever been knocked out or unconscious?   _____   _____
     Have you ever had a seizure?   _____   _____
     Have you ever had a stinger, burner, or pinched nerve?   _____   _____
7.   Have you ever had heat or muscle cramps?   _____   _____
     Have you ever been dizzy or passed out in the heat?   _____   _____
8.   Do you have trouble breathing, or do you cough during or after activities?   _____   _____
9.   Do you use any special equipment?   _____   _____
     (pads, braces, neck role, mouth guard, eye guard)
10. Have you had problems with eyes or vision?   _____   _____
     Do you wear glasses, contacts, or protective eyewear?   _____   _____
11. Have you ever sprained/strained, dislocated, fractured, broken, or had
     repeated swelling of any bones or joints?
     ___ Head   ___ Shoulder ___ Thigh ___ Neck   ___ Elbow ___ Knee   ___ Chest
     ___ Forearm ___ Shin/Calf ___ Back   ___ Wrist ___ Ankle ___ Hip   ___ Hand   ___ Foot
12. Have you ever had any other medical problems?
     (infectious mononucleosis, diabetes)
13. Have you had a medical problem since your last evaluation?
14. When was your last tetanus shot?
     When was your last measles immunization?
Female athletes:
15. What was the longest time between menstrual periods in the last year?

Signature of Parent/Guardian: _____   Date: _____

Signature of Student: _____   Date: _____

Figure 4.1   Medical evaluation form addressing an athlete's personal history.

Figure 4.2 illustrates the rules and guidelines that I have set for my players.

There have been several times when players have committed minor rule violations and the coaching staff has brought them to the attention of the team captains and asked for feedback. Often, captains can share with coaches the sentiments of the team. As coach, you might be fighting hard to save a player and never notice that the rest of the team is ready to move on without her because they believe she's become detrimental to the team. The feedback you receive from captains can provide valuable insights into the chemistry of your team.

Rule/Guideline	Failure to follow rule/guideline may result in all or some of these consequences:
1. Players will adhere to all Oak Ridge High School athletic policies. Regarding training rules, players are prohibited from smoking, drinking alcoholic beverages, and/or using illegal drugs.	Extra conditioning/reduced playing time/ suspension from team/dismissal from team.
2. Players will adhere to all Oak Ridge High School field trip policies.	Extra conditioning/reduced playing time/ suspension from team/dismissal from team.
3. Players will learn the Lady Wildcat Success Plan.	Extra conditioning.
4. Players will attend all required basketball functions. This includes but is not limited to practices, games, and team activities.	Each absence handled individually by the coaching staff.
EXCUSED absence—cleared by a coach prior to the absence.	
UNEXCUSED absence—not cleared by a coach prior to the absence. This includes but is not limited to absences as a result of detention, suspension, or other school disciplinary action.	Extra conditioning/reduced playing time/ suspension from the team/dismissal from the team.
5. Players will report to basketball functions on time. This includes but is not limited to practices, games, meetings, bus trips, and other basketball activities.	Extra conditioning/reduced playing time/ suspension from the team/dismissal from the team.
6. Players will wear appropriate basketball clothing when involved in basketball functions. This includes but is not limited to practice gear, game gear, travel suits, and bus attire.	Extra conditioning/reduced playing time.
Players will return basketball equipment at the end of the season.	Player charged appropriate amount for lost or damaged equipment.
7. Players will be respectful toward coaches.	Extra conditioning/reduced playing time/ suspension from team/dismissal from team.
8. Players will represent themselves, the Lady Wildcat Basketball program, and Oak Ridge High School in an appropriate manner at all times, as outlined in the Lady Wildcat Success Plan.	Extra conditioning/reduced playing time/ suspension from team/dismissal from team.
9. Players are required to ride the team bus to and from all away games. Players will sit alone or with a teammate. Special situations may allow a player to ride home with her parent if a coach is notified on the front end.	Extra conditioning/reduced playing time/ suspension from team.
10. Players will maintain satisfactory academic progress.	Weekly grade check/daily grade check/tutoring /study sessions/reduced playing time/suspension from team/dismissal from team.

Figure 4.2 Rules and guidelines.

Electing Captains

Leadership within a team is essential. Developing leadership is a coach's challenge. Born leaders are a blessing for a team. Some players lead by action, others by word. If you get a player that can do both in a positive manner, you have a player who can be a great leader.

You might elect captains before the season or once the season has begun. In our program, we elect captains after preseason conditioning and the first month of practice is completed but before our first game. I want to wait long enough to give players an opportunity to lead in the preseason if that's their calling. Captains might be senior members of your squad or might be freshmen, although the latter case is rare.

You might elect captains by vote of the team, vote of the coaching staff, or a combination of the two. In our program, we choose to combine votes. I definitely want the players' feedback, so they participate in the vote, but I also value my coaching staff's input. Not surprisingly, in all my years of coaching, players and coaches have not disagreed on whom to elect as captains.

If you feel you have several good leaders on your team, you might want to increase the number of captains. This year we had game captains and practice captains. My two seniors who received most of the players' votes for captain were named as practice and game captains. My two juniors, who received slightly fewer votes, were elected as practice captains only. I really liked the idea of four people leading in practice and sharing in the responsibility of the quality of our practices. Some coaches might rotate captains each game as a way of rewarding positive individual performances.

Remind your captains that they are in leadership roles and are expected to be leaders on and off the court. This is a responsibility that comes with the title and the territory. They are role models and are often quite visible in the community. Let captains know their status can be rescinded if they act in a manner unbecoming to the program. Being a captain is a privilege, not a right.

Determining Starters and Nonstarters

Be careful thinking that it really doesn't matter who starts but who plays and gets the job done. I was once naive and thought that. As a coach, you might feel that way, but over the years I've found very few players or parents who agree. You'll need to share with your players the criteria for being in the starting lineup. Let them know what they need to do in order to start, and also tell them how they could lose their starting position.

I believe practice productivity is extremely important, because so much time is spent on the practice floor. In my program, a starting position is usually won or lost on the practice court. This can become a problem for the "gamers"—those players who are quite talented and turn it up for a game but loaf through practice. You need to challenge these players to raise their performance in practice. If they don't, they can be a cancer on your team and cause ill will. If your best players can get the job done in practice, their impact won't go unnoticed by others.

Injuries and illnesses can affect a starting lineup. We spend most of our practice the day before a game preparing for our opponent. If a starter is absent, excused or unexcused, she doesn't start the next game. She has not been there for the preparation. If the absence is excused, the player will still get considerable playing time, but she won't start. This is not seen as a punishment but as a way to be fair to all team members.

Sometimes your opponent dictates your starting lineup. For example, your usual five starters might be smaller than what you need against a larger team, requiring a change in the usual starting lineup. If this happens, be sure to let all players know the reason for the change.

Your starting lineup might also be affected by a reward system you have in place. For instance, you might be playing a tournament that calls for playing several games in a row, with little or no practice time between games. A player off the bench might have had an outstanding game, and you want to reward her with a start. On the other hand, a player might go into a shooting slump in the middle of a tournament. Maybe you think she would respond better coming off the bench. In either case, share your decision with the affected players.

Nonstarters need to know that the coaching staff and their teammates value them. In many cases, nonstarters aren't going to get the recognition from the public, and often their efforts go unnoticed. As coach, you need to set an example

Players contribute in many different ways on the court. A player off the bench ignites the team with hustle plays.

in how you treat your bench personnel. In our program, we have instituted a Big Six award to present to a player after each ball game. At the conclusion of our postgame meeting, players vote for a teammate who did not start but made significant contributions coming off the bench. We also present a Big Six award to a player at our end-of-the-year banquet. We hope this sends a message that regardless of the minutes played, all players can and do contribute.

Sometimes it doesn't take long to realize that some players come off the bench better than others. Try to get a feel for those players who struggle with confidence. You might ask a player to describe her feelings when she starts a game compared to how she feels when she comes off the bench. Often players will be quite honest, and you can make adjustments accordingly. Sometimes you learn through trial and error. I've observed players who never seem to get out of the gates at the opening tip. However, if I sit them for a minute or two at the start, they come into the game focused and ready to

contribute. Often these players enter a game with such a negative mindset that it's hard for them to perform to their potential. See if you can place positive thoughts in their mind. One year I asked our bench players to enter the game with the thought, *I am going to make a positive contribution.* I didn't want them to feel they had to conquer the world, but I wanted them to make some positive plays. This focus on a positive mindset worked for many players.

One of the hardest awards for me to hand out at the end of the basketball season is the Most Improved Player Award. The problem is that there are usually several players who have really improved their overall game. This is a good problem to have. To accommodate overall team improvement, it's a good idea to add some new wrinkles to your system at the end of the year, before postseason tournaments begin. Usually, players get excited about the new strategies. Some fresh plays might provide your team with a much-needed spark at the end of your season.

Heart of a Champion

My 1990 team was one of the best teams I've ever had at playing their roles. They were also one of the most coachable teams I've ever had. They weren't as talented as some other teams, but they played with great effort and pride. The starting lineup was composed of one "horse" (whom we had rode all season), one good outside shooter who was extremely competitive, one athletic complementary inside player, one player who was not allowed to shoot (ever), and a right-handed-only point guard (that is, no skills with her left hand) whom I had to beg to shoot. We had no bench. We were in the regional finals, playing a team who had a wealth of talent and appeared ready and willing to mow us down. We decided to pick up their point guard full court just to see if we could get into her head—and we did. They pressed our point guard, so our horse had to bring the ball up the floor and then give it up. It was a matter of giving it up and getting it back. She and our outside shooter took the majority of the shots. The others played their roles—rebounding, making great passes, and playing excellent defense. We really had no bench. Our philosophy—team play, role play, and unselfish play—worked. Their point guard couldn't hit a shot because she was so mental about getting picked up full court. Our horse never batted an eye about having to bring the ball up the court as our point guard looked on. Every time our non-shooter got an offensive rebound, she kicked the ball back out—and she was an excellent offensive rebounder. That night they played with the hearts of champions, and it earned them a regional title. That game is one of my fondest memories in coaching. It's been more than 10 years since, but that special team still gets together as friends off the court.

ESTABLISHING PRIDE AND TRADITION

Pride and tradition are intangibles that can separate the great programs from the good ones. Former coaches and players can help you instill pride and team spirit in your program. If your school enjoys a rich tradition of success, sometimes that tradition alone can give your team an edge over an opponent. Not only does your team feel confident, but your opponent might sense your team is invincible. If your program has no tradition in place, challenge them to be the foundation players for building a rich tradition.

One way to instill a sense of pride and tradition in your current team is to bring back former players. Former players are often very motivational and sentimental about your program. They can share what it meant to them to put on the uniform.

Our community takes a lot of pride in our program. One way they showed this was by donating generously to the rebuilding of our team room. We now have one of the nicest team rooms I've seen in a high school program. Our room displays trophies, plaques, and pictures of former players. Our current players are proud to show off this room. They hope one day they will contribute to the wall of champions and have their picture displayed. This room is a source of pride for all current and former players.

I want our players to know and understand the Lady Wildcat tradition that has been evolving for years (figure 4.3). This is something they are a part of just by playing in the program. I tell each team they will leave their mark. I challenge each group by asking them, "How do you want to be remembered? What will be your legacy?"

Class On and Off the Court

If you want to run a first-class program, you must instill class, demand class, and demonstrate class. As coach, you are the model for your players to follow. There's a classy way to win a game and a classy way to lose a game. Your players will take their cues from you, so conduct yourself in the way you want your players to conduct themselves. Being able to handle adversity is a life lesson, not just a basketball lesson. Help your players feel good about giving their best, regardless of the ultimate result.

Try to help your players understand that class goes beyond the confines of the court. There is a way we act in the classroom and in the community that exudes class. There's a certain image you want your team to portray. You might have to paint them a picture for them to understand.

Lady Wildcat Tradition

What is it? How do I become a part of it?

- It is a tradition of *excellence* that has been demonstrated through the years and is expected of *all Lady Wildcats.*
- In part, it is a *free gift* you have not earned.
- In part, it is a *standard* others before you have set.
- *You* are expected to learn the *tradition* and through your actions be part of the *tradition.*

One day you will be expected to teach the tradition to new Lady Wildcats.

As a Lady Wildcat:

1. I strive to be the best I can be—In the community, classroom, and on the court.
2. I take pride in my appearance—My dress on and off the court.
3. I am well mannered—I am respectful of others. I show respect by addressing others with "please," "thank you," "yes sir/ma'am," and "no sir/ma'am."
4. I am appreciative—I show my appreciation for all I receive from my coaches, teachers, and parents.
5. I recognize I am a part of a first-class program—Boosters, budget, practice gear, meals, etc.
6. I practice a certain way—Intense, competitive, defensive, fundamental.
7. I play a certain way—Team oriented, coachable, disciplined.
8. I recognize I am a part of a family and have a big support system.

To those who are given much—much is expected.

Figure 4.3 The Lady Wildcat tradition.

I tell my players that the little things as well as the big things display class in a person. It's how we dress, how we speak, how we handle the tough times, and how we handle success. It's how we carry ourselves when no one is looking and also when all eyes are on us.

Alumni Importance

Former players can be terrific ambassadors for your program. Find ways to keep in touch with them, especially those who have added something special during their time on the team. We have a Tip-Off Club at Oak Ridge, which is a booster club comprised of many former players. This club gives to our program monetarily and receives a monthly newsletter that helps them keep up with each year's season. This is an easy way to stay connected with alumni and form lasting bonds. Some programs hold alumni games, which are truly enjoyable and meaningful events. The mingling of former and current players can be quite special.

Giving Back

A couple of summers ago, Jennifer Azzi, a former player at Oak Ridge, was in town visiting her parents. She stopped by the gym to visit during a summer camp session. She was eager and happy to take the time to talk with young campers about her experiences at Oak Ridge High School and Stanford University and as a member of the USA Olympic team. She talked about hard work, not cutting corners, and being the best you can be. She had a captive audience. Those campers were able to see and hear a wonderful success story. I was so proud that Jennifer still considers herself a member of the Lady Wildcat family. She still felt the pride and tradition she had carried during her high school days.

Feeder Programs

Your feeder programs are part of your basketball program and should be treated as such.

Feeder programs can include your community youth programs, middle school or junior high programs, and your freshman and junior varsity squads. There might also be special programs in your community that involve youths, such as summer basketball camps or fall youth clinics. As the head coach, try to reach out to all these groups and show your support by finding ways to get involved. Doing so tells the youngsters who belong to these groups that you have an interest in them and their future. If you can hold camps and clinics, you can teach these youngsters your philosophy, as well as the skills of the game. You can get your players to be a part of your camps and clinics, too. Youngsters love to interact with current players.

Find ways to get involved in your middle school or junior high programs. Watch a practice or attend a game. Let those coaches and players know you have an interest in them. Each year I send our middle school coaches the same coaching packet that I give to my staff. In this packet is our system—our philosophy, style of play, points of emphasis, and offensive and defensive strategies. I want our schools' coaches to be familiar with our program, and I would love for their program to implement as much of our system as possible.

Getting many players involved in your program is a plus. Each year we hope to fill a junior varsity squad and a freshman squad. Time spent with each of these coaching staffs and teams is time well spent for your program. Try to find time to visit their practices; attend as many games as possible. Seek out ways to get your players involved. Maybe your players can act as Big Sisters to the younger players in the feeder programs. If you want these players to move to the next level and continue in your program, show them you care about them.

Ideally, your junior varsity and freshman teams will run your system. Of course each team needs to adjust to the players they have, but they can still be running your system. If you have a system that works and which you believe in, try to get your feeder clubs to buy into it. This will make your job easier, and your teams better, in the long run.

As I've mentioned in a previous chapter, if a freshman is good enough to contribute on the varsity team, I give her the opportunity. I would hesitate to move a player up if we're going to use her only sparingly. She'd get much more playing time, and thus more helpful experience, as an impact player on the junior varsity or freshman squad. Still, you might want to reward your younger players by giving them a chance to earn varsity playing time. This is a great motivator for younger players. Along the same lines, this year I moved up three freshman players at the end of their season but before our tournaments began. They had earned a chance to move up, plus I felt the tournament experience would be very beneficial to them down the road.

Also, encourage your freshman and junior varsity coaches to be as much a part of the varsity program as their schedule allows. Some coaches love to sit on the bench during games. Some might even be willing to do some scouting for you. If they want to get plugged in, consider it a blessing and make it work.

GAINING SYSTEM SUPPORT

Wouldn't every coach want his or her team to be the talk of the town? That takes more than just winning games. People watch how you win and how you don't win. They watch how you and your team carry yourselves. There are many groups out there you'll want to win over and thereby gain support for your program. I believe that support starts in your own building, with your administration. Share your philosophy and goals with your administrators. Administrators like to be informed. If you have a first-class product, your principal will be proud to mention your program when he or she has opportunities to speak to community groups. Let administrators know your program is not just about winning. Show them you are a team player. You can do this by showing your support for academics, clubs, and other athletic teams. If your team has a great opportunity to travel, for instance, let your administrator know the benefits your players can gain through such an experience. Invite your administrators to your games. Ask them to travel with your team on one of your away trips. Let them see your team up close, off the court.

You can reach out in the same manner to your central office staff, your assistant superintendent, and your director of schools. Make them aware you have a good product and that you want to show off that product to them. School board members might attend a game if invited.

We're fortunate at Oak Ridge to have a very supportive group of administrators. Our principal, Ken Green, is a former athlete and understands the value of athletics in a young person's life. He attended college on a scholarship and understands athletics can open doors for many young people. Our assistant principal, Chuck Carringer, traveled with us this past season to the Nike Tournament of Champions in Phoenix, Arizona. He wanted not only to attend our games but to travel with the team and be a part of our experience. This show of support really meant a lot to our players and staff. Rarely a home game goes by that we don't have in attendance our assistant superintendent and our director of schools. Yes, we are a one high school town, but the support our administration gives us is wonderful.

If you don't have your administration's support, maybe it's time to step back and reevaluate. It is important to be open and up front with your administrators. If there's a problem, let them know you're anxious to work it out. Keep your lines of communication open.

Student Support

There's nothing in basketball like a home-court advantage when your stands are filled with a spirited student body. Find ways to get the students out in numbers. Some schools have a student section. At our school we give students free T-shirts and rope off a section for the students to sit at each home game. The students have fun dressing up in crazy gear and painting up in school colors. They add a lot of excitement to the game atmosphere. Our players really enjoy the show of support. A free night's admission might bring out students who otherwise couldn't afford to come. As I've mentioned, at our school we offer a free night to each grade (9th, 10th, 11th, 12th) for the first four home games. We hope to get some students hooked on the game so they'll come back. On some game nights when the weather is mild, students tailgate in the parking lot. They come to the game early and cook out with their peers before tip-off. This pregame get-together becomes quite an event, and student numbers start to increase. It's amazing the response you can get from your players when their peers come out in numbers. Having them there is not only a source of motivation but instills pride in the players. Everyone wants to play well in front of their peers.

Community Support

Fill your stands not only with students but also with fans and supporters from your community. If you have a local paper, make sure your game schedule and roster get printed at least once early in the season. At home games, you can admit special community groups free of charge. Maybe make one night senior citizen night and another middle school night. There are endless community groups you could invite in hopes to hook them on your basketball team. If they like the product, they'll be back.

Local media can provide an avenue to promote your program and gain support. Most local newspapers will print your schedule, a roster, and perhaps a team picture if you provide them with those items. Newspapers are always looking for great feature stories for their sport's section. You might have to write the article, but that's not too time consuming, especially if you can send it off through e-mail. Getting your game scores and statistics in your paper might take only a phone call on your end. Great coverage helps your community keep up with your team and perhaps can form a following. In Oak Ridge we have a local paper, *The Oak Ridger,* and our sports writer, Mike Blackerby, gives the Lady Wildcats excellent preseason, season, and postseason coverage. He not only covers our games but also writes many feature articles about players, past and present. He's also quite willing to help us with our promotions, clinics, and summer camps.

Some communities have local radio programs that carry ball games live. In Oak Ridge, all our games are broadcast live, and coaches do a postgame show on the radio. This allows fans who can't attend games to follow your team. Additionally, our radio voice of the Wildcats, David Clary, hosts a weekly cable TV show called "Off the Glass," a coach's show that includes game commentary and game footage. Throughout the season players are special guests on the show.

This show runs weekly in our community and is another way fans can get an up-close look at the Lady Wildcat program. The more fans see our faces, the more familiar they become with our program. Over time, the same can happen for your program.

Faculty Support

If you can gain the support of your school's faculty, you have gained a lot. To help this process, let teachers know that academics are important to you and that teachers have your support. I think this needs to be a two-way street. If you have a good working relationship with the faculty, help seems to come easier, whether that means in making up missed work, a missed test, or scheduling a tutor. If you can be flexible with teachers, they tend to be more flexible with you and your players.

One of the first things our players do is introduce themselves to their teachers and give them a game schedule. This way, teachers know at the outset about any class time a player might have to miss. Our coaching staff communicates frequently with teachers. We have an understanding that players are expected to do their best in class, which includes their behavior. If a teacher tells me about a behavior problem with one of our players, we address it immediately, and corrections are made. I want teachers to be excited to have a Lady Wildcat in their class.

PROMOTING YOUR BASKETBALL PROGRAM

Basketball is now a 12-month season. This might not be true for players, but it's more and more true for coaches. If you have a great product, you want to maintain that level of success. You want to share your product with others as much as you can to gain further support.

Booster Clubs and Fundraising At Oak Ridge we have a very active and supportive booster club. For a small membership fee, anyone can join, but our members are primarily parents and a few community members. Their main function is to help raise funds to add to our athletic budget, but they also provide manpower at many of our basketball functions. We try not to involve players or coaches in fundraising during the season, so much of this is done before the season begins. Once the season starts, you and your players have enough work to do. Plus, parents want to sit back and enjoy the games without having to think about raising money. One of our best sources of revenue has been the printed programs for our basketball games. We sell program ads to businesses to raise these funds. If you can get a lot of businesses to reply, which is likely once your teams become successful, you can raise quite a bit of money for your program.

Additional fundraisers our basketball boosters have helped with include our yearly golf tournament, Thanksgiving Hoop Classic, and our annual fall coaching clinic. These events raise funds and are also great sources of PR for our program and team travel.

Youth Clinics Holding a free clinic for girls in your community is a great way to work with local youths and get them into your gym. They get a chance to see your facilities and to work with you, your staff, and your players. They learn some skills and are introduced to the success of your system. Each fall in Oak Ridge our team holds a free youth clinic for girls in grades one through six. In addition, our youth coaches are invited to watch the clinic and stay afterward for a question-and-answer session with our staff.

The clinic is a super opportunity for our current players to teach future Lady Wildcats, and the parental feedback has been very positive. We try to make the evening instructional by teaching fundamental skills such as dribbling, shooting, passing, and defensive footwork. We add a competitive component to the evening with dribbling relays and shooting competitions. We want youngsters to enjoy the clinic while they're learning. Our players do an excellent job of interacting with the youngsters—you can tell by the laughter heard throughout the gym. At the end of the evening we award T-shirts to competitors in our Lady Wildcat name recognition contest and other games.

Summer Camps Summer camps give you and your staff another opportunity to connect with the youths in your community. At Oak Ridge, we offer a variety of camps for ages 10 through 17.

We hold shooting camps, position camps, youth coed camps, and weeklong individual camps. I have been amazed how eager young girls are to learn the game. We staff our camps with high school coaches and players, coaches from our feeder programs, and former players.

Charity Events When opportunities arise, playing in a charity event can be good PR for your program. Plus, participating in these events is a good way to give back to the community. Find events that you, your staff, and your players can be a part of. There are many good causes to which your program can contribute.

Hosting a charity event is a great way to get a large number of people into your gym. Each year our community Boy's Club holds their fundraiser basketball game in our gym. The place is usually packed with fans as well as community dignitaries. Our players and coaches are very visible, sometimes taking part in the game. The Boy's Club is appreciative of the use of the gym, and we get a chance to help raise some needed funds for a worthy cause.

Team Meals Taking your team out into the community to eat a team meal is a lot of fun and also a chance for you to establish some PR with community restaurants. There are ways to get these restaurants to feed your team at no expense. One method we use is to offer restaurants a full-page ad in our basketball game program in exchange for a team meal. Our community has responded very generously. We eat some meals out and eat some meals at the gym after practice. This is good PR for the restaurant, and the girls enjoy a fun, relaxing time with their teammates. We try to spread these meals out throughout the season to offer breaks and rewards for our team. Judging by the number of restaurants willing to take part, these ventures are win–win situations for the restaurants and our team.

SUMMARY

- Good teams come and go. Great programs last.
- Personnel may dictate your team's style of play.
- Surround yourself with quality people—staff and players.
- Develop rules and guidelines for your team. Let the punishment fit the crime.
- Have and communicate your criteria for starting a player.
- Captains provide excellent leadership for your team.
- Instill team pride in your players; teach them the tradition of your program.
- Class is important on and off the court.
- Alumni can give back and help connect the past to the present.
- Incorporate feeder programs into your program.
- Share your team's system with your feeder programs.
- To gain support for your program, reach out to the various factions you interact with, including administrators, faculty, student body, and community members.
- If you have a first-class program, find ways to promote it.
- An active booster's club can help you with fundraisers and special events.
- Give back to your community by participating in charity events.
- Let your local media help you spread the good word about your program.
- Connect with the young people in your community through summer camps and youth clinics.
- Seek opportunities to meet with civic organizations and talk about your program.
- Plan fun events for your team, such as team meals and other outings.

PART II

COACHING PLANS

CHAPTER 5

PLANNING FOR THE SEASON

It seems just as one season draws to a close, it's time to start planning for the next season. Part of that planning is enjoyable. You look at current personnel and upcoming players and begin to discuss coaching strategies with your staff. The plotting and scheming are fun. But there's also the paperwork and the busy work involved in planning for the next season. You must collect forms, organize meetings, and devise a timetable to address all the responsibilities for next year's season.

One thing I have found helpful is to organize my program by months of the season and the off-season. I plot out my "to dos" on a calendar as well as plan out the teaching parts of my season. As I look at each month, I first identify what needs to be accomplished in the program, and then I consider what needs to be accomplished by our team. I have found this to be a helpful way to organize my staff, my players, and myself.

YEARLY TIMETABLE

As school begins in August, so does basketball. Much of the planning for the upcoming season is already under way. Ideally at this point most of the paperwork is completed on your players. I usually give our players a few weeks to get acclimated to their new school year and class load. Players need to be reminded of the importance of academics. We begin our weight program about two weeks after school has begun. Our actual conditioning and preseason program doesn't begin until six weeks before our first official practice. Our first practice date is set by our governing body, the Tennessee Secondary Schools Athletic Association (TSSAA). They dictate the date for our first game, and our first practice is 21 days before that. Usually, that means our first practice is in early November. Each state and association has their own guidelines.

When planning for the upcoming season, I find it helpful to divide the season into three parts. The first part begins with day one of practice and runs until Christmas break. During this time we introduce our system to our players and begin its implementation. We're trying to complement our talent. We cover all situations that might be encountered in a game. By Christmas break, we will have played approximately 10 games. As a coach, I think this is a good time to meet with your staff, reflect on and evaluate the start of your season, and plan any changes that need to be implemented in the next part of your season.

The second part of our season runs from Christmas break through the end of the regular season. This is usually the most difficult part of the year. The newness of the season has worn off, and tournaments seem far away. I refer to this part of the season as the "dog days." As a coach, I try to shorten my practices when possible or give players a day off. The challenge here is to keep players hungry and competitive. In this segment, we try to add to our playbook because we will play our district teams (league teams) for the second time. We want to be somewhat unpredictable—unless we're by far the stronger team. Ideally, by this time of the year you will have built up some depth and can begin to incorporate more players into your game strategies. By the end of this part of the season, we have likely played about 30 games.

The third and last part of our season we call "tournament time." This time usually rejuvenates both players and coaches, and most of us consider it the best part of the season. Prior to our opening tournament game, we add a few wrinkles to our system. Again, this keeps the juices flowing for our players and helps prepare us for anything our opponent throws our way. We also might add players to our roster to reward them and strengthen our numbers. Tournament time can be as short as a single game or as long as 10 games. By dividing the season into three parts, I find it easier for my staff and me to narrow our focus and cover all our bases.

To Do List by Month

One way to help you organize yourself and your program is to place your monthly basketball reminders in your calendar or daily planner. In addition, your "to dos" can be divided up. In our program, the boys' basketball staff will sometimes take the lead on a project, or sometimes it's one of my assistants. Regardless of who gets the job done, there's always another "to do" waiting in the wings. Without the help of others, all these projects could never be completed. On the other hand, I believe there's more to a first-class program than just the work done on the basketball court.

If you sit down and look at what you need to accomplish each month, you can come up with your own to do list (figure 5.1). You might be surprised at all you and your staff do to make your program a success.

Monthly To Do List

March
Individual player meetings
Senior meetings
Attend state tournament
Thank you cards mailed
Equipment inventory
Team camp letter
Brochure for summer camps
Scheduling begins
Begin budget work
Final Tip-Off newsletter
Organize team banquet

April
Finish scheduling
Submit budget
Mail team camp information
Mail summer camp brochures
Visit middle schools
Devise summer calendar for team

Identify next year's clinic speakers
Hire camp workers
Meet with staff to plan spring practice
Team banquet

May
Call middle school players
Call rising seniors
Articles in newspaper about summer camps
Hold spring practice and tryouts
Finalize summer plans for players
Seek out new fundraising ideas
Jr. Wildcat flyer
Visit coaches
Officials for team camp
Workers for individual camp
Prepare free-throw fundraiser
Mail team camp schedules
Call vendors about equipment
Weights

Player free physicals
AAU games
Meet with booster president
Travel plans for Christmas
Golf tournament

June
Weights
Team camps
Open gym
AAU games
Team room ideas
Summer camps

July
Weights
Tip-Off brochure to printer
Open gym

August
Letters to teachers
Mail Tip-Off brochure
Finalize game promotions
Order new stationary
Schedule coaches retreat
Prepare booster budget
Prepare conditioning program
Copy of players' schedule
Team room work
State tournament motel reservations
Junior Wildcat mail out
Jr. Wildcat and Tip-Off info sent to
    newspaper
Game corporate sponsors
Player meetings

September
Program ad committee meeting
Call restaurants for meals
Schedule bus times
Order coaching clothes
Begin conditioning program
Select ball girls
Finalize freshman and JV games
Tip-Off newsletter
Type schedule Varsity, JV, and Freshman
Mail out scrimmage information
Get scrimmage day officials
Complete eligibility forms
Order nameplates

Attend a clinic
Host coach's clinic
Pregame music selection
Work on staff notebook
Organize equipment room
Order workout gear
Promotional nights

October
Devise scouting calendar
Organize Tip-Off lunch
Tip-Off newsletter
Prepare master list—Xs & Os
Visit college practices
Early dismissal times to office
Opponent file folders updated
Individual player meetings
Conditioning workouts
Grade check

November
Tryouts for new students
Scrimmage days
Eligibility sent for all players
Holiday schedules made
Packet sent to middle schools
Shirt sent to middle schools
Receive middle schools rosters and game
    schedules
Youth clinic
First practice

December
Tip-Off newsletter
Winter camp
Tip-Off night/Jr. Wildcat night
Game promotions
Travel plans secured
Team travel

January
Tip-Off luncheon
Tip-Off newsletter
Set camp dates
Organize golf tournament information

February
Tip-Off newsletter
Select camp dates

Figure 5.1 Example of a monthly to do list.

Conditioning Your Athletes

A well-conditioned athlete has a better chance of performing closer to her potential than a poorly conditioned athlete. Basketball today, with AAU and summer camps, is nearly year-round. Thus, conditioning should be nearly year-round. Your well-conditioned athletes will likely perform better and will be less likely to be injured.

Preseason Conditioning   Players often think of preseason conditioning as a necessary evil. It's important to make this time of year productive for your players but also enjoyable. Not all hard work has to be dreadful. Explaining to your players the benefits of conditioning might help ease some of the pain. I remind my players that getting in shape is harder than staying in shape. Once they get in decent shape, staying there is not so tough. As a coach, ask yourself what you want this time to produce.

In our program, we have outlined four areas we hope preseason conditioning can enhance: physical fitness (increased strength, speed and agility), mental toughness, leadership development, and team bonding. To accomplish our goals in these four areas, we run hills, distances, and sprints; incorporate agilities and footwork exercises into our training; and implement a weightlifting program (figure 5.2).

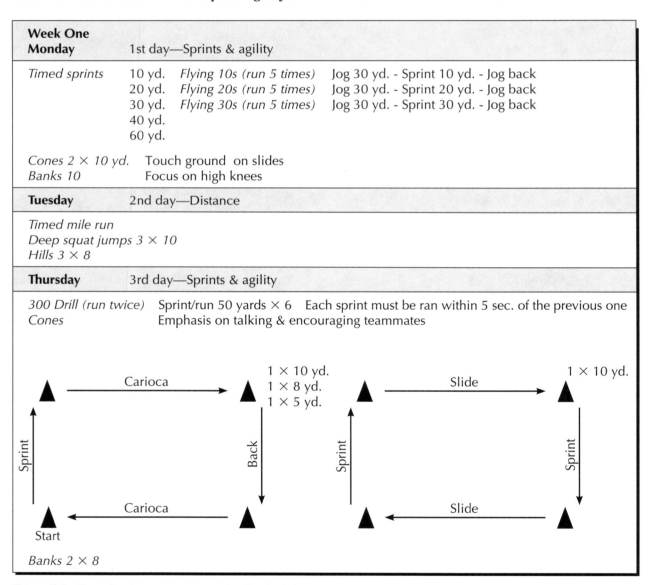

Week One		
Monday	1st day—Sprints & agility	
Timed sprints	10 yd. *Flying 10s (run 5 times)*	Jog 30 yd. - Sprint 10 yd. - Jog back
	20 yd. *Flying 20s (run 5 times)*	Jog 30 yd. - Sprint 20 yd. - Jog back
	30 yd. *Flying 30s (run 5 times)*	Jog 30 yd. - Sprint 30 yd. - Jog back
	40 yd.	
	60 yd.	
Cones 2 × 10 yd. Touch ground on slides		
Banks 10 Focus on high knees		
Tuesday	2nd day—Distance	
Timed mile run		
Deep squat jumps 3 × 10		
Hills 3 × 8		
Thursday	3rd day—Sprints & agility	
300 Drill (run twice) Sprint/run 50 yards × 6 Each sprint must be ran within 5 sec. of the previous one		
Cones Emphasis on talking & encouraging teammates		

Carioca   1 × 10 yd.
            1 × 8 yd.
            1 × 5 yd.

Slide   1 × 10 yd.

Sprint   Back   Sprint   Sprint

Carioca   Slide

Start

Banks 2 × 8

Figure 5.2   Sample of a preseason workout schedule.

Our preseason conditioning is usually a six-week program—the six weeks prior to our official first practice. Weightlifting is the one element we incorporate into our program year-round. During our season, we cut back on the number of days we lift as well as the number of repetitions in our weight workout. The focus of our weight workout is to maintain the strength acquired in our preseason weight-training program.

Off-Season Conditioning   The off-season is that time just after the season ends and before your fall preseason conditioning program begins. Off-season conditioning will vary for your players, depending on other commitments they have. For example, some might devote much time to AAU practice and games, whereas others might be out of town a good deal because of summer vacations.

In our state we are allowed 15 days of off-season practice with our teams in the spring. In addition, our school board implements their guidelines, and they limit us to 10 days of spring practice. We use this time for tryouts for next year's squad and for practice time. Of course any student who is new to our school in the summer or fall will have an opportunity to try out. Two to three days are used to try out players. The rest of the time we spend on fundamental skill work, team play, and implementation of new strategies to complement our new roster. These 10 days are actually part of our off-season conditioning program and usually occur in early May.

Summer month workouts often vary from year to year, depending on numbers in the program (freshman, junior varsity, and varsity players) as well as the number of players in town. In our state we're allowed unlimited practice time, with the exception of a two-week dead period. June is usually our busiest month with our players. During June we have additional practices, open gym sessions, and weight workouts; we also host a couple of team camps and travel to team camps.

During the summer months, weight workouts are offered for players three times a week (figure 5.3). Players have several options to work out in the weight room because basketball and football coaches work together to open the weight room at different times and athletes can choose a time that fits into their schedule. Our assistant athletic director, Mike Mullins, organizes the weight workout for our players. Mike is extremely knowledgeable in this area, and his expertise and assistance are always eagerly welcomed and appreciated.

Early practices in the summer are geared toward getting players into shape and preparing them for June team camps. Once camps are over, open gym sessions are made available to players. I want players to have an opportunity to get into the gym and work on their game.

It can be very beneficial to give post players and perimeter players a summer workout plan. If you decide that a summer plan would be helpful for your players, make sure to encourage

Summer Weight Workout

Hang clean	2 × 6 @ 60%	2 × 5 @ 68%
Back squat	2 × 10 @ 60%	2 × 8 @ 68%
Bench	2 × 10 @ 60%	2 × 8 @ 68%
Big 40	Front, side, upright row, power press	
Lat pulldown	3 × 10	
Leg extensions	3 × 10	
Triceps or biceps	3 × 10	
Crunches in between EACH set		

Figure 5.3   Summer workout plan for the weight room.

them to stick to it as many days as they can throughout the summer. A plan should focus on developing the skills needed for each position (figure 5.4).

Your school might have limitations on summer workouts. It's my belief that players are made in the off-season, so I strongly encourage all our players to work on their game during the summer months. Players can work during open gyms but are strongly encouraged to work on their own.

PRESEASON PLANNING

As I mentioned, the preseason is the time to get some of the tedious but necessary paperwork in order and to make sure your program is ready to roll once the season starts. There's rarely enough time to get everything done before the season begins, so get a jump on these tasks as early as you can. Most of what needs to be done falls under the categories of medical planning and consent, academic support, scheduling of games, and providing proper equipment and facilities.

Medical Planning and Consent

Medical support personnel are extremely important in a contact sport such as basketball. Most coaches today don't have the training to address player injuries. Plus, in this age of rampant lawsuits, it's smart to have trained personnel to work with injuries.

A certified athletic trainer is a welcome addition to a basketball team. Ideally, this individual is available before and after practices for treatment of injuries and during practice time should an injury occur. Perhaps your school can supply your team with student trainers in addition to a certified trainer. Student trainers are helpful in assisting with minor injuries. If money is an issue, perhaps your school system or the professionals in your community can help with funding.

At Oak Ridge we're fortunate to have a full-time athletic trainer plus several student trainers. The athletic trainer is available to many sports at one time; however, each sport has its own student trainer. With this setup, the certified trainer is available to handle specific injuries or rehabilitation needs, and the student trainer can assist on a daily basis and be at the practice sight to treat minor injuries.

For a player to participate in your program, she must complete and turn in a parent or guardian permission form. This form serves several purposes. First, the signing of the form acknowledges the player's desire to participate in your sport and gives a parent's or guardian's consent. Second, all athletes need insurance, and insurance information needs to be provided by the parent or guardian to the coach. Finally, any specific rules your school might have for team travel can be outlined on this form. At Oak Ridge we call this form a Sports Information and Permission Form (shown in chapter 4) Each athlete must complete this form and have it signed by a parent or guardian.

Academic Support

I strongly recommend having an academic support system in place to help your athletes. At Oak Ridge, the registrar helps inform coaches of a player's eligibility status as well as her current grades. Teachers are contacted at the midterm of each nine-week grading period to check on each player's academic status. Teachers are also encouraged to e-mail coaches at any time should they have a concern about a basketball player in their class. It's important that teachers know you support their efforts. Tutoring might be a beneficial tool for a player falling behind in a class or achieving less than desired results. Try to work out a time for your player to attend tutoring sessions. Most schools offer tutoring opportunities. At Oak Ridge we offer tutoring before and after school and during lunch. Tutoring might be done by a teacher or by an honor student. Our guidance department offers all types of academic aids to help prep our students for college entrance exams. Students are also assigned a counselor who is actively involved with helping each student prepare for her post–high school career choice, be that college or work. If one of our players is interested in playing basketball after high school, I will sit down with that player and her parent or guardian and help them in their decision making. This process can be overwhelming for players and

Summer Workout for Post and Perimeter Players

Ball handling	Stationary	2 minutes
	Seven full court and backs	1. Speed 2. Hesitation 3. In and out 4. Stutter step 5. Stutter crossover 6. Between legs 7. Choice
	Weak hand	5 × speed dribble 10-second rest
Footwork	Lane slides	4 × 30 seconds (gym)
	Rope skip	4 × 30 seconds (gym) Right leg, left leg, both legs, jogging
	Banks	3 × 10 (hills) 2-minute rest between sets
	Lines	10/22/33 × 2 (gym) 30-second rest between each 1-minute rest between sets
	Sprints	110 jog, 110 sprint, 110 jog, 110 sprint (track) Run 4 of each 2-minute rest between sets
	Agilities	Length of court (gym) 1. High-stepping 2. Backward 3. Carioca 4. Forward Run 3 of each 30-second rest between sets
Shooting: Post players	Layups	X-outs × 10 3 sets 1-minute rest between sets
	Back to basket	Drop step baseline; make 20 both sides Pivot middle; make 20 both sides Crossover; make 20 both sides
	Free throws	Make 25
	Face-up shots	Elbow; make 20 both sides Lag; make 20 both sides
	Shots off dribble	Power layups from high post; make 20 both sides
Shooting: Perimeter players	Layups	X-outs × 10 3 sets 1-minute rest between sets
	One on one	Start at half court; make 10 × 3 1-minute rest between sets
	Shots off screen	1 dribble shot, left and right; make 10 × 3
	Free throws	Make 25
	Shots off pass	Wing; make 10 × 3 Top of key; make 10 × 3
	Threes	Make 25
Workout order	1. Ball handling 2. Shooting 3. Footwork	

Figure 5.4 Example of a summer workout plan for post and perimeter players.

families, and they might benefit much from some good advice.

When freshmen enter our program, they are made fully aware of the importance of academics, which include class work, course selections, and college entrance exams. Remind players they are students first and athletes second. As the coach, you might have to be the one who seeks out the academic support available in your school.

Game Schedule

Each coach has his or her own philosophy on what opponents to schedule or not schedule and when to schedule certain games. Talent, depth, and experience are always factors to consider as you begin scheduling opponents. If you have a young team, or a marginally talented team, you might want to ease up on the competition for the year. If your team is talented and experienced, you might put together an extremely competitive schedule to prepare them for tournaments down the road. If you're in a district or conference, you will have teams you have to play each season. Placing these teams strategically into your schedule might help your team. For instance, if your team is young and fragile, scheduling your toughest opponent late is often a wise decision.

Your state might have travel rules for your team that affect whether you can travel to tournaments. Many teams try to play in holiday tournaments over Thanksgiving or Christmas. If you can travel, these tournaments are a wonderful opportunity for your team to see the world (or at least other parts of the country) and compete against quality competition. In Tennessee, we are in a state that allows us to travel. We've tried to play in a quality tournament over each holiday. The travel is great for team bonding, and the level of competition makes us better in the end. There are so many quality tournaments; if you can attend one, the rewards are tremendous.

We schedule varsity and junior varsity games in the spring. By the end of the school year, our schedule is complete. The only games left to schedule are our freshman games, which we schedule in the fall. Our governing body stipulates how many varsity and freshman games we can play in the regular season and how games are counted in tournament play. You'll need to abide by your state's guidelines, if any, for scheduling games.

Equipment and Facilities

A final element in preparing for your season is providing your players with the proper equipment. One of my jobs in the spring is to inventory equipment so that I can order what we need for the next season. After taking inventory, I put together a basketball budget and submit it to our athletic director. Our school system uses a bidding process when ordering equipment—a process that I highly recommend. Sporting equipment representatives bid on the products a coach wishes to purchase. Once all bids have been received, the coach decides which bid is the best deal. For example, if a coach wishes to purchase a new set of uniforms, through a bidding process he or she can find out the lowest price for those uniforms. We saved our budget a lot of money by using this process. If you can use the bidding process, keep in mind service as well as price. The lowest bid does not always mean the best bargain. If we need items that exceed our budgets, we either raise the funds or call on our boosters to help us out financially.

Uniforms Players want to feel good about putting on their uniform. Feeling good and looking good can be catalysts for playing good. The game uniform also sends a message to fans. First-class uniforms portray a first-class image. You can have a first-class uniform without paying top dollar. Style and fit don't necessarily equate expense. If you're willing to look, you can find affordable uniforms that look first class but that fit your budget.

Because uniforms can be one of the greatest expenses in your budget, it pays to shop around. We order new uniforms about every three years. Our players have a home uniform and an away uniform. When the varsity team gets a new uniform, we pass their old uniforms down to the junior varsity for additional wear. The freshman players get new uniforms every four or five years. To make these uniforms last, I don't let players take them home. I launder them myself. One mistake in laundering can ruin a uniform. Laundry duty is a small inconvenience for me but beneficial in the long run.

Players appreciate and enjoy the opportunity to give their opinions on uniform styles. I have even taken groups of players to the uniform plant to see the latest styles. The players are the ones who will be wearing the uniforms, so I want their input. Plus, they like having a voice in the decision.

Practice Gear   Along with ordering new uniforms now and then, you also have to order practice gear. To make the word "team" the focus of our practices, all our players dress alike each day in their team practice gear. Practice gear is a budgeted item. Our varsity gets two new sets each season so they can wear them every other day. Players are given the responsibility of washing them. After the varsity wears a set for a year, they are passed down to the junior varsity for a season, and then passed down to the freshman squad. Every four or five years, the freshmen receive their own new set of practice gear.

For us, practice gear is a reversible jersey and a pair of shorts. The reversible jersey makes it easy for players to switch teams during a scrimmage. Our players wear their game shoes for practices. Game shoes are of high quality. Because many players go through one pair of shoes before the season is complete and the school doesn't have the money to purchase an additional pair for them, our players are given the option of purchasing an additional pair of shoes at the bid price. I want our players to wear our practice clothing the way the gear is made to be worn, regardless of the current styles. We want our players to look good in their practice gear, just as they do in their game gear. We pay a little more for our practice gear, but I believe it's well worth it. Players are proud and appreciative of the practice gear they receive.

Teaching Aids   Many teaching aids are available that you might find helpful in your program. Over the years we've purchased several such aids, including heavy balls for upper body strength, dribble goggles for improved ball handling, and shooting disks and straps to improve shooting form. A few years ago our booster club helped us to purchase a Shoot-a-Way machine, which enabled players to get to the gym and work on their shot. Which teaching aids you'll want to consider depends on the needs of your basketball team. You can find teaching aids in physical education equipment ordering catalogues, often in the basketball or game section.

Basketballs   Each year we order the basketballs our state has adopted for use in the state tournament. They are usually a high-quality leather basketball. Because we hold a number of summer camps and use our basketballs frequently, we order new balls each season. When our balls become a little worn but remain in fairly good shape, we offer them to our feeder programs. Because of their limited budgets, they are usually quite appreciative.

First-Aid Supplies   You never know when an injury might occur, so your team needs to be equipped with appropriate first-aid supplies for practices and games. At Oak Ridge we have a certified athletic trainer who's very knowledgeable about necessary equipment, so we let her provide us with a list of first-aid supplies to order. Then we include her first-aid order in our total budget. The first-aid supplies are easily accessible at both practice and games.

Safety and proper care of injuries need to be a priority in your program. When I first started coaching, we didn't have an athletic trainer. Volunteer trainers from our local therapy center helped us out for games and practices. You might want to look into this if your school system doesn't have a certified trainer on staff.

Facilities   Your facilities, such as your gym, are usually provided by your school system. Some coaches are fortunate to have a new or renovated facility, but in middle schools and high schools that's far from the norm. If you're not among the fortunate in this respect, you must work with what you have. To make your gym look the best it can look, add some touches to it. A new coat of paint before the opening game might be the cheapest and easiest way to give a fresh look to your gym. New nets, cleaned backboards, and a waxed floor also add a new feeling to an older gym. If you have artists in residence, they might agree to paint your school's mascot on your floor or to draw an athletic mural on your gym wall. Creativity can produce wonderful results.

Players nowadays take pride in their dressing facility. We call this their "team room." Again, you might have little input on what this room is like, so chances are you'll need to take what you're given. However, with a certain amount of creativity and time, you can customize this room to suit the style of your team. When our team room was renovated a few years back, we were given a new, clean, but very generic team room, which our parents and boosters promptly decided to upgrade. Because of their money and manpower, we now have a beautiful team room that reflects the pride and tradition in our program.

IN-SEASON PREPARATION

After taking care of some of the much needed housekeeping duties, you are now ready to attack the "joy" of the preseason, the actual game plan preparation. This usually gets me excited as I envision the upcoming season.

Tactical Planning

Tactical planning can be one of the most enjoyable parts of planning for your season. Having assessed your talent and put together your offensive and defensive schemes, now it's time to implement your Xs and Os. It's a good idea to ask yourself several questions: What plays will you run to complement your team's talent? What defenses will bring out the best in your players? What drills should you use to improve skills? How and when should you introduce them? These are just some of the questions you'll want to address during tactical planning. Bring out your drawing board—this is where the fun begins!

You might want to start with your offensive game plan. Your offensive package might include man-to-man offenses, zone offenses, set plays and continuities, quick hitters, isolation plays, three-point plays, delay game, zone press offenses, man press offenses, transition offense, special situations, and other systems or strategies. You'll have your own timetable for implementing each part of your plan. Sometimes I have an assistant teach part of our plan to the players so they hear a new voice. This also builds the assistant's credibility in your players' eyes. Specifically, you might want to assign your assistants an area that they focus on and can be in charge of. Match their knowledge and strengths to their teaching roles. For example, if an assistant coach has a good perimeter background, have her work with perimeter players while you work with post players. Head and assistant coaches can share in teaching parts of the offenses and defenses. If an assistant has a good grasp of the defensive aspects of the game, perhaps she can introduce various facets of your defensive system.

You and your staff need to decide how and when your offensive segment is implemented into your practices. In our practices, we usually work on offense at about the midpoint. Prior to our offensive segment in practice, we either do some shooting drills or offensive position work. If an area of our offense is not clicking, screening for example, then we'll break that offense down into parts and build it back up. We usually spend 30 to 40 minutes on our half-court offenses each practice. Early in the season, we spend more time on man-to-man offenses and teach zone offenses afterward. We practice some type of special situation daily so that players get familiar with as many different scenarios as possible.

When you're ready to implement your defensive schemes, you might include half-court man-to-man defenses, half-court zone defenses, combination defenses, full-court man defenses, full-court zone defenses, three-quarter-court man and zone defenses, transition defense, and special situations. In our system, we teach basic defenses first. We also teach several variations of our base defense. Depending on our talent, we might add other defenses. Defense is one of the early parts of our practices, and we practice it each day, usually for 30 minutes or so. Again, teaching is shared by the staff, although I introduce most of the defenses myself. Defense is broken down similar to offense, and much of the breakdown work is addressed in position work. Again, you and your staff will need to decide how and when to introduce your defensive system.

Scouting

I recommend gaining every advantage you can before playing a game. Spend time on game preparation, including scouting your opponent. If you can get a feel for their style of play, as well as their defensive and offensive tendencies, you'll be much better prepared to play them. These days, there are many ways to scout a team. The good old-fashioned way is to attend one of your opponent's games, which is ideal, if time allows. I try to see as many teams in person as I can. If time or travel doesn't allow you or an assistant to attend a game, you and your opponent can exchange game tapes. Most teams today videotape their games. Another alternative is a well-organized scouting report, done over the phone, faxed, or mailed. Getting a good scouting report on an opponent before you play them makes a huge difference in your preparation.

I use a calendar to organize scouting. I plug in my games for the first few months. Next, I receive all opponents' schedules so I can plug their games into my calendar. Then I meet with my coaching staff to plot out which games one of us can attend for scouting purposes. If a team can be scouted in person, we use a scouting form. Initially, as a game is being watched, a coach might handwrite the scouting report. Then, whichever coach watches that game transfers her notes to a scouting form to be shared with the entire coaching staff (figure 5.5). If there are teams whose games none of us can attend, we try to get film on that team. If you're willing to exchange tapes and build a relationship with other coaches, exchanges can be easy. If you're willing to help others, most will help you. As coaches, we owe it to our staff and players to be as well prepared as we can be going into each game.

Travel to Away Games

Your school system might dictate how your team travels. Most teams travel in school buses. As you complete your game schedule, it's helpful to also make out a bus schedule for your season. Let your school's transportation department know your busing needs as early as possible.

Our school system supplies school buses for all athletic transportation. Most of our regularly scheduled games are within an hour's time from our school, so a school bus is appropriate. Our team rule is that we all travel to and from the games as a team, so all players are required to ride the bus. I believe this is important for team

unity. During our travel to the game, players may study, talk softly, or listen to music on a headset. The bus remains fairly quiet. The image we want to portray on the road is important. We dress up for away games or wear our travel sweats. Either way, we want an image of first class.

If we have a tournament game to which travel is significantly longer than one hour, we upgrade our transportation to a coach bus. Our school pays the cost of what a regular bus would charge, and our boosters pay the difference. This upgrade is a welcome treat for a long trip.

Today, more than ever, teams travel over the holidays. We try to take a trip over our winter break, either before or after Christmas. This has been a wonderful experience for our teams. Before we head out of town, we remind our players that they are role models both at home and on the road. For many people, their only impression of Oak Ridge basketball will be what they see during our short visit to their city. Last year we traveled to Phoenix, Arizona, for the Nike Tournament of Champions, which was as much an educational experience as a basketball experience. Some of our players had never been away from their families for more than a weekend. Many of our players had never flown. Most had not seen the Grand Canyon. This trip afforded them all these opportunities and made for great bonding for our team. We enjoyed our basketball experience and also had fun traveling and sight seeing. A bonus was that this tournament was during open recruiting time for college coaches (as many are nowadays), so some of our players had the opportunity to be seen by college representatives.

To make our trip to Phoenix happen, we had to do many things on the front end. Our administration was extremely supportive. To afford such a trip, players raised funds, and some community businesses chipped in. It was a total town effort. The town was excited that these young ladies had such an opportunity. Of course, players had to take care of their schoolwork before we left. Teachers were notified well beforehand that the team would miss two days of classes. All schoolwork was completed before we left town.

If you can afford to travel with your team, the rewards are numerous. The planning might take a lot of work, but the benefits are well worth it.

Scouting Form

Date _____   * _____ vs. _____

STARTERS

Our matchup   #   Position   Strengths/Weaknesses

_____ _____ _____ _____

_____ _____ _____ _____

_____ _____ _____ _____

_____ _____ _____ _____

_____ _____ _____ _____

_____ _____ _____ _____

BENCH

_____ pos. _____ _____   # _____ pos. _____ _____

_____ pos. _____ _____   # _____ pos. _____ _____

Jump ball alignment
court diagram

Defenses

Q1 _____

Q2 _____

Q3 _____

Q4 _____

Defensive Summary

_____

Offensive Style

_____

Half-court sets
court diagrams

Go-to player(s) _____

Inbounds   Delay game
court diagrams   court diagram

Keys offensively _____

Keys defensively _____

Strengths _____

Weaknesses _____

In order for us to win: _____

_____

Figure 5.5 Sample scouting form.

For many players, such a trip with their team is a once-in-a-lifetime experience.

SUMMARY

- A yearly timetable is very helpful in planning your season.

- If you work at your program throughout the year, your workload is easier to manage.

- Make sure all your players are cleared medically to play.

- Keep parent or guardian information, permission, and insurance forms on file.

- Certified athletic trainers or student trainers can help you with injuries or rehabilitation of your players.

- For best results, and to minimize injuries, have a plan for preseason and off-season conditioning.

- Remember your players are athletes first, so have an academic support system in place.

- Schedule your games to fit your team's needs.

- Scouting your opponent might be the best way to prepare for an upcoming game.

- Providing your team with proper equipment helps establish pride in your players and your program.

- Team travel over holidays can provide a rich, unforgettable experience for your players.

CHAPTER 6
PREPARING FOR PRACTICES

Developing a master plan for your basketball program can be quite beneficial (figure 6.1). Through meeting with your assistants you will have already identified your offenses, defenses, and various components of the game you will use for the upcoming season. Your master plan serves as a guideline for implementing all the components of your system. Once you have developed this plan, it won't vary much from year to year unless a rule change requires you to alter it.

Once we have our master plan in place, we work on developing a monthly practice plan, which identifies the components of our system we want to introduce during each month of the season (figure 6.2). I like to include my coaching staff in developing this plan. The first month's plan will be slightly more detailed than those of the months to follow. This allows for flexibility. Not all plans go as expected. I don't want to waste time detailing plans for the future that need to be adjusted and reworked. Consequently, the plan for November is the most detailed. In developing our monthly plans, we break each month down into four weeks and complete weekly plans. Our staff identifies what we want to teach out of our system within each week.

Once the weekly plan is outlined, we draw up an individual daily practice plan for each practice (figure 6.3). Practice segments for teaching are identified and time allotments assigned. Usually, our early-season practices are longer than our practices after Christmas. Our early-season practices might last two and a half hours. Practices the day before a game are shortened by 30 to 60 minutes. Toward the end of the season, practices might last a little over an hour, depending on the content that needs to be covered in that practice. If a late-season practice runs over an hour, some of that time is spent talking or going through a "walk through," neither of which requires a great deal of energy from players. At this stage we are working on fine-tuning various elements of our game. We hope our conditioning is already in place. Practices are briefer at this stage in the season because we want to keep players fresh, both physically and mentally.

We also might add a new wrinkle or two. For instance, we might try a new quick hitter for our best player—a play we've not used before that our opponents could not have scouted. Defensively, a new wrinkle might be a new trapping defense, something else opponents haven't seen. These new elements might be just what we need to catch our opponent off guard.

Master Plan

I. Conditioning
   A. Physically
   B. Mentally

II. Offenses
   A. Team
      1. Versus man to man
      2. Versus zone
      3. Versus combination
      4. Versus pressure
      5. Delays

III. Defense
   A. Team
      1. Man to man
      2. Zone
      3. Combination
      4. Pressure
   B. Individual
      1. On the ball
      3. Away from the ball
      4. Perimeter and post

IV. Fundamentals
   A. Footwork
   B. Passing
   C. Dribbling
   D. Shooting
   E. Rebounding
      1. Offensively
      2. Defensively

V. Transitions
   A. Offensively
   B. Defensively

VI. Out-of-Bounds Situations
   A. Defensive end
      1. Full court or three-quarter court
      2. Sideline
      3. Under opponent's basket
   B. Offensive end
      1. Full court or 3/4 court
      2. Sideline
      3. Under your basket

VII. Free-Throw Situations
   A. Offensive alignment
   B. Defensive alignment

VIII. Jump Ball Situations
   A. Offensive alignment
   B. Defensive alignment

IX. Time and Score Situations
   A. Delay game when ahead
   B. Quick hitters for points when trailing

   C. Defensive strategies
      1. When and who to foul
      2. Defensive gambles

X. Player and Team Evaluation
   A. Our team
      1. · Charts and stats
      2. Film breakdown
   B. Opponents
      1. Charts and stats
      2. Scouting
      3. Film breakdown

XI. Rules
   A. Team
   B. Game

XII. Game Organization
   A. Night before game
   B. Day of the game
   C. Pregame
   D. Game strategies
      1. Game plan
      2. Player assignments/personnel
      3. Bench
      4. Timeouts
      5. Half time
   E. Postgame

XIII. Trip Organization
   A. Schedule
   B. Players
      1. Rules
      2. Finances
      3. Packing
      4. Equipment
      5. Academics
      6. Emergency numbers
   C. Staff
   D. Parents/guardians
      1. Information packet
   E. Travel party
   F. Lodging
   G. Transportation
   H. Meals
   I. Fundraising

XIV. Public Relations
   A. Parents
   B. Administration
   C. Faculty
   D. Feeder programs
   E. Community
   F. Media
   G. College coaches

Figure 6.1 Example of a basketball program's master plan.

Monthly Practice Plan

October–November 2003

First Game Is on November 18th

Week 1 October 27– November 1

- Scrimmage at Oak Ridge November 1st

Offensive
1. Fundamentals:
   - Ball handling
   - Passing
   - Footwork
   - Shooting form; Passing; Dribbling
   - Position work
   - Defensive slides
   - Defensive rebounding positioning
   - Offensive rebounding triangle
2. Man inside offense: Georgia
3. Man quick hitter: Stack
4. One shot: Clear
5. Delay: Tennessee
6. Zone offense: UCLA
7. Transition:
   - Primary
   - Secondary

Defensive
1. Man: 5
2. Press: 1-2-1-1; 11
3. Transition defense: 5

Special
1. Inbounds under basket: Box
2. Inbounds side: Duke
3. Press O: Belmont Box 25
4. Free throw
5. Jump ball
6. Subbing
7. New game rules
8. Conditioners

Week 2 November 3–November 8 (Review)

- Scrimmage at Heritage November 8th
- Youth Clinic November 4th
- Meet the Wildcats November 6th

Offensive
1. Fundamentals
2. Position work
3. Offensive breakdown
4. Man offense: Triangle; Double high
5. One shot: 4 down
6. Zone offense: Over
7. Secondary options: Come back; Fist

Defensive
1. Zone: 2
2. Man inside: 5 cat
3. 3/4 press: 13

Special
1. Inbounds under basket: UCLA
2. Inbounds side: Clemson
3. Press O: 2 guard
4. Conditioners

continued

Figure 6.2 Example of a monthly practice plan.

Monthly Practice Plan, *continued*

Week 3 November 10–November 15 (Review)

- Scrimmage at Oak Ridge November 15th

Offensive
1. Fundamentals
2. Position work (together)
3. Man offense: USA; Wildcat
4. Zone offense: Break; 2 guard
5. Delay: Tennessee; Stop-and-go
6. Secondary: Switch and step out
7. One shot: Fade and isolate

Defensive
1. Man-to-man variations
2. Zone: 3 down
3. Press: 1-2-1-1

Special
1. Full court: Freight train; Ladder; Diamond
2. Conditioners

Week 4 Monday, November 17th

- First game versus Heritage is Tuesday, November 18th

Offensive
1. Review offenses
2. Position work
3. Offensive game plan vs. Heritage

Defensive
1. Defensive transition
2. Defensive rebounding
3. Defensive game plan vs. Heritage

Special
1. Scouting report
2. Game plan
3. Inbounds review

Daily Practice Plan

2003–2004 Practice Plan
Practice 10   Date 11/07/03

Areas of focus: Offensive—easy shots; zone offense; review man-to-man offense
Defensive—half-court traps; rebounding; switching defenses; man-to-man defense
Special—inbounds without defense
Announcements—letters to middle school; scrimmage 9:30

3:05–3:10	Prepractice routine
3:10–3:15	Easy shots: layups; bank shots (competitive finish)
3:15–3:25	Stretch
3:25–3:35	Circle wagons: boards! Transition decisions: 2× beat; sprint/keep score (Coach T)
3:35–3:40	Angles of traps (Coach P)
3:40–4:00	Teach 33 half-court trap: whole team, then break down into groups (Coach P)
4:00–4:10	Review 13 trap: focus on second trap coverage (Coach T)
4:10–4:25	Man-to-man breakdown; pick-and-roll; cut cutter
4:25–4:30	Pressure free throws
4:30–4:45	Position work (Coach T, perimeter; Coach P, post)
4:45–5:00	Zone offenses (Coach T, defense; Coach P, offense)
5:00–5:10	Man-to-man review (Coach T, defense; Coach P, offense)
5:10–5:20	Changing defenses in the middle of a possession (Coach P)
5:20–5:30	Shell inbounds under goal (Coach T)
5:30	Conditioners: ball-handling challenges; pressure free throws

Figure 6.3 Example of a daily practice plan.

CONDUCTING A PRACTICE

In some years I have posted the agenda for practices in the team room for players to view before the start of practice. In other years, I have met with the team as a group before practice to share the main focus of practice that day. Either way, I think it's important to have a plan for how you'll inform players of the focus of practice each day. This helps them prepare mentally for the work ahead. It also lets them know what areas you think need the most improvement.

Regardless of the length of practice, each practice is broken into time segments. As players step onto the court each day, they are greeted by one or more coaches, and they begin their prepractice routine. This lasts about five minutes and generally consists of some full-court ball-handling warm-ups, form shooting, and a shooting routine specific for each player. After this warm-up, we circle up for announcements and discuss our focus for the day. This is followed by 10 minutes of stretching led by our captains.

The next segments vary day to day in length depending on what we need to cover and how much breakdown drilling we need. We usually open up our practices with some fundamental work, which lasts about 15 minutes. Normally, our next segment involves full-court work, which I call the "transition decisions" segment. Here we work on our primary fast break, secondary breaks, and defensive transition. This segment typically lasts 20 to 30 minutes.

We usually address defense in the middle of practice. Depending on how many breakdown drills we need to do and whether we're working on full- or half-court defenses, the defense segment lasts from 30 to 45 minutes. Defense has always been a focus for our program, so even if the length of these segments varies, the intensity is always the same—very intense and competitive.

We usually cover special situations at the beginning of practice, when players are the most alert and rested. However, after the initial teaching is done, we work on these situations when players are the most tired. I believe that we need to be able to execute when we're in the fourth quarter and tired, so why not simulate that in practice? We also throw in special

situations sporadically throughout practice to keep players sharp and prepared for gamelike encounters.

The final segment of our practice is devoted to offense. Before we begin this segment, we usually do anywhere from 10 to 20 minutes of position work, which includes shooting and offensive breakdown drills by position. Post players work at one end of the court and perimeter players at the other end. Our offensive segment usually lasts between 30 and 45 minutes. Free throws and competitive shooting are interspersed between segments. The same is true of conditioners. Sometimes we run a "gut check" sprint followed by a "pressure free throw."

We end our practices in a variety of ways. Sometimes we run sprints, with or without basketballs. Sometimes we divide up for team shooting and running competitions. Whether we do this usually depends on the amount of running we've already done in practice. If we can condition primarily through our drills and scrimmage work, we condition very little at the end of practice.

Player Preparation

I recommend giving your players little time between the end of school and the beginning of practice. I've found that the less free time you give them, the fewer opportunities they have to get involved in mischief. We give our players 15 minutes from the last bell to be dressed and on the practice floor, ready to begin their prepractice routine. Exceptions to this rule are players who need to go to the training room for taping or treatment and those who are attending a tutoring session. Most players head to the team room after school to change into their practice gear. Each day I post on the dry erase board the focus for the day and any important announcements for the day and the week. The time in the team room is used for socializing with teammates and mental preparation for practice. Once players are greeted by coaches and step onto the practice floor, their work begins.

After completing their prepractice, players circle up for announcements. At this time I do a quick check of the team's attitude and energy level. Announcements posted in the team room are reviewed. The more chances they have to hear or see the announcements, the better chance they'll remember them.

Next, players participate in a stretching routine that is taught to all players by the captains. To encourage players to be vocal during practice, players count out loud during their stretching. We put 10 minutes on the clock for stretching. After they have finished stretching, players huddle up. This is their time to get themselves mentally and emotionally charged up for practice. After a minute of huddling and talking among themselves, players break their huddle and hustle over to the coaching staff, and we're ready for practice to begin.

Practice Outline

Each coach has a practice outline sheet on which drills are listed, as well as offensive, defensive, and special situation segments. Each drill or segment is allotted a set amount of time. A student assistant places this time on the score clock so that both players and coaches can see it. Putting the time on the clock helps us be efficient and organized in our practices. If coaches believe additional time is needed on a drill or in a segment, time is added. Even water breaks are timed on the clock. Players hustle, not only from drill to drill, but from drill to their water break, and back to their drill again. If players do not hustle, we have "running reminders" or "frozen push-up reminders." A couple of those can get a player's attention quickly. We try not to waste any time.

I write a coach's name next to each segment or drill on the practice outline. This lets coaches know if they are the lead in a drill or the teacher in a segment. Especially early in the season, I want my assistants in the teaching or leading position often in practice. I think players respond more positively to assistant coaches if they are given leadership roles.

Quality Versus Quantity

"Quality versus quantity" is a phrase my players are very familiar with. They understand that this means if we have quality in our practices, the quantity—that is, the *length*—will be shortened. This is especially effective as a reminder when practices are dragging or as an incentive toward the end of the season. Sometimes I open up our practice by telling our players, "Quality versus quantity." Usually they respond with a very spirited, enthusiastic, and energetic beginning. Most players want short practices. I have found this to be quite an effective form of motivation.

Practices usually have more than one focus. Often, we're trying to teach an aspect of the game. But more than that, we're teaching our players how to practice and the discipline involved in practicing. We're teaching life lessons such as teamwork, accountability, and time management. Before each practice my staff and I identify what we want to get out of it. When I ask players their main objective for practicing, the first word I hear is "fun." Keeping this in mind, we try to keep practices upbeat and competitive, and we try to vary how we approach segments. However, I tell my players that I don't plan my practices first and foremost to be fun. I believe fun can occur during each practice. I try to show them how much fun it is to enjoy the fruits of their labor. When they have mastered the breakdown drills of an offense, and suddenly that offense is clicking on all cylinders, that is *fun*. When they understand angles involved in pressing, and suddenly they press their teammates into turnover after turnover, that is *fun*. Working on your shot and having it pay great dividends in a ball game is a *lot* of fun. Getting your teammates to become like family is also fun. Each time I see someone having fun in practice or in games, I try to point it out to our players. I want them to understand that fun doesn't have to be "programmed" into practice. Of course, *some* fun can be programmed into practice. I love humor as much as anyone, and I'm always looking for ways to get us to laugh at ourselves in a healthy way.

SUMMARY

- Take the time to develop a master plan for your season.
- Break your master plan down into monthly or weekly plans.
- Make each minute of your daily practices count.
- Involve your coaching staff in leadership roles for planning and implementing your plans.
- Help players enjoy the fruits of their labor.

PART III

COACHING OFFENSE

CHAPTER 7
TEACHING OFFENSIVE POSITIONS AND SETS

For success in basketball, a player needs a variety of skills. She may excel more in ball handling, three-point shooting, or defense, but she needs a wide array of skills to be able to play effectively on both ends of the court. These skills can be divided into offensive skills and defensive skills. Players need solid abilities in their basic individual basketball skills as well as sound fundamentals in order to put together effective team offensive and defensive schemes.

Offensively, all players need repetitions on basic skills such as ball handling, dribbling, passing, catching, footwork, shooting, and offensive rebounding. After they learn the basics, players need to understand how to best use these skills in a variety of situations as they execute the offensive game plan.

Defensively, the basic required skills are defensive footwork (such as stances and slides), defensive rebounding, and taking a charge. Defensive footwork is complex and can cover many aspects of defense, such as on-the-ball defense, denial, and help-side defense, as well as defensive positioning in zone defenses.

As a coach, strive to identify your players' offensive and defensive strengths, work on their weaknesses, and find roles they can play on your team so that all players and the team as a whole can be more successful.

POSITION SKILLS

In addition to basic skills such as shooting, passing, dribbling, and rebounding, all players have a different combination of secondary skills. Offensive frameworks are designed around these skills, and players are assigned offensive positions according to which skills they possess. Terminology might differ from coach to coach, but in our system the five starting offensive positions are divided into "perimeter" players and "post" players. Although there are many exceptions and different things occur within different game plans, perimeter players tend to play farther from the basket, whereas post players play closer to the basket ("in the paint").

Perimeter players are divided into a point guard and two wings. Post players make up the other two positions. We give players numbers to quickly identify their positions. The numbering system also helps in diagramming plays and scouting opponents. In our system, the point guard is one, right wing is two, and the left wing is three. The point guard is the main ball handler for the team and, we hope, a good floor leader. The wings are the perimeter players, ideally with skills that complement play away from the basket. These players might be long-range shooters, perimeter drivers, or good passers into the posts. The right wing and left wing can be positioned to suit the offensive game plan and according to their individual strengths. If one of your wings is right handed and the other left handed, it's often natural for them to play the right side and left side of the court. Posts are numbered four and five. If I have a post who is better at stepping out of the paint and has extended shooting range, that player is the four in our system. If I have a player who is stronger and more effective in the paint area, closer to the basket, that player is the five.

You have to adjust your coaching to your personnel. Your best five players might all be perimeter players, in which case you might not have a true post player in your lineup. On the other hand, your best five players may be three posts and two perimeter players. Let's call our team the "ideal team" and say it consists of one point guard, two wings, and two post players.

Point Guard

In our system, the point guard needs to be an extension of the coach, a leader in voice and actions. She is the coach on the floor. If your point guard happens to be a natural leader, this is a real bonus. A point guard needs to be a player who can take charge and get her teammates into the correct offense. The point guard needs to be a good communicator with both her teammates and her coaches. Good point guards understand game fundamentals, game strategy, and game flow. The point guard is usually the best ball handler on the team. She needs to be able to handle the ball when facing defensive pressure, in a full-court transition setting, or in a half-court offensive set. Handling the ball with confidence provides excellent leadership.

The point guard might or might not be your main scorer. This depends on her particular skills, the needs of the team, and how your opponent plays her defensively. If your opponent plays off this position, the point guard will need to be able to knock down perimeter shots. If the point guard is played tightly, her ability to drive to the hoop creates offensive opportunities. If your point guard is your leading scorer, be cautious. This means you're depending a lot on the skills of one player. If she's shut down by the defense, what do you do? A point guard needs to pride herself on getting her teammates involved in the offense. Even if she's a terrific

shooter and scorer, there needs to be a blend of shots from her and her teammates. She needs to make sure to spread the ball around.

Point guards must be good passers. They need the ability not only to run a play but also to *make* a play. If a play breaks down, a point guard needs to be able to create a scoring opportunity for herself or for a teammate. Point guards need to be able to make the easy pass in transition to set up players to score. If a point guard has the ability to read defenses in a half-court setting, she can help make the necessary adjustments offensively for her plays to work. The point guard needs to be a good decision maker.

Good point guards strive to bring out the best in her teammates. She strives to get the ball to the right person, in the right place, at the right time.

Wing Players

Wing players and where they play on the court are defined by the coach's system. In our system, transition is a big part of our offense. If I have a right- and a left-handed wing player, we would have them on the right and left sides of the court, respectively, so they could use their dominant hand away from the defensive player in a transition attack. If both wings are right-handed or both left-handed, it doesn't matter in our system which is the left wing and which the right. Ball handling, passing, rebounding, and shooting are devised for the system and for each player; it makes no difference who is the 2 player and who is the 3. In our system, they are interchangeable.

Right Wing The right wing tends to be more comfortable on the right side of the floor, especially in transition situations. In transition, the right wing would run the right side of the floor and dribble with her outside hand (her right hand). More players are right-handed than left-handed. In transition, the ball stays on the right side of the floor more than on the left side. Consequently, the second best ball handler should be the right wing. In a half-court setting, players move from one side of the court to the other often, so being right- or left-handed would not necessarily dictate where they might play. If the better post player plays on the right block, the right wing needs to be a good passer to that post. Whenever possible, we like to have our best scoring post and best scoring wing on the same side of the floor. If our strongest scoring post is on the right block, our best perimeter shooter is on the right wing. When this happens, it makes it hard on the defense to double down on the post or to play off the wing shooter. This is especially true if the right wing is a good percentage three-point shooter. If the right wing shoots more than the left wing, rebounding is not as big a role for the right wing as it is for the left wing. If the left wing is the better perimeter scorer, the right wing needs to be a good rebounder.

Left Wing   If most of your perimeter players are right-handed, you'll run a greater percentage of offenses on the right side. Keeping this in mind, the left wing is often the weakest perimeter ball handler. If the best inside player plays on the left block, the left wing needs to be a good passer. In addition, the left wing needs to be a good shooter, to eliminate double-downs on the post player. If the right wing is the better shooter, the left wing needs to be a strong rebounder. Again, the roles of your 2 and 3 players can vary according to your system and to complement your inside post play.

Post Players

Post players used to refer to those players who scored primarily in the paint. Nowadays, coaches love a post player who can step out of the paint to score and thus stretch the opponent's defense. Post players can play with power or finesse. How you define your post players depends on their skills and abilities.

Low Post   The low post is called the 5 player and is usually the most dominant inside player. This player needs to be able to play with her back to the basket to become a solid inside scoring threat. Consequently, these players need to work on post moves with their backs to the basket. Besides a layup, a post player's shot is closest to the goal. Consequently, a post player needs to take high percentage shots and make them on a regular basis. Often a low-post player by size alone might be your strongest, most physical player. If a post player can also play facing the basket, this is a bonus. Size and strength can help low-post players become

good rebounders. Teaching them correct rebounding techniques can help them become *great* rebounders. A post who can both score and rebound has increased her stock considerably.

If five is your go-to inside player, she will probably be fouled more than your other players. This player needs to shoot a good free throw percentage. If your 5 player is double teamed a lot, being a good passer is also important. The ability to read the defense and make the extra pass can make for a powerful offensive weapon.

High Post   The high post is called the 4 player. "High post" means a post player with extended shooting range. This player might be able to shoot a consistent 15-foot shot or even have the ability to step out and nail a three-pointer. The 4 player can be effective not only by having extended range but also by her ability to slash within an offense. If the 4 player has good size, she becomes the second inside scoring weapon. The more skills she has, the more of a challenge she becomes to guard, and the more she can help her team offensively.

If the 5 player is the dominant scorer inside, the 4 player needs to be a good rebounder. The ability to pass from post to post also helps make this player effective offensively. If she can score off the dribble, she will need to be an adequate ball handler as well.

OFFENSIVE SETS

Offensive sets are primarily used in half-court basketball games. If your style of play is mainly a full-court transition game, you will use few half-court sets. Some coaches rarely want to set up in an offense. Other coaches might want to "run their stuff" and use a half-court attack much of the game. Regardless of whether your style of offensive basketball is full court or half court, you always want to create a numerical advantage. Good passing and good player and ball movement can create offensive situations in which your team has a two-on-one or perhaps a three-on-two situation. This can happen in a full- or half-court setting. As much as I enjoy the tempo of a run-and-gun offense, this style cannot be used an entire game. We must be prepared to set up in an offense when needed. Offensive basic sets can be structured in many forms, versus either zone or man defenses.

Zone Sets

When setting up zone offensive sets, you set up your offense opposite of how the defense is aligned. If the defense is set up in an even guard front, the offensive should set up in an odd guard set. For example, if the defense is a 2-1-2 zone, the offensive should have an odd guard front such as a 1-3-1 (see figure 7.1). If the defense is set up in an odd guard front such as a 1-3-1 zone, the offense should have an even guard front such as a 2-1-2 (see figure 7.2). You want to place your offensive players in an area where the defense is not. You are always looking to create numerical advantages.

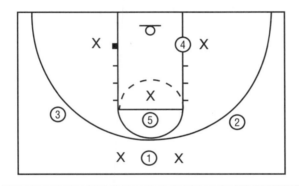

Figure 7.1 Defense in an even guard front, offense in an odd guard front.

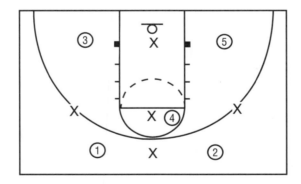

Figure 7.2 Defense in an odd guard front, offense in an even guard front.

Man Sets

Decisions on your man-to-man sets are dictated by your players' strengths and weaknesses as well as those of your opponents. For example, if

you have a dominant point guard, you might run sets in which she can be isolated. An example of that would be a 1-4 low offensive set in which four players line up along the baseline and the point guard has the freedom and the space to go one on one versus her defender.

If you have three perimeter players and two strong posts, a 1-2-2 set might be effective for using the strengths of your players. Posts can set up double low or in a high-low formation out of a 1-2-2 set. Perimeter players can have their own movement outside the lane area without infringing on the inside post play.

If your team has a dominant post player and four perimeter players, a four-out set with one post inside may be the best way to use your players. This set spreads the defense out and allows the post player to be isolated inside. Another set to spread the defense out is a 1-4 high set. This set starts out spread and then can finish in a variety of ways using drives, back screens, overloads, and so on.

If you have a dominant inside post player and a good high-post scorer, a 1-3-1 set takes away the backside defensive help on your low-post player. For this to be effective, the perimeter players have to entertain their defenders.

Offensively, you want to place your players where they are most effective and to take advantage of any mismatches you might have with your opponent. Take size, speed, strength, and skills into consideration. For example, you might rotate a tall perimeter player inside if she has a considerable size advantage on the player guarding her.

Court Balance

Court balance refers to offensive floor balance. Regardless of what set you run your offenses out of, spacing is important for your offense to be effective. By using good spacing in your offenses, you spread out the defense (figure 7.3). If you bunch players up in an offense, sometimes one defender can guard two offensive players. Poor spacing can also take away a player's main weapon. A good post player might find she has little room to work when too many players cut through the paint. An effective perimeter player who scores well off the dribble might have no room to drive if other perimeter players play too close to her position. Part of understand-

Figure 7.3 Good offensive floor balance.

ing offensive spacing comes when you teach fundamental skills such as passing, cutting, handoffs, and penetration concepts. Players need to understand what to do in each of these situations.

Floor balance is also important when a shot is taken. Players need to understand offensive rebounding responsibilities. Who's responsible for going to the boards and who's responsible to be the safety, the first part of your defensive transition? Make sure players know their job.

SUMMARY

- All players need basic skills to play both ends of the floor.
- Offensive players are divided into two positions: perimeter players and post players.
- Perimeter players play primarily outside the lane; post players play primarily inside the lane.

- Positions are determined by a player's skills and abilities, strengths and weaknesses, and size.
- A point guard is usually the best ball handler, an effective leader, and a good communicator; she has the ability to make her teammates better.
- Wing players are interchangeable and are used according to their abilities and the needs of the team.
- A good low-post player is your go-to inside player.
- An effective high-post player can stretch a defense.
- Offensive sets are designed to create mismatches for the defense and advantages for the offense.
- For any offense to be effective, floor balance and court spacing are critical components.

CHAPTER 8

TEACHING OFFENSIVE SKILLS

Developing good, fundamental offensive basketball skills requires proper execution and repeated practice. These skills are the foundation on which you build your offensive system. Fundamentals are the little things that make the big difference in how effective and efficient your offense becomes. A sound fundamental team can run an offense like clockwork.

Offensive skills are divided into two categories: playing with the ball and playing without the ball. Playing with the ball involves stationary moves, moves while dribbling, ball handling, passing, and shooting. Playing without the ball involves footwork, screening, and cutting.

PLAYING WITH THE BALL

Most players are more comfortable with the ball in their hands than not. Usually, once you add defense, it becomes obvious who has the skills and confidence to attack the defense and who doesn't. Every player needs to learn to be an offensive threat on the court. To do that, players must square up, or face the basket, each time they receive the ball in a half-court offense.

A good offensive ready position with the ball is called a triple threat position (figure 8.1). Feet are about shoulder-width apart and

knees bent in an athletic position. If a player is right-handed, her right foot should be slightly ahead of her left foot, with the right foot acting as the pivot foot. Reverse the footwork for players who are left-handed. In either case, the feet and shoulders should be facing the basket so that any move is in the direction of the goal. From this triple threat position, a player can dribble, pass, or shoot.

When receiving the ball, the player needs to protect the ball. Placing the ball on the back hip (the right hip for a right-handed player) away from the defense protects the ball. Players should stay in their low athletic position, which allows them to make their move more quickly and explosively, giving the defense less time to react.

When driving to the basket, players should attack the goal in straight lines. Once the defender is beaten, the shortest path to the basket is a straight line. Players often drive in a curved line, known as a "banana cut" to avoid their defender. This type of cut is not as efficient and gives the defense time to recover from the initial move, negating its effectiveness. Driving in a straight line also helps the offensive player keep defenders behind her. Once the player has beaten the defense, she shouldn't allow defenders to catch her. She should limit the space she creates as she makes her move past her defender. Closing the gap minimizes the

Figure 8.1 Triple threat position.

defender's chances of recovering and getting back into the play.

Stationary Moves

On receiving a pass, a player squares up to the basket and gets in a triple threat position, from which she is ready to attack the defense. Stationary moves refer to the initial moves a player makes from this triple threat position, prior to putting the ball on the floor. Reading the defense, she uses a stationary move to gain an advantage over her defender. Basic stationary moves include the jab step and shot; jab step and drive; crossover step and dribble; and jab step, drive, and pull-up jumper. All these moves are dictated by the strengths of the offensive player, and, more important, by the defense being played. The jab step used before a move gives the offensive player an initial read on her defender's decision to play tight or guard loosely. The stationary moves used after the jab step are a reaction to the defender's play and the offensive player's ability to read her defense.

Jab and Shot The jab step is used after a player assumes the triple threat position. The step is done with the right foot for a right-handed player and the left foot for a left-handed player (if she's using a permanent pivot foot). The purpose of the jab step is to get the defense to react.

The jab step is a short (2- to 4-inch) step done directly at the player's defense. The offensive player then reads her defender. If her defender responds to the jab step by taking a step back, thus playing off the offensive player and giving her space, the offensive player immediately takes a shot. Of course, the shooter needs to shoot on balance, and the shot must be within her shooting range.

Jab and Drive After a player receives a pass in a half-court set, she should assume the triple threat position. Next, she executes a quick jab step (a right-handed player makes a right-foot jab). If the defender does not retreat and is overplaying the shooter's left side, the offensive player takes a longer step with the same foot. (If the defender overplays the offensive player's right side, the right-side jab and drive is not the best move to take.) In taking this longer step, she is trying to get her second step past her defender. When teaching this move, I say, "short–long" to remind players the jab step is short, followed by a longer second step taken to pass their opponent's back foot. Once the offensive player beats her defender with her long step, her body should cut closely past the defender. She then finishes the move with a hard dribble to the basket. She should use as few dribbles as possible to get to the basket so that her defender has little time to recover.

Players need to learn to be efficient and effective with their dribbling. Getting to the basket with the fewest possible dribbles helps prevent defenders from getting into the play and stopping their drive. Court vision is also important when dribbling. If a player keeps her head up while dribbling, she can see both her defender and her own teammates. She then puts herself in

a position to read the defense and the offensive situation and decides whether to continue to drive or pass to an open teammate.

When teaching the jab and drive, I have players practice the short–long footwork that the move requires. This is awkward for players, and they often lose balance. Repetition can help with this.

Crossover Step If a right-handed offensive player executes a jab step, and the defender responds by sliding to her left, the offensive player can then go in the opposite direction with a crossover step. If a defender has previously been beaten by a jab-and-go move on the strong side (for a right-handed player, her strong side is her right side), there's a good chance this countermove will be open.

When the defensive player overplays the strong-side drive, the offensive player crosses her right foot over to her left side, making sure her crossover step passes the defender's foot, thus putting the defender on her right hip (figure 8.2). While this footwork is occurring, the offensive player rips the basketball across

Figure 8.2 Crossover step.

her stomach, low and tight, to protect the ball before putting it into her left hand. The offensive player keeps her defender on her right hip as she puts the ball down on the floor with her left hand to protect it from the defense. Once the offensive player has beaten her defender with the crossover move, she drives in a straight line to the basket, limiting the defender's angle for recovery. The fundamentals of effective dribbling apply to the crossover as well as to the strong-side drive. The offensive player should keep her head up, keep the ball close to her body, and limit her number of dribbles.

If the defense reacts to the offensive player's jab, and the correct footwork is executed by the offensive player (either a crossover or go move), this can lead to a layup or jump shot or a pass to a teammate.

Jab and Pull-Up Jumper If an offensive player beats her defender and continues driving to the basket with either a go move or a crossover move, the other defenders will eventually adjust to cover her. The offensive player reads this defensive adjustment. As she starts to drive and sees that her defender is retreating, she picks up her dribble and takes a pull-up jumper (if she's on balance and within her shooting range).

Moves on the Move

Moves on the move occur when an offensive player is in the act of dribbling as she reaches her defender. To beat her defender, she might change speeds or direction or both. One of an offensive player's weapons when dribbling is her unpredictability. If she rarely changes direction or speed, she becomes quite predictable and easier to guard. With changes in speed and direction, she can catch her defender off guard. An average ball handler or a player with average speed can use change-ups in her dribbling to counteract an aggressive defender. There are several good moves a good offensive player can use to beat her defender.

Hesitation Dribble The hesitation dribble is also known as the stop-and-go dribble. For this move to be effective, changing speeds is essential. The offensive player begins by dribbling hard in one direction, protecting the ball with her off hand, and keeping her head up. To disrupt her defender, she slows down quickly

and dribbles once or twice in place while protecting the basketball. As the defender stops or becomes off balance, the offensive player explodes past the defender, pushing the ball out in front of her, slicing past the defender's body to keep her behind her.

Again, the dribbler must stay low as she explodes past her defender and pushes the ball out in front of her. This move can't be done too far from the defender or she will have time to adjust and make the move ineffective. A good player must be able to do the hesitation dribble with either her weak hand or her strong hand.

Crossover Dribble Changing speed is an effective weapon when dribbling, as is changing direction. If a dribbler can't change direction, she's usually easy to defend. A defensive player can keep the dribbler on one side of the floor and limit her options. A crossover dribble is an effective way for ball handlers to change directions.

Similar to the hesitation dribble, the offensive player begins the move by dribbling hard in one direction. To execute the crossover, the dribbler plants her outside foot (the right foot if dribbling with the right hand) and crosses the ball in front of her body to the other hand, away from the planted foot. The ball is crossed low and kept close to the body. After the ball has changed hands, the offensive player steps with the opposite foot, pushing off with the planted foot, and slices past her defender. Once the dribbler is past her defender, she keeps her on her hip, closes the gap, and pushes the ball out in front of her.

In-and-Out Dribble This dribble is an excellent complementary move to the crossover dribble move. The in-and-out dribble fakes the crossover dribble and keeps the ball on the same side of the floor in the same hand. The offensive player begins the move by dribbling hard in a direction with her right hand. As if she's going to cross over, she leans with her left shoulder and at the same time takes one dribble toward the midline of her body. She wants to catch the defense reacting to her lean and sliding toward her left hand. When this happens, the dribbler takes one hard dribble away from the midline of her body and pushes the ball out in front of her. At the same time, she pushes with her left foot and with her right foot takes a big step past her defender. This move is called "in and out" because the dribbler takes one dribble in toward her midline and then one dribble out past her defender. Once she has beaten her defender with her right hand, she keeps the defender on her hip, closes the gap, and pushes the ball forward with her right hand.

Speed is not a critical factor in making this move. You need to give the defense time to react and "bite" on the move that looks like a crossover. Players should practice this move with both the strong hand and the weak hand.

Reverse Dribble Whereas in the crossover dribble the ball is presented to the defense if not well guarded, in the reverse dribble, the ball is shielded from the defense throughout the move. To execute a reverse dribble, the offensive player plants her left foot (if dribbling right-handed) and does a reverse pivot on that foot. While pivoting, the player takes one hard dribble backward with her right hand so the dribbler's body protects the ball. This position puts the defender on the dribbler's hip. Next, the dribbler changes her dribble from her right hand to her left. Once the ball has changed hands, she can push the ball out in front, close the gap, and beat her defender.

The move takes a lot of practice because beginners tend to carry the ball or lose control of it in an effort to go too fast. As with all moves, the dribbler needs to stay low and keep the ball close to her body when changing hands. A difficulty encountered in this move occurs when the ball handler reverse pivots, thus turning her back not only on her defender but also on her own teammates. During this brief lack of vision, the ball handler might not see an open teammate. In addition, a dribbler who turns her back to the defense is susceptible to defensive traps and offensive charging fouls.

Control Dribble The control dribble is used primarily by point guards. It can also be beneficial for a dribbler who is receiving defensive pressure and is trying to buy herself some time before making an offensive decision. A right-handed dribbler turns her left shoulder and left hip toward her defender. She stays low in an athletic position. As she dribbles the ball behind her right hip, her footwork is similar to that of a defensive slide forward. Her head is up, looking down the floor. In this position she is protecting the ball as she surveys the court. A guard receiving pressure in the backcourt might use this move, as might a point guard trying to set her team up in a half-court offense.

There are several other effective moves a player might use to free herself from her defender. Executed properly, a behind-the-back dribble, between-the-legs dribble, or fake-reverse dribble can all be effective. Remind players that these moves are used to beat a defender, not to showcase their ball-handling abilities. Sometimes the simplest move is the best. The more comfortable a player becomes with the basketball, the more weapons she'll have when dribbling the ball. The following checklist reinforces the importance of sound ball-handling fundamentals.

Dribbling Reminders

1. Always keep your head up for court vision.
2. Stay low in an athletic position for explosive power.
3. Dribble the ball with your finger pads, not the palm of your hand.
4. Dribble with a purpose as you attack the defense.
5. Keep your dribble close to your body.
6. Attack the basket in a straight line.
7. Protect the ball with your body and your off hand.
8. Changes of speed and direction are dribbling weapons.
9. Make your weak hand a weapon, not a liability.

Passing

Passing is such an overlooked and underpracticed skill in basketball. Just the right pass often leads to easy baskets in your transition game. Making the extra pass in your half-court game can produce easy scoring opportunities. On the other hand, poor passing leads to turnovers and easy baskets for the opponent. Timing, passing angles, the ability to read a defense or handle defensive pressure are all factors to consider when teaching players how to make and receive a pass.

Basic Passes The three basic passes are the chest pass, the bounce pass, and the overhead pass. Of course there are several other kinds of passes, but these three are used the most. The chest pass is often used as an entry pass from a point guard to her wing without a defensive player in the path of the ball. A strong chest pass might also be used in a transition game. A player sees her teammate ahead of the defense and makes a full-court chest pass to her running teammate to advance the ball. This pass is often initiated off the dribble to add momentum and power in the pass.

The bounce pass is effective when there's a defender between the offensive player and her teammate. The bounce pass might be used in combination with an offensive pivot to evade the defender. Perimeter players often use a bounce pass as an entry pass to a post player on the block.

The overhead pass is an excellent pass to use as an outlet pass from a rebound because it allows you to keep a rebounded ball high and away from defenders. If a player has a strong upper body, her outlet pass can be deep up the floor to start a fast break.

Making the Pass Players need to recognize what pass is best in each situation. They also need to learn not to telegraph their passes. We teach our players to "fake a pass then make a pass." The right pass at the right time, having been telegraphed, becomes the right pass at the wrong time. I have found the most difficult pass for players to make is the entry pass from a perimeter player to a post player. We spend a great deal of time teaching our perimeter players how to read post defense.

Footwork is important when passing. Players want to step into their passes to make them strong. Players who shy away from defensive pressure find themselves back on their heels when passing, resulting in a weak pass that's easily stolen.

As much as possible, we teach our players to pass using both hands. I'm not a fan of the one-handed pass. Players try to imitate what they see professionals do. I find our players make fewer mistakes when they have two hands on the ball.

Receiving the Pass Players must be good at receiving as well as at passing. I'm constantly reminding my team that we want players with good hands. Of course there's more to catching the ball than just using their hands. Players must always be ready to receive a pass. They do this by getting open on offense and showing their teammates a target with the position of their hands. Once the player is open and showing a good target, she's ready to receive the pass. Once the pass is thrown, the receiver needs to watch the ball into her hands. Clinic speakers refer to "catching the ball with your eyes first." Second, a player catches the ball with her feet. She needs to move in the direction of the pass. We often tell our players, "step to meet the pass." Finally, the player catches the pass with her hands. Eyes, feet, hands, in that order. Coaches love a player who can pass the ball to the right player at the right time. The following passing reminders help offensive players become fundamentally sound passers.

Passing Pointers

1. Make the easy pass.
2. Don't telegraph your pass.
3. Fake a pass, then make a pass.
4. Step into your pass.
5. Read the defense.
6. Receive a pass first with your eyes, then with your feet, then with you hands.

Passing Drills

As coaches, we need to remind ourselves that if we want our players to become better passers, we better spend practice time on the improvement of passing skills. A little bit of practice each day on passing drills can improve not only a player's passing skills but also her focus on the importance of *effective* passing.

Four-Corner Passing Players form four lines in the four corners of a half court. They take three dribbles in rhythm, jump stop, reverse pivot, and make a chest pass to the teammate in line to their right. They then follow their pass to the back of that line (figure 8.3). Dribbling, jump stops, pivots, and passes are all done in rhythm with each line. Use four balls. Reverse directions.

Star Drill Starting under a goal, players form five lines in the shape of a star. Each player is a point on the star. They make chest passes to the

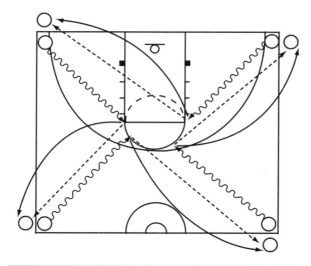

Figure 8.3 Four-Corner Passing Drill.

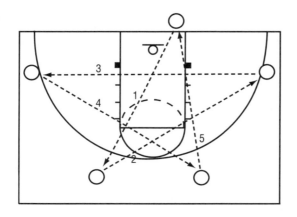

Figure 8.4 Star Drill.

next player in the star and follow their passes to the end of their line (figure 8.4).

Two-Ball Passing Drill This drill requires two balls and two players 10 to 12 feet across from each other. They make right- and left-handed chest passes and right- and left-handed bounce passes simultaneously. Players need to pass quickly without making a turnover.

Bad Pass Drill This drill requires two players and one ball. Players throw bad passes back and forth to each other. The receiver moves both feet to the ball to get into position to catch the ball with two hands.

Three-Man Weave Players form three lines across the baseline, executing chest passes as they weave down the length of the court. The

rules are no dribbling, no walking, and no passing behind a player. Encourage players to pass ahead and catch with two hands.

Ball Handling

Regardless of the style of basketball your team plays, all players need to be able to handle the ball. The best way for a player to gain confidence in ball handling is through hours of practice. When doing ball-handling drills I have my players first work on technique, second on speed, and third under pressure or gamelike conditions. This can be done first with stationary ball-handling drills, then with basic dribbling drills, and finally with advanced dribbling drills. While working on their ball handling, players need to incorporate other fundamentals of the game. They need to keep their heads up as if they were in a game. I remind our players to work in an athletic position as if they were playing the game. Start out easy to build and gain confidence. Then I tell them to challenge themselves. Go at a pace or speed that's almost frantic. I want players to push themselves in all areas, including with their ball handling. If they never get past the easy stage, they never improve. As I tell my players, basketball is not a game of horse. Add pressure and challenges to your workouts to simulate game conditions. Your players should work daily on improving their ball-handling skills. Just 10 to 15 minutes each day can really improve all areas of a player's game, especially her confidence.

Stationary Ball-Handling Drills

There are hundreds of ball-handling drills players can use to improve their ball handling. Sometimes you'll need to tailor the drills to the weaknesses of the player. Ball-handling drills can be done stationary, while dribbling, or with two balls. Frequency, duration, and intensity all affect what a player gets out of her ball-handling practice. The best ball handlers I've coached put together their own ball-handling routines to improve their skills. The following basic drills have been proven effective in improving a player's ability to handle the ball.

Ball Slaps A player holds the ball in front of her in one hand and slaps it with the other hand. Then she switches hands and repeats.

Body Circles Using both hands, players take the ball around their head, then around their waist, and then around their knees, each time completing a full circle. Have them repeat this routine in reverse order, then change directions.

Figure-Eight Around the Legs Players weave the ball between and around their legs in a figure-eight pattern.

Straddle Flip With feet shoulder-width apart and knees bent, players start with the ball in front of their knees, held in both hands. They drop the ball and catch it with two hands behind their knees before the ball hits the ground. With their hands behind their knees, they drop the ball and catch it before it hits the ground as their hands change to the front of their knees. The ball stays between their legs and the hands continually go in front of their legs, knees, then behind their legs, knees. Hand position keeps changing.

Blur Players put the ball between their feet and grab it with both hands. They start with the left hand behind the left leg and the right hand in front of the right leg. They then drop the ball and let it bounce once. They quickly move their left hand in front of the left leg and the right hand behind the right leg and catch the ball as it bounces up. They drop the ball again and switch hands back to the original position (left behind, right in front) and catch it. Have them repeat this action. To add difficulty, have players catch the ball before it hits the ground.

Double Leg–Single Leg Players start with feet shoulder-width apart and knees bent, holding the ball in both hands in front of their knees. They take a side step with the right foot and circle the right leg. They then bring the right foot back to a shoulder-width position and circle the ball around both legs. Next, they take a side step with the left foot and circle the left leg. They then bring the left foot back to a shoulder-width position and circle both legs. Have them continue this pattern, circling one leg, both legs, then the other leg, always remaining in an athletic position.

Spider Players start with feet shoulder-width apart and knees bent. The ball is to be dribbled between the feet and under the body. Hands are in front of your body. Players start with a

right-handed dribble and then do a left-handed dribble. Then they put their hands behind the body and take one dribble with the right hand and one dribble with the left hand. Ideally, the ball stays in the same place as the hand position moves from in front of the body to behind the body. The dribbles are low and quick.

Dribbling Drills

Dribble Figure-Eight This is done in the same way as the stationary figure-eight pattern except the ball is dribbled throughout the movement.

Dribble Attack Place five or six players in the free-throw lane, each of them with a ball. Players begin dribbling within the confines of the lane, trying to maintain their dribble while attacking the other players within the lane and trying to knock their ball away. Players are eliminated if they lose their dribble, kill their dribble, or cross the lane lines.

Get There Start at the free-throw line. Players get one dribble to score a layup. From half court they get two dribbles for a layup. From three-quarters they get three dribbles for a layup. From baseline to baseline they get four dribbles for a layup.

Pete Maravich Drill Start in the center circle with two minutes on the clock. Players dribble in the circle using all the dribbling moves they know, such as the in and out, crossover, behind the back, and so on. They do not leave the circle. Have them do the drill as rapidly as they can without rushing. Add a minute to the clock each day until they can dribble for five minutes straight.

Speed Drill This drill is done full court. Four cones divide the court equally into quarters. At each cone the player is required to perform a different dribbling move, predetermined before the drill begins. At the whistle, players dribble full court, executing a move at each cone. They should dribble right hand down court and left hand back. Accuracy and speed are important.

Two-Ball Dribbling Drills

Stationary Dribbling With Two Balls All dribbling is done in a bent-knee athletic stance. A coach calls out the dribble to be executed, using these commands: "same" (balls dribbled at the same time); "alternate" (balls dribbled out of rhythm); "side to side" (balls dribbled from side to side); "forward and back" (balls dribbled on the side of the knees, forward and back); and "one high, one low" (one ball dribbled high while the other ball is dribbled low).

Full-Court Dribbling Coaches call the same commands as in the previous drill, but players go full court and back with each type of two-ball dribbles.

Half Court and Back Players turn sideways with their shoulder facing half court. Dribble commands are the same as for the previous two drills. This time players slide to half court. This requires the player to push and pull the ball as she dribbles to half court and back.

Zigzag Dribbling Cones are placed on the court in a zigzag position. Players dribble two balls from cone to cone using dribble moves such as the hesitation, crossover, and in and out.

Shooting

There is a big difference between a shooter and a scorer. Most players are shooters. It's our job to help them become scorers. Becoming a good scorer is more than just the ability to shoot the ball—it requires a combination of skills. There's a technique, an attitude, and an ability to use other skills, such as dribbling and screening, that make a shooter a great scorer. There are many types of shot in basketball—the layup, free throw, jump shot, hook, and so on. There are also many ways to shoot each shot. However, there are some basic fundamentals in the art of shooting that can increase a player's ability to successfully shoot and score.

The jump shot is the most popular shot in the game today. You can teach the jump shot literally from the ground up. Initially, a shooter's stance should be square to the basket with feet about shoulder-width apart. Of course, all shooters tailor their stance to their comfort level. However, when too close together the feet don't allow balance or provide a strong base of support. Knees should be flexed, ready to extend as the shooter jumps. When the shooter jumps to shoot, the shot should be released at the peak of the jump. Often the shooter's toes point to the ground as she jumps into the air to shoot.

The ball rests on the pads of the shooter's shooting hand, not on the palm of the hand. The shooting elbow is bent about 90 degrees. The shooter's wrist is cocked back. The nonshooting hand is placed on the side of the ball, with its main purpose being to help balance the ball in the shooting hand. The fingers of the nonshooting hand point to the ceiling in preparation for the shot.

As the shooter jumps, her legs extend, as does her shooting hand. Her elbow should be higher than her eyes on the release of the shot. This encourages the shooter to lift the ball and straighten out the shooting hand. As the ball is released from the shooting hand, the shooting wrist snaps down. This wrist snap imparts backspin on the basketball, which helps to cushion a shot and increases its chances of going through the basket.

Where's the BEEF?

BEEF is an acronym for a checklist of reminders for shooters and those teaching correct shooting form. It's a simple way to teach or remember the fundamentals of shooting:

- **B**alance. Shoot on balance, not while falling forward, backward, or sideways.
- **E**lbow. Line your shooting elbow under the ball, parallel to the floor. The elbow should not point downward.
- **E**xtend. Extend your shooting arm as you shoot. Elbow is higher than your eyes.
- **F**ollow through. As you release the ball, snap your wrist on your follow-through so that your palm faces the floor.

Shooting Drills

Great shooters spend hours in the gym, "grooving" their shot. Here are some drills to demonstrate to your players for them to do independently or with a partner to improve their shooting technique and scoring ability.

Beat the Pro A player starts with a shot from the free-throw line. If she makes the free throw, she receives one point. If she misses the free throw, the pro receives three points. Thereafter, the player tosses the ball to herself and shoots field goals (10 to 15 feet from the basket), scoring one point for herself if she makes the shot and two points for the pro if she misses. Play continues until either the player or the pro has 10 points. The player's goal is to shoot 66 percent or better. Younger players may substitute one layup for one of their missed field goal attempts.

Beat the Pro Off the Dribble This drill is the same as the previous drill, but the shooter starts behind the three-point line, tosses the ball to herself, and then takes one dribble before she shoots.

Four Up A player shoots against another player from designated spots. The first player to get four baskets ahead wins.

Steve Alford Drill A player starts in the lane with the ball. She passes the ball back to herself 10 to 12 feet out on the floor. She catches the ball, pivots, and shoots. She then gets her own rebound and back passes to another spot on the floor (figure 8.5). The goal is to make eight shots in one minute. Dribbling can be added to this drill.

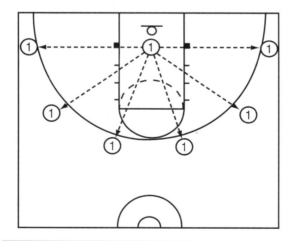

Figure 8.5 Steve Alford Drill.

Run-the-W A shooter will need a partner to be the passer for this drill. The shooter starts in the corner, then sprints to midcourt and back to the corner for a catch and shoot. She then sprints back to midcourt and then to the wing for another catch and shoot. She continues around the court to the other sideline, shooting from seven spots (figure 8.6). Dribbling can be added to this drill.

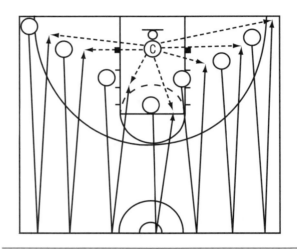

Figure 8.6 Run-the-W.

PLAYING WITHOUT THE BALL

When I watch players run the offense, they seem to be more comfortable with the ball in their hands than without it. Even good players often stand when they don't have the ball, which causes the offense to break down. Players need to know how to get open on their own when pressured defensively, how to get a teammate open with a screen, and how to use a screen to get themselves open. Teaching proper footwork, understanding angles, and being able to change speeds help players learn to be successful without the ball.

Footwork

Some players are naturally quicker than others. However, a player's effective quickness can be greatly enhanced if she uses proper footwork. A naturally quick player who lacks good footwork skills can be beaten or perhaps contained by a player with solid footwork fundamentals. Offensive footwork includes a player's stance, pivoting, starts and stops, changing speeds and directions, jumping, faking, and cutting.

Players need to play in a good basketball position or stance. This improves their ability to start and stop, change speed and direction, jump, shoot, pass, and dribble. A player's weight should be on the ball of her feet with feet about shoulder-width apart and knees flexed. Her head should be centered above her lower body.

Pivoting in basketball involves keeping one foot planted on the floor while moving the other foot, thus turning the body. All players need to know how to pivot both forward and backward on the balls of their feet. When pivoting, it's important to protect the ball and keep the head up. The pivot foot can't change from one foot to the other, nor can the pivot foot slide.

There are two ways to stop in basketball—either a one-two step stop or a jump stop. When executing a one-two step stop, one foot lands first and then the second foot lands. The foot that hits the floor first is the designated pivot foot. When executing a jump stop, both feet land simultaneously. In a jump stop, the last step should be a hop, and the landing should be on bent knees for balance. After a jump stop, the player is free to use either foot as the pivot foot.

When changing directions in basketball, a player plants the opposite foot (that is, the foot opposite of the way she wants to cut) and then pushes off the inside part of that foot in the direction she wants to go. For example, if a player wants to make a sudden cut to her left, she should plant her right foot and then push off from the inside part of her right foot, changing direction to the left.

Almost every offensive move is set up by a good fake to get the defender leaning in the wrong direction. This is true whether a player is making an offensive jab step, coming off a screen, or preparing to pass.

V-Cuts Changing speed and direction is important when using a V-cut, whether it occurs in the lane or on the perimeter. This cut is one of the most effective ways for players to free themselves from defenders. A "cut" is a step or steps taken in the opposite direction from which the player wants to get open. This cut is called a V-cut because a V is the path a player uses to free herself. If she's on the perimeter, she jogs to the block and then sprints back to the perimeter using a different path but in a straight line like a V (figure 8.7). With this move she wants to get the defender off balance or out of position, thus giving herself an advantage. The V-cut can also be used to set up backdoor cuts, screens, or basket cuts.

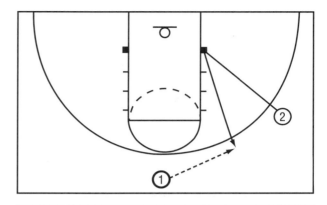

Figure 8.7 V-cuts.

The V-cut can also be used in the post area. A post player on the right block who wants to cross the lane to the left block would use a V-cut. Starting on the right block, she would take one or two hard steps in the middle of the paint and then finish her V with one or two hard steps to the left block. She wants her defender to believe she's really cutting high out of the lane in a straight line instead of going to the opposite block. Again, this move is done in straight lines with an explosive change of speed after the initial setup.

Backdoor Cuts The pop out is an excellent way to set up the backdoor play. On the perimeter, the player makes a hard cut to receive a pass. If being tightly overplayed by her defender, she plants her outside foot, pushes off with that foot, and makes a strong backdoor cut to the basket (figure 8.8). Changes of speed is again important for the move to be effective. For this move to work in the post area, the post player needs to stretch out her defense. She might do this from the high-post area or out on the perimeter if she has extended range. The footwork is the

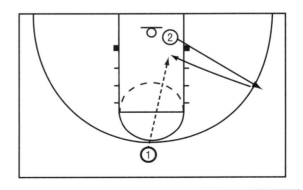

Figure 8.8 A pop-out cut sets up the backdoor play.

same, and she needs to be overplayed for this move to work.

If the backdoor cut is denied by the defense on the perimeter, the offensive player can turn the backdoor cut into a V-cut that can help her get open. She does this by popping out to make a backdoor cut, seeing it's not there, then making a V-cut to the block and out to the corner (figure 8.9). The offensive player is worried about getting beat to the basket, which sets up this V-cut flare move.

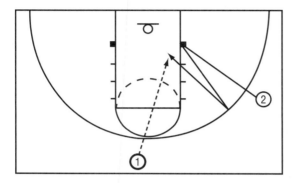

Figure 8.9 A backdoor cut turns into a V-cut.

Screens

A screen, or a "pick," happens when an offensive player attempts to block a defensive player away from the player she is guarding, thereby freeing up that offensive player for an open shot or pass. All offensive players should realize that both the screener and the player being screened for are options to receive a pass.

The screener needs to make contact with, but not foul, the defender she's trying to block. The screener needs to be strong. Feet need to be shoulder-width apart and knees bent to make a strong base (figure 8.10). The screener can't move as she makes contact with the person she's screening or she'll be called for a moving screen. Coaches vary on hand and arm position. Some have players cross their arms over their chest. Others have players hold their own wrists. Regardless of the position, players can't use their arms or hands to grab or hold the defender.

The angle or direction of the screen and the timing of the screen are two of the most overlooked factors when setting a screen. The screener must anticipate the direction her offensive teammate wants to go and then screen her

Figure 8.10 Setting a screen.

defender in a position that directly blocks the defender so that she can't get around her.

After setting a screen successfully, the screener needs to open to the ball. In doing that, she can see how her defender and her teammates played the screening action. If there's a switch, or help on the screen, the screener might be the open player.

Timing is important when using a screen. The player receiving the screen must be patient and wait for the screen to arrive. I tell my players to wait for the screener to jump stop and plant her feet for the screen. The player receiving the screen must cut hard and close to the teammate setting the screen. Tell your players to "go shoulder to shoulder" as they rub off each other during the screen.

The most often used screens to get teammates open are the front screen, back screen, and down screen. On the front screen, the screener is facing the defender that she's setting the screen on. This screen is most often used in the open court. In the back screen, the screener sets the screen on the defenders "blind" or backside. Usually, the screener is facing away from the basket. This is an excellent screen to use when the defender is closely guarded and a lane is open to the basket for the player being screened. When executing the down screen, the screener sets the screen down low for a player near the block, and she's usually facing the basket with her back to the ball. Down screens are often used to initiate an offense with a pass to the perimeter.

SUMMARY

- For offensive success, break the whole down into parts and drive home the importance of fundamentals.

- Drills provide opportunities to work on individual and team skills.

- The better your team can dribble, pass, and shoot, the greater chance your team has of being successful on offense.

- Learning to play without the ball is as important as playing with the ball.

- Playing with the ball includes moves from a stationary position as well as moves while dribbling, passing, and shooting.

- Moves from a stationary position include the jab step and shot; jab step and drive; crossover step and dribble; and jab step, drive, and pull-up jumper.

- Moves while dribbling include the hesitation, in and out, crossover, reverse, and control.

- Playing without the ball includes screening and cutting to get open.

- Players need to be taught the proper technique of setting screens and using screens.

CHAPTER 9 DEVELOPING A RUNNING GAME

If you ask players what style of play they prefer, they'll tell you they like to play up tempo, otherwise known as the running game. As a coach, you have to decide if that style best suits your personnel and your philosophy. If you have the players to push tempo, and you believe transition baskets can be a weapon for your team, a running game can be fun and exciting. The important thing is to play and coach to the strengths of your player personnel. To run, you need not only quick players but players who can control the ball while moving quickly. Both must be present—speed and skills. There have been years when I believed we had a dominant inside game offensively. With those teams, we were best off attacking our opponent in a half-court game, pounding the ball inside.

The ability to run with the ball can create several advantages for your team. First, by pushing tempo you're constantly putting pressure on your opponent's defense. If you run on most offensive possessions, you allow the defense little time to rest, relax, or regroup. Thus, your team dictates the tempo.

Second, offensive transition can lead to easy scoring opportunities. Players need to get out early on the break and run the floor hard. I believe transition opportunities are created in the backcourt, not the frontcourt. If your players will run hard in their own backcourt, by the time they cross the half-court line, they can have a significant jump on their opponent.

Many times players wait until they get to half court to decide if they need to run hard for a transition basket. Players waiting to run the floor hard blow many opportunities. I'm constantly reminding players to get out early on the break. If all offensive players run the floor hard, they can create a numerical advantage for your team on the offensive end. When you have a numerical advantage over the defense, you can get some high-percentage baskets.

Finally, the fast break is an effective way to break or beat full- or three-quarter court defensive pressure. If your team runs on a missed or made basket, you often can push the ball up the floor before a defense has time to set up their press. I've found when we run on a made basket, fewer and fewer teams press us. They become more concerned about defensive transition and getting back to protect their basket. Often, we have the ball down the floor before the opponent's defense can get into their correct defensive positioning. We might not always get layups, but we often have the numerical advantage and can get a high-percentage shot. Along with all of these reasons for playing a running game, I simply like that we're dictating the pace of the game.

Pushing the offensive tempo too often can lead to sloppy play. Sometimes players can get in too big a hurry, especially the player with the ball, and this can lead to costly turnovers. I remind my team that the players without the ball should run the floor hard and the player with the ball should take her speed down just a notch.

A second possible disadvantage to a running game is that up-tempo play might complement your starting players but not your bench. Be sure to change gears offensively if the fast pace is not best suited for your players on the court.

I have a rule: When a team fast breaks on us, we do not fast break back. If we have just given up an easy score, I want my team to get settled, slow down and regroup mentally, and then get a high-percentage shot in our half-court offense. I have found when we do run after a team has just run a fast break on us that we tend to get into a helter-skelter type of game. This frantic pace often leads to poor offensive decisions.

Finally, there are times as a coach when in controlling the tempo you need to control the clock. Many times maintaining possession of the ball is more important than trying to score quickly. In these situations, playing the running game is not to your team's advantage.

PRIMARY FAST BREAK

To create a primary fast break, players need to be drilled to get the ball up the floor the quickest and safest way. The primary fast break is designed for players to create numerical advantages offensively, thus getting into position to shoot a high-percentage shot. Here are numerical advantages to be gained via the fast break and the typical result:

- 1 on 0: layup
- 1 on 1: layup or foul
- 2 on 1: layup or foul
- 3 on 2: layup or short jumper
- 4 on 2 or 5 on 2: layup or short jumper

One on Zero   When your offensive player runs the floor hard, and the defense has no safety back, your player can get a breakaway score. After a heads-up pass from a teammate, your player might get an easy layup opportunity or, with luck, a layup and a foul with a chance at a three-point play. Some teams automatically have a player "run out" when the shot goes up. If this player can get ahead of the defense, she has a good chance of scoring an uncontested layup.

One on One   A one-on-one situation should result in a high-percentage shot—either a layup or a short jumper. Encourage your players to attack the goal initially to put pressure on the defensive player. Force the defense to take away the highest percentage shot first. If a player is given a chance to shoot a layup, and she anticipates a foul, she should focus on making the layup. Then she can step to the line to finish the three-point play.

If the defense has a good angle to take away the layup, your player should pull up for a short jump shot. The best angle to shoot a layup is a 45-degree angle. This is the path the defender tries to cut off. The defender wants the offensive player to attack the goal using a wider lane, one that is not straight or direct, which takes longer and is slower. If the defender is successful in accomplishing this, it buys her some time, and maybe her teammates can catch up to the play. Depending on how much time is remaining and the score, the offensive player might pull the ball out to set up a half-court offense.

Two on One   In a two-on-one situation, players need to attack the goal. It's important to get a shot off, because you still have a rebounder if the shot is missed. To maintain this advantage, players need to get a shot off quickly, before additional defenders catch up.

In a two-on-one situation, offensive players must spread far enough apart that the defender can't guard both of them at once (see figure 9.1). If one offensive player can get ahead of the defender, she needs to cut hard to the basket, and her teammate needs to pitch the ball ahead of the defender for a high-percentage shot. If the defender is ahead of both offensive players, the offense stays wide until they cross half court and are in scoring range just outside the three-point line. At this point, it is the job of the offensive player with the ball to make the defender guard her or her teammate, read the defensive player's decision, and create an easy scoring opportunity for herself or her teammate.

For the ball handler to make the defense commit to guarding her, she must be a scoring threat. If she's not, the defender will ease back off the dribbler, fade to the second offensive player, and, in essence, guard them both.

The ball handler should not predetermine what she'll do with the ball. It's important that

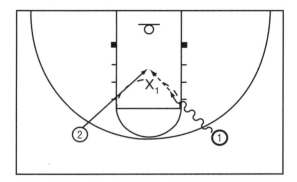

Figure 9.1 Two-on-one situation.

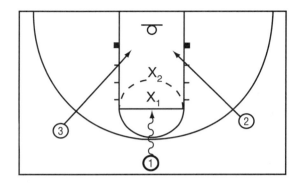

Figure 9.2 Three-on-two situation.

she make the right read on the defense. Getting in a hurry and predetermining a pass or shot can lead to a turnover.

The key to the two on one is for the ball handler to keep possession of the ball until the defender has decided to either guard the ball handler or drops off to guard the other player. The ball handler then makes the quick decision to either dump the ball off to her teammate for a layup or a drive or take the shot herself. Two-on-one situations should always result in a high-percentage shot.

Three on Two   In a three-on-two situation, many of the principles in the two-on-one situation apply. Players need to be thinking of attacking the goal. To maintain their advantage, they need to run the floor hard and attack aggressively.

As players run the floor, the ball should be in the hands of the player in the middle, and her two teammates should fill the left and right wing positions. The wing players need to spread the court so no single defender can guard two players at once. As players cross half court and approach the three-point line, the key is the middle player with the ball.

The player with the ball wants to attack the defense and make one of the defenders guard her. If neither defender guards the ball, and the dribbler has a good angle to the goal, she needs to drive hard to the basket for an easy score. If neither defender guards the dribbler, and both slough off into the lane area, it's important for the dribbler not to penetrate farther than the foul line. Too much penetration (without a shot) by the middle player can result in a three-second call, an offensive foul, or a poor passing angle to teammates (see figure 9.2).

If the defenders stay back in a three-on-two situation, the dribbler should pass to an open wing and then step to the opposite elbow. I have the middle player fill to the opposite elbow so there's still a two on one on the weak side. If player 1 passes to wing 2, wing 3 needs to read the defense and decide if she needs to make a basket cut to receive a pass from wing 2. Ideally, if the defense guards the dribbler, player 1, there's only one defender left to guard wings 2 and 3. If the second defender guards wing 2, and the first defender is slow to react or reacts poorly, wing 3 should make a basket cut and receive a diagonal pass from wing 2 for an easy score. Thus, a three on two becomes a two on one. If the top defender who had guarded player 1 reacts quickly, sinks, and takes away the pass from wing 2 to wing 3, then wing 3 should look for her own jump shot or make a pass to player 1 at the opposite elbow for a short jumper. This is considered a high-percentage shot for a couple of reasons. First, it should be an uncontested shot. Second, it is a 15-foot shot. Third, if the shot is missed, teammates are in excellent rebounding positions. Again, if the defense reacts quickly from the pass from wing 2 to player 1, player 1 might have a dump pass to wing 3 on the block. The defense can't guard all three players if the offense makes smart, quick decisions.

It's important not to overpass in a three-on-two situation. If the defense can make the offense pass more than twice on the offensive end, the defense has done their job of buying time for teammates to hustle down the court and help make a play. If the offense can get a high-percentage shot off with two passes or less, most defenses will not have caught up in time.

Four on Two and Five on Two These numerical advantages are rare in primary breaks. Usually the 4 and 5 players are more involved in secondary fast-break opportunities. If your team has a four on two or a five on two fast-break opportunity, the first three players down the floor attack the defense as if it were a three-on-two situation. The ball needs to get to the middle of the floor, and the next two players fill the wing spots. The wing players want to stay wide until they cross half court and get near the three-point line. If the wings see or hear a post trailing the play, they need to stay wide to open up a lane for the post in the paint. At this time the 4 and 5 players finish as they would in a secondary break.

Once the dribbler gives the ball up to a wing player, the trail post (player 4) makes a strong cut to the ballside block, looking for a pass or getting into rebounding position. The last player down the floor offensively (player 5) makes a read. She might be the safety, trail post, or a lag perimeter player.

Again, the numerical advantage won't last long. Players should have a scoring mentality but not be in a hurry. Playing too fast or making the wrong decision can lead to a turnover.

Transition baskets are a fun and exciting part of the game. Players need to practice all primary break situations to learn how to make smart and efficient decisions. We spend 20 to 30 minutes each practice working on some aspect of our running game.

SECONDARY FAST BREAK

If you lose your numerical advantage but still have the basketball, you can move right into your secondary fast break. You're still looking for quick scoring opportunities, but now it's probably a five-on-five situation.

Secondary fast-break sets are determined by the coach. We finish our secondary break with a four-out look. In a four-out look, four offensive players are placed on the court in perimeter positions, all outside the free-throw lane. They can be inside or outside the three-point line. One offensive player is positioned inside the free-throw lane. This inside player is usually a post player, and the other four players have perimeter skills. Our point guard, two wings, and a lag player fill the four-out spots. The four spots are the right and left wings and the lines of the free-throw lane extended.

The fifth player is the lag player and is in the last spot filled, which is usually opposite the low post and above the free-throw line extended. There is already a post filling the block area. Our lag player can be a post or perimeter player, depending on personnel. From this four-out look, we can run several options to play to the strengths of our players on the court (see figure 9.3).

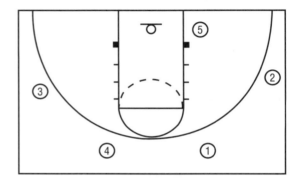

Figure 9.3 Four-out secondary fast break.

Players get into their secondary fast-break positions when they recognize that (1) there's no primary break opportunity, (2) the defense has three or more players back defending their goal, and (3) the coach or point guard calls out the secondary set options. Players can quickly go from primary to secondary positions. Secondary sets can also be run as half-court offenses.

FAST BREAK AFTER THE OPPONENT SCORES

A third type of fast break is transition after an opponent's made basket. I refer to this as a "made fast break." We run a made fast break as a sideline break. Each player has a spot on the floor to fill and a job to do. We won't run this sideline break if any of three scenarios holds true: (1) our opponent just scored a transition layup on us, (2) we're playing too fast and are out of control, or (3) we need to change tempo or run some clock.

For our made fast break to work, the ball must be inbounded quickly. We designate a player, usually our 5 player, to inbound the ball. If our point guard is right-handed, the 5 player steps out of bounds on the right side of the basket.

We will run a right sideline break (see figure 9.4). The 1 player sprints to the right sideline free-throw line extended to receive the pass from the 5 player. The 2 player sprints up the right sideline and looks over her left shoulder to receive a pass from the 1 player. Ideally, the passing goes from 5 to 1 to 2. The 2 player should be across midcourt when she receives the pass. The 3 player is on the left side of the

floor. She makes sure the 5 player can safely enter the ball to the 1 player and then runs the left sideline. If 1 is denied the pass from 5, 3 is 5's second pass option. If the ball goes from 5 to 3, 1 cuts to the middle of the floor to receive a pass back from 3. Player 1 would then throw the ball to 2. As soon as the opponent scores their basket, the 4 player is sprinting up the floor to the right block. The 5 player lags the play and goes to the secondary spot. Once player 1 gives the ball up, she fills her secondary position. Once players cross the half-court line, they need to make decisions. Players might have primary break opportunities. If no primary break opportunities exist, players go immediately into their secondary break options.

If the defense overplays the right sideline and takes away passing opportunities to the 2 player, the 1 player can crosscourt the ball to the 3 player on the left wing. This then becomes a left break, and the 4 player crosses the court to the left block, and secondary spots are filled on the left side of the court if no primary action occurs.

The sideline break is a great attack weapon against an opponent who lets up after a score or uses some time and energy in celebrating a score. It also gives the opponent little time to set up a full-court defense. In our system, we have a cue when the made fast break is on and when it's off.

FAST-BREAK DRILLS

Fast-break drills can help players work on fundamentals and decision-making skills and can also be a great way to condition your team. You want your players to develop good habits of getting the ball up the floor quickly and safely, recognizing the opponent's defense, and responding with good offensive decisions.

Two-Player Drills

This is a series of full-court two-player drills. These drills can be done simultaneously using both sides of a full court. Once two players have done the drill on the right side of the court, they get in line and, when it's their turn, make their return trip down the left side of the court.

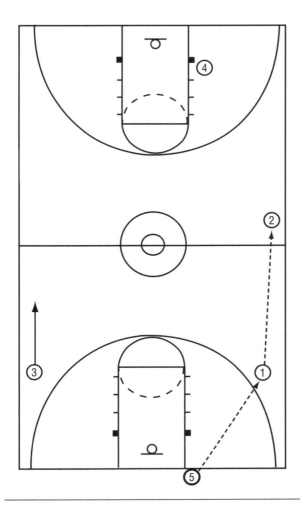

Figure 9.4 Sideline fast break.

Full-Court Layups

Purpose: To practice layups at game tempo. This drill teaches players to run the floor hard with their heads up, verbally communicate, run lanes wide, and incorporate such fundamentals as jump stops, cuts, pass fakes, and layups.

Setup: Three cones are placed with equal spacing along the right free-throw lane line. Two lines are formed. All line 1 players have a ball and line up behind the endline behind the first cone. All line 2 players line up behind the baseline behind the right sideline.

Procedure: The drill starts as player 1 weaves in and out of the cones and then speed dribbles to the opposite end. She jump stops at the free-throw line, fakes a pass, and makes a pass to player 2 for a right-handed layup. While dribbling she keeps her head up and uses as few

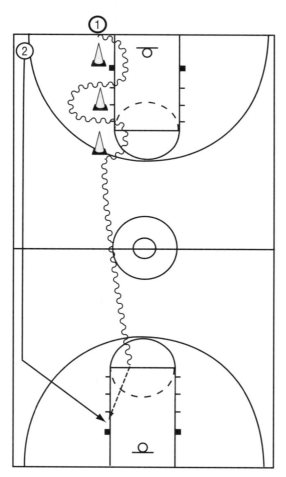

Figure 9.5 Full-court layup.

dribbles as possible to get to the free-throw line. Player 2 sprints the right sideline as soon as player 1 begins dribbling. She is running her right lane wide and is calling out her lane ("Right!") to the 1 player. She stays wide until she reaches the free-throw lane at the opposite end. At this point, she plants her right foot and makes a hard cut directly to the basket. She runs in a straight line. She receives a pass from the 1 player for a layup (see figure 9.5). If the layup is missed, player 1 puts in the rebound. Positions are exchanged on the return trip. This drill is run simultaneously down the right and left sidelines.

Full-Court Jumpers

Purpose: To practice jump shots at game speed in a transition setting.

Setup: The setup for this drill is the same as the Full-Court Layup Drill (see previous drill).

Procedure: When player 2 crosses half court, she stays wide and heads toward the baseline, taking two or three steps past the three-point line. Next, she plants her right foot and makes a strong cut back to the 1 player at the free-throw line. Player 1 fakes a pass and makes a pass to player 2 for a jumper. If the shot is missed, player 1 puts in the rebound. Player 2 needs to step to meet the pass from player 1.

Full-Court Fade

Purpose: To practice a fade shot at game speed in a transition setting.

Setup: The setup for this drill is the same as in the previous two drills.

Procedure: When players are executing the fade shot, player 2 cuts to the basket at the opposite-end free-throw line extended, touches the right block, plants her left foot, and pushes off hard to the corner, thus executing a flare move. Player 1 fakes a pass and makes a pass to the shooter who has flared. If the shot is missed, player 1 puts in the rebound. Player 2 needs to make her cut to the basket and her fade cut in straight lines with changes of speed.

Three-Player Drills

This is a series of full-court three-player drills. These drills can be done full court and back, or one time down the court, depending on numbers and time.

Touch-and-Go Drill

Purpose: This is a full-court drill for three players. The emphasis is on passing, catching, running the floor, and scoring. This drill is an excellent conditioner.

Setup: The team forms three lines. Players in the first line are rebounders, players in the second line are outlets, and players in the third line run the sideline looking for the pitch-ahead pass.

Procedure: Player 1 rebounds a shot off the backboard. She yells "board!" and turns to her outside to outlet the ball to player 2. Player 3 steps to meet the outlet pass. After the pass, player 1 sprints up the floor.

Player 2 squares up after receiving the pass, takes a couple of dribbles with her inside hand, and passes to player 3, who has sprinted the floor and is making a basket cut as player 2's pass comes to her. Player 3 shoots a layup and then becomes the outlet player (see figure 9.6a). Player 1 gets the ball out of the net, steps out of bounds, and inbounds the ball quickly to player 3. Player 2 touches the baseline and then sprints to the opposite end along the sideline. When player 2 gets to the free-throw line extended, she makes a basket cut and receives a pass from player 3 (see figure 9.6b). Remind players to call their lanes, run the floor hard, and step to meet passes.

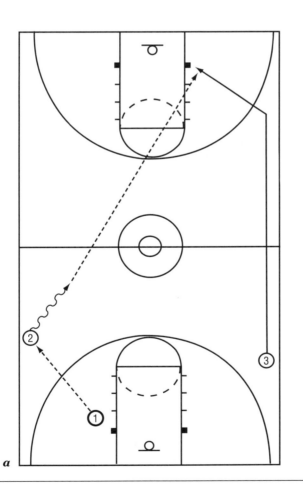

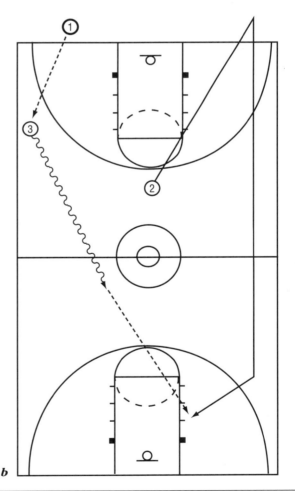

Figure 9.6 Touch-and-Go Drill.

"11 Man" Full-Court Fast Break

Purpose: This drill is designed to practice three-on-two situations.

Setup: The drill is set up with two defenders at each end positioned in a tandem defensive alignment. Three offensive players are at the half-court line with the ball in the hands of the girl in the middle position.

Procedure: These three players attack one end at which a tandem defense is set up. This initial set has three offensive players on the court and two defensive tandem sets, for a total of seven players. All other players are out of bounds in four lines on the sideline. These players are outlet players and become offensive players as the drill progresses. The first three offensive players on the court attack a tandem using three-on-two guidelines (see figure 9.7). They

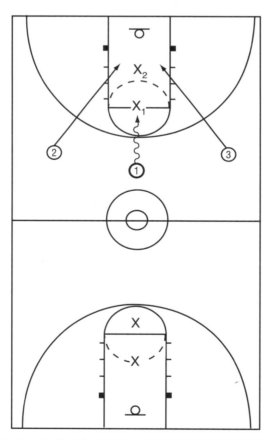

Figure 9.7 "11 Man" Full-Court Fast Break.

want a high-percentage shot. Whether the shot is made or missed, the two defensive players become offensive players as they advance the ball to the other end. The third offensive player comes from the out-of-bounds line on her half of the court, on the same side the outlet pass should occur. Of the three players who were on offense, two become tandem defensive players, and the third goes to the out-of-bounds line to replace the player who just joined the offensive group. Again, there is a three-on-two situation. This is a continuous drill with only one shot allowed at each end.

Three-Man Weave Drills

The Pitch Drill along with the Tip Drill, the Three Man Weave Into Two on One, and the Three-Line Fast Break are a series of drills that can be run from a three-man weave setup.

Pitch Drill

Purpose: These drills are excellent for working on offensive transition. Players work on the offensive skills they need to play up tempo as well as practice reading defenses and making quick and accurate decisions against differing defensive alignments.

Setup: A three-man weave.

Procedure: Players line up in three lines across the baseline to execute a full-court three-man weave. Player 1 shoots a layup at the opposite end. Regardless of whether the shot goes in, player 1 sprints the full length of the court to the other end to shoot another layup. Player 2, who made the first pass for the layup to player 1, follows her pass and makes the outlet pass to player 3. Player 3 receives the outlet pass and makes a pitch-ahead pass to player 1 for a layup (see figure 9.8). Players 2 and 3 must sprint the full court and should finish in the paint as the ball goes through the net on the layup.

When executing the three-man weave, players never throw behind a player. This is also true in the Pitch Drill. If need be, the player with the ball dribbles in for the shot. Players need to run the floor hard, keep their heads up, and communicate with their teammates. Players need to lead their teammates on the pitch pass.

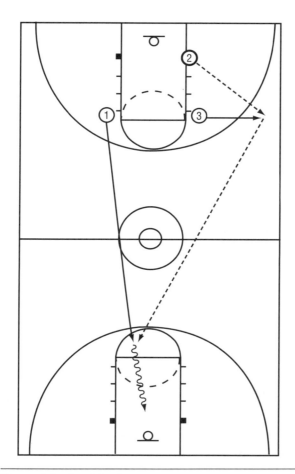

Figure 9.8   Pitch Drill.

Tip Drill

Purpose: To improve passing, catching, and scoring in a fast-break setting.

Setup: A three-man weave.

Procedure: Instead of player 1 shooting a layup, she tosses the ball up on the backboard. Player 2 follows with a backboard tip (the ball must not hit the ground). Player 3 finishes the play with a tip in. Player 1 tosses, player 2 tips, and player 3 scores.

Three-Man Weave Into Two on One

Purpose: To improve offensive decision making when playing with a numerical advantage

against the defense. Also, to improve player defense when playing against an offensive numerical advantage.

Setup: A three-man weave.

Procedure: Players form three lines on the baseline to execute a three-man weave to the other end to shoot a layup. Regardless of whether the shot goes in, whoever shoots the ball hustles back to the other end and becomes the sole defender. The other two players become the offensive players. They get the rebound (or get the ball out of the net on a made shot) and begin their two-on-one attack against the defender at the opposite end of the court. The offensive players are encouraged to attack the defense with good two-on-one fundamentals. Encourage the defensive player to be active, not to commit too early to the ball, and to try to get a deflection, steal, or rebound. This drill is a three-man weave down court and a two on one back up court.

Three-Line Fast Break

Purpose: To improve the initial steps of an offensive transition—the rebound, the outlet pass, and the middle pass.

Setup: Players form three lines on the baseline. One line is the rebounding line, one the outlet line, and one the middle line. The three lines are spread out equally across the baseline.

Procedure: Players in the outlet line toss the ball up on the backboard and rebound the missed shot. They yell "board!" as they rebound the ball and turn to the outside to make their pass. Remind them to "catch it high and keep it high." Players in the outlet line take a step or two toward the opposite baseline and then, yelling "outlet," make a hard cut toward the rebounder. The outlet catches the ball and squares up. As this is happening, the player in the "middle line," calling "middle," is making a cut toward the middle of the court. The outlet passes to the middle player, who squares up and begins dribbling to the opposite end (see figure 9.9). She jump stops at the free-throw lane, fakes a pass, and then makes a pass to one of the other two players cutting to the basket for a layup. The rebounder makes her pass and fills the lane opposite of where she just threw the ball. The outlet player continues running the lane on the same side of the floor she is on. This becomes a three-player fast break, with the ball in the middle of the court and the two outside lanes filled.

Variation: For variation, the drill can end with a jumper or a layup. We use this drill to remind

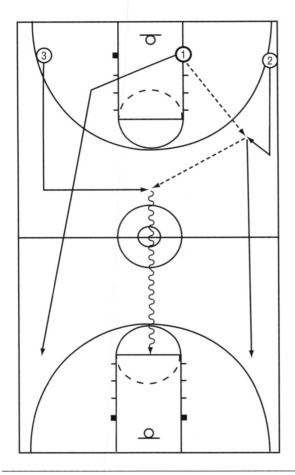

Figure 9.9 Three-Line Fast Break.

players of spots filled in a primary fast-break situation.

Four-Player Drills

This is a series of full-court four-player drills. These drills can help your team build numbers into their transition offense.

Four on Three Plus One

Purpose: To work on player positioning offensively as a fast break develops and to improve offensive decision making when playing with a numerical advantage over the defense.

Setup: Four offensive players are spread across the baseline. Four defensive players are spread across the free-throw line to the sideline (see figure 9.10a).

Procedure: A coach throws the ball to one of the offensive players and, at the same time, calls out the name of one of the defensive players. The four offensive players run a primary or secondary fast break. The player whose name was called out must run and touch the baseline and then sprint up the floor to help the other three defenders who are retreating and defending the opposite basket (see figure 9.10b). The defense must communicate. The offensive players try to score while they have a numerical advantage; the three defensive players try to buy some time until their fourth defender joins them.

Offensive players must run the floor hard, get the ball into a ball handler's hands, and make good decisions on the other end. The defense must stop an easy or quick score and then match up.

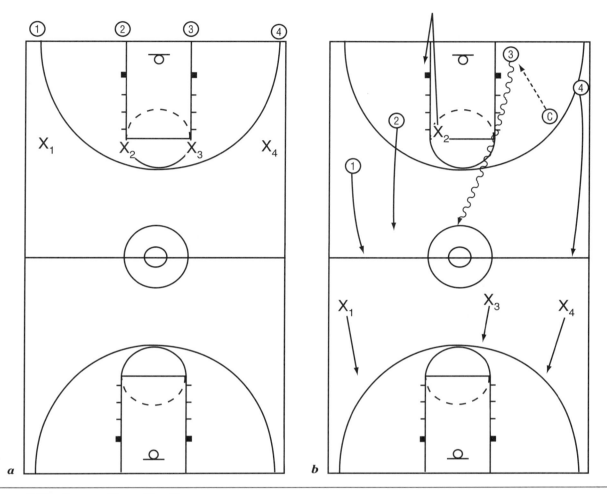

Figure 9.10 Four on Three Plus One.

Four on Two Plus Two

Purpose: This drill is designed for players to make quick offensive reads and decisions when they have numerical advantages over the defense.

Setup: Players are divided into three teams of four players. Team 1 plays against team 2, team 2 plays against team 3, and team 3 plays against team 1. The first team to score 10 points wins.

Procedure: Team 1 sets up at half court, as shown in the diagram. Team 2 has two players setup in a defensive tandem. Their other two players are out of bounds in each corner. The two players out of bounds enter the game on team 1's second pass across half court. If team 1 shoots before team 2 passes, those players out

of bounds can enter only after the shot is made. Team 1 tries to take advantage of their four-on-two advantage. If team 1 makes a second pass, or any additional passes, all of team 2's players are now involved. Play continues until team 1 scores or team 2 gets the ball.

Whether a shot is made or missed, team 2 must advance the ball up the court and attack team 3's tandem defense. As team 2 works to advance the ball up the floor, team 1 pressures them in the backcourt. If team 1 forces a turnover, they get the ball right back, and the game becomes four on four with team 1 versus team 2 again.

If team 2 successfully advances the ball across half court, they are ready to attack team 3. The same rules apply as in the first game. Whether a shot is made or missed, team 3 advances the ball up the floor to attack team 1.

There are four key points to emphasize in this drill: (1) the game is four on two until the second pass that occurs across the half-court line, (2) players need to make quick decisions to get a high-percentage shot, (3) defensive players need to match quickly on the second pass, and (4) great backcourt pressure can give teams additional offensive possessions.

SUMMARY

- Executing a primary fast break correctly can lead to high-percentage shots.

- Don't get in a hurry when executing your transition game.

- Secondary fast breaks are used when the defense has three or more players in position to defend.

- Made fast breaks can keep the pressure on the defense and make it difficult for the defense to set up full court.

- Players need to practice making quick and correct decisions in their transition game.

CHAPTER 10

DEVELOPING A HALF-COURT OFFENSE

If I have the players, I prefer to play an up-tempo game with transition offense as my main offense. However, there are times when a half-court offense is needed. To be effective in a half-court game, your team needs to have designed offenses to run against the two most common defenses played: man to man and zone. In man-to-man defenses, players are each assigned a player on the opposing team to guard. You can design your offenses to take best advantage of your players' strengths and your opponent's weak matchups. In zone defenses, players guard an area on the court. They guard players on the opposing team who enter their area. Zone offenses are run to attack the zone area in which the offense thinks they can take best advantage. With some small adjustments, some offenses are effective against either a man or a zone defense. However, most coaches have both man offenses and zone offenses in their offensive system.

MAN-TO-MAN OFFENSE

Our team faces more man-to-man defenses than zone defenses. To prepare for this, we spend a great deal of time on our man offenses, break-down drills of the offenses, and position work addressing parts of the offense.

Each year at the beginning of the season our coaching staff sits down to evaluate our team's personnel and devise an offensive system that we believe best suits our players. Thus, our offenses change year to year. If our main strength is our post players, we implement power offenses. If we're guard oriented, we look to spread the court and open up space for our guards to operate. Plays might change, but our overall package stays the same. Our package consists of continuity offenses, some set plays, and some quick hitters. Some plays are designed to milk the clock and others to take off little time.

With each man-to-man offense, players must understand the philosophy of the offense and their role in the offense. All roles might not appear equal, but it's as important to set a good screen as it is to use the screen correctly for the high-percentage shot. Offenses are taught in the whole-part-whole method. For example, if we're teaching a power inside offense, we discuss the purpose of the offense. Next we teach the offense in its entirety. Then we add defense so our players understand correct spacing, screening, and so on, and then we break the offense down into its smaller teaching parts. Much of the smaller teaching part work is done in position work.

Breakdown Drills

Breakdown drills allow players to practice running an effective offense. A breakdown drill works on one portion of the offense at a time. For example, if you have an offense that uses the pick and roll, a breakdown drill focusing on the pick and roll is quite helpful. Sometimes players become robotic in their play. They don't understand choices or options in an offense. During position work, players can put together the small parts of the offense, focusing on the little things that make the offense work. We divide our position work drills into two groups: perimeter and post players. After both groups have worked separately, we bring them together to work. Perimeter and post players need to know how to be efficient in their part of the offense as well as complement the other position.

Perimeter Drills

We usually divide our perimeter drills into a number of parts. In our position work, perimeter players work on individual skills, two- and three-player situations, and team concepts.

We almost always incorporate some ball-handling drills into our position work. Point guards need to be able to initiate an offense against pressure. Wings need to be able to make an entry pass to a post player against pressure or make a good pass to another perimeter player. We practice these situations in our two-man drills. We start with an offensive point guard with defense at half court and an offensive wing player with defense on the perimeter. In this simple two-on-two drill, point guards work on handling the ball against pressure, protecting the ball from the defense, and making the open

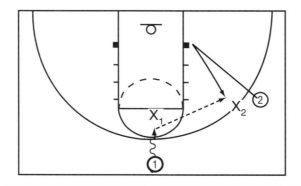

Figure 10.1 Two-on-two pass drill.

pass to a teammate (figure 10.1). We emphasize the timing of the passes and an effective use of the dribble.

The wing players on the perimeter work on getting open, stepping to meet the pass, protecting the ball in a triple threat position once the pass has been received, and preparing to make the next move, whether it's a shot, pass, or dribble. The specific offense we're practicing dictates how the wings get open and what options they'll use from their triple threat position. Typically, perimeter players work on V-cuts to get open (see figure 10.2). They complement the V-cut with backdoor cuts (see figure 10.3). We work on both of these cuts in drills. Once a perimeter player receives the ball, she needs to be able to execute any of the three triple threat actions: pass, shoot, or dribble.

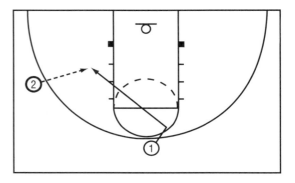

Figure 10.2 V-cut.

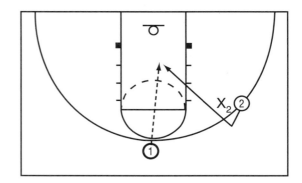

Figure 10.3 Backdoor cut.

Passing is another key element of the offense drilled in perimeter work. Perimeter players need to be good passers, whether the pass goes inside or stays on the perimeter. In the two-man drill, players work on timing of passes and learn to read defenses. On the perimeter, player and ball should arrive at the spot at the same time. Too often, players stand to receive a pass, and a good defender steps into the passing lane for an easy steal. Players need to know how to read the defense as well as read their teammates. We practice this in our two-man drill by having the defense slough off at times, play denial defense, or overplay defensively. This is where we incorporate our backdoor action. We work on backdoor cuts from the top of the key, from the wing, and from the baseline. We work on passing to the post player during the practice segment in which position work is combined.

Shooting is usually a routine part of our perimeter position work. Shots are practiced for each player and for each offense. Not all players are good three-point shooters, and not all players excel in putting the ball on the floor. However, all the shots we use in our offenses are practiced in perimeter position work. On receiving a pass, perimeter players need to know how to protect the ball and read their defense. All players practice shots off a pass with and without a screen as well as shots off the drive. Shots off the pass might be made to a player coming off a screen, a stagger screen, from a pop out, from a clear-out (see figure 10.4a), or from an overload. Shots off a ball screen start the same way, with a strong swinging motion that allows the player some space and helps protect the ball. Perimeter shots off the dribble include layups, pull-up jumpers, change-of-direction moves, go-to moves, countermoves, power layups, and dribble hops. Early in the season, we practice moves in a shooting repetition series that includes each move without defense and then with defense. As we get into the season, we incorporate moves specific to an offense. For example, the day we work on our delay game, perimeter players practice layups, power layups, pull-up jumpers, and dribble hops. All these moves are a part of our delay-game offense. When we work on perimeter quick hitter offenses, we work on shots off a stagger screen (see figure 10.4b), clear-outs, and overloads, which are all components of one or more of our quick hitters. To simulate screens, we set up chairs, and players make their cuts off the chairs.

Setting good screens and using screens effectively are difficult for many players. When we teach offenses that involve screening, I believe

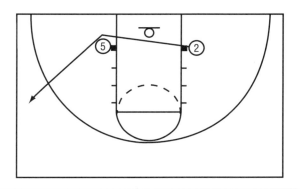

Figure 10.4a Setting up the shot by passing to a player after a clear-out.

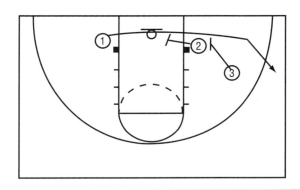

Figure 10.4b Setting up the shot from a stagger screen.

it's very important to teach screening with defense guarding the offensive players so they can understand how to set screens and how to use the screens according to defensive positioning. We practice setting and using screens in our perimeter three-on-three drills. We practice screens off the ball such as cross screens, down screens, and back screens as well as screens on the ball. We emphasize correct technique in setting a screen and help players learn to read the screen. By reading the defense, players practice executing the correct move, whether it's a backdoor cut, a curl (see figure 10.5), or a flare move (see figure 10.6).

Offensive rebounding is another area we focus on in perimeter breakdown drills. From a three-on-three perimeter set with a point guard and two wings, a coach shoots the ball, and offensive players are taught to slash into the lane. The slash is designed to avoid their defense, thus avoiding contact, and pursue the loose ball.

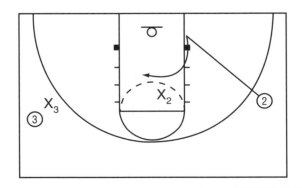

Figure 10.5 A curl move.

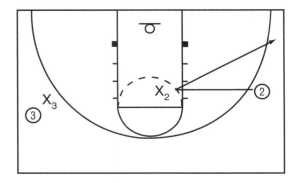

Figure 10.6 A flare move.

Once we've worked on perimeter breakdown drills, we join the perimeter players with the post players and continue to drill parts of the offense. Inside players and outside players need to understand how to complement each other.

Post Drills

Similar to perimeter position drills, post drills are designed to complement the players we have and the offenses we run. We run several offenses that include a post-to-post high–low game and a couple of offenses that begin in a four-out look with a post isolated. With either look, our dominant post player needs to learn how to work with her back to the basket.

We begin our post drills teaching a simple post-up position along the lane line. Our players post up on the first hashmark above the block, which gives them more room to work. From this posting position, we add defense to help players learn how to use their body to their advantage in the post area. We work daily one on one, offensive post player with a defender,

for good posting position. A post player can have wonderful post moves, but if she can't get open to receive a pass, she'll never be able to use them. A good post player likes contact. If a player doesn't like contact, don't play her in the post. The post defender plays defense behind the offensive post player, on the side of the post, or directly in front of the post so that the offensive post player can work on positioning and moves. We teach our offensive post players to keep defenders on one side, behind, or in front of them, to create passing angles and to safely receive passes. We start this drill with our posts executing a reverse pivot to get into their posting position, adding a defender, and entering the ball to the post. We stress the little things such as calling for the ball, assuming a wide and strong low base, chinning the pass, and checking for their defense. We explain the difference between posting up and pinning. Because we run a high–low game, we teach our post players to pin if the post-up position is denied by the defense.

Our next set of drills involves basic post moves. We try to teach a go-to move along with a countermove. Initially, we practice moves without a dribble. Our shooting series includes pivoting on the inside foot and shooting a bank shot and pivoting on the high foot and shooting a short jumper. When we add a dribble, we begin by teaching a drop step baseline with a power dribble. Players step toward the basket with their inside foot. We finish the shot by jumping off two feet to emphasize it's a power shot. The last basic move we work on is the up-and-under move. Once the post player has received the ball, she squares up to the goal using a forward or reverse pivot on her high foot. If her defender backs off her, she shoots a jump shot. If her defender guards her tightly, she executes a jab with a shot fake to see how her defender reacts. If the defender continues to play her tight, the post player executes a crossover move or an up-and-under move. This move can be done as a layup with no dribble or with a power dribble followed by a two-foot jump shot. Our shooting series is pivot and score, drop step, and a crossover or an up-and-under move.

We teach post players to recognize when and how they can pin their defender in the post area. If we can teach our players to use their bodies and maintain contact, the pin can be an easy way to set up an inside score. We drill the pin position teaching the offensive player to hook her post defender who has committed to playing defense on a side of the offensive player. If a post defender commits to a side, the post player wants to keep her on that side. As the post player executes the pin, she maintains contact throughout the hook movement. Once she has correctly executed the pinning position, she extends her inside arm and hand for a target to receive a pass. If the pin is successful, and the pass to the post player is completed, the post player should have inside position on her defender and no post move is required other than a jump shot.

For post players to learn to work together, we teach the high–low game in a two-on-two drill. We allow the low post to be fronted defensively, thus setting up the pin. We teach the high post to read the low post's defense and to throw to the inside hand of her teammate after the pin has been executed. The high-post player should not lead the low-post player with her pass because the low-post player is trying to maintain contact with her defender throughout her pin.

We drill post moves away from the basket. Our offenses bring one of our posts away from the basket. Depending on her ability and shooting range, she locates at either the high post or close to the three-point line. Players get to the high post from various positions. They might get to the high post from a V-cut (see figure 10.7), a flash, or a transition trailing position (see figure 10.8), or they might come off a screen. We practice each of these in our breakdown drills. Next, we work on high-post moves. Some of the moves are similar to those taught to perimeter players. We work on a jump shot, a jab and shot, a jab-and-drive "go move" on the strong side, and a crossover dribble move to the weak side. We teach a dribble hop from the high post as a power move with an explosive finish. This can be done on the strong side or as a crossover move. All shots are practiced first without defense, then with defense. We practice low-post and high-post moves daily during position work.

Similar to perimeter players, post players are taught how to set a screen and use a screen. We teach this out of our two-on-two post drills. Post players practice setting cross screens (see figure 10.9), down screens (see figure 10.10), and

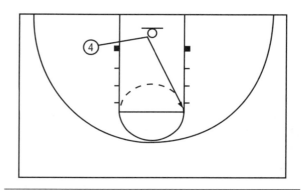

Figure 10.7 V-cut to high post.

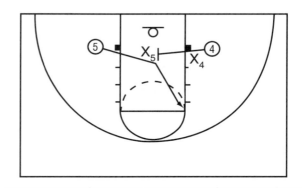

Figure 10.8 Trailing position to high post.

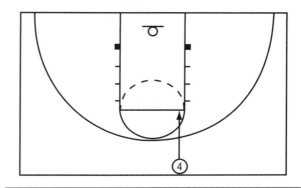

Figure 10.9 Cross screen.

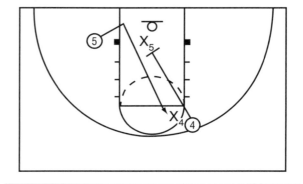

Figure 10.10 Down screen.

back screens off the ball (see figure 10.11). We teach players how to read the screen and their defender and how to make an appropriate move. We teach the screener how to set a legal screen, emphasizing the importance of not setting an illegal moving screen. As we drill screens, we also show post players how to open up after they have set a screen. In many cases, the screener is the open player in the offense. We teach players to reverse pivot and step to the ball after they have set a screen. An exception to this is screening on the ball. We have several offenses in which the post player sets an on-the-ball screen for a perimeter player. We teach the post player how to roll to the basket (see figure 10.12) or pop out to the perimeter after setting the screen (see figure 10.13).

We work on offensive rebounding in our post position drills. Our offensive philosophy on rebounding involves forming a triangle in front and on the side of the basket (see figure 10.14). Post players, if they are closest to the basket, normally fill one of the three positions. Often a post player is already in the low-post area, in perfect rebounding position. To practice offensive rebounding, we drill posts from a one-on-one post position. We allow the post defense to play behind the post in the block area. A coach tosses up a missed shot, and the offensive post player rolls off her defender and hooks around her to gain the inside rebounding position. Too often, we find that the offensive post player is content to stay behind her defender and reach over her back to get the rebound, which usually results in an over-the-back foul. The offensive rebounding technique is similar to the technique used in pinning, so we hope that learning transfers from one skill to the other.

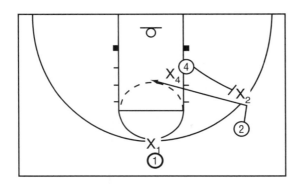

Figure 10.11   Back screen.

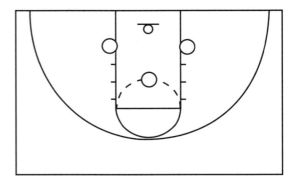

Figure 10.13   Screen and pop out to the perimeter.

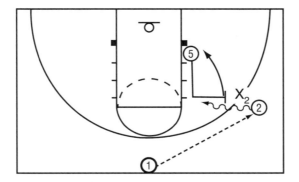

Figure 10.12   Screen and roll to the basket.

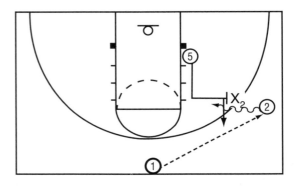

Figure 10.14   Triangle rebounding positions.

Team Drills to Build Up the Offense

To build up our offense, we combine perimeter and post play and continue to work on parts of our offense. Almost daily we drill entering the ball from the perimeter to the post area. We do this with and without defense on the perimeter players and with and without a dribble from the perimeter players. Posts start with defense. They work on posting and pinning, and together the two groups try to make the right read on the post defense and thus the correct entry pass. We divide our team up and play on the right and left sides of the court. This is our basic Post Entry Drill (see figure 10.15).

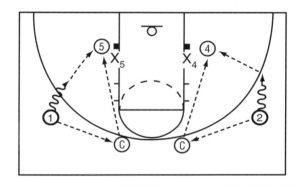

Figure 10.15 Post Entry Drill.

Next we break down our offense into smaller parts. If the offense calls for a post and guard pick and roll, we practice this in a two-on-two drill. If the offense, for example, is a continuity offense, we break it down into its parts and run one option at a time. Each part is practiced separately and then put together.

We work on our offenses with and without defense. Sometimes players just need to shell the offense to understand the pattern of the offense. Once we add defense we talk about "running" plays and "making" plays. Players who know how to read defenses have no trouble making plays. They can break the pattern of a play because they see an option that's better than the option the play calls for. When we practice the play as a whole, we try to help players recognize when they need to make a play and when they should run the play. I don't want players to be robots, with no creativity

of their own. On the other hand, if players are always making plays, there's no need to have set plays. We want our players to learn a balance in running plays and making plays.

Once we've run our offensive plays in a half-court set, we practice getting into our offenses out of our transition game. Some of our offensive sets flow smoothly from our secondary offense into our half-court offense. Others require a change of gear or pace from our transition game to our half-court game. We practice the transition from full-court offense to half-court offense with and without defense.

Set Offenses

Set offenses are designed to complement the players you have on your team. If your team is strong inside, your offense should be inside oriented. If your team is small and quick, you'll probably want to spread the court and use your speed as a weapon on offense. You can put set offenses together in such a way to teach your players their roles in the offense and how to play them to the best of their abilities.

We run a set offense out of a 1-4 high look (see figure 10.16). I like this set because it spreads the floor and makes it difficult for defensive players to help. I also like the set because you can run many options out of it, which makes your team less predictable and harder to scout. In addition, if you have weak offensive players, they can be used as passers and screeners.

Whether you have primarily perimeter players or post players, you can take advantage of their strengths in a 1-4 set. If we have a strong post player, we'll run the post option out of the 1-4 (see figure 10.17, a-c). If we have two really

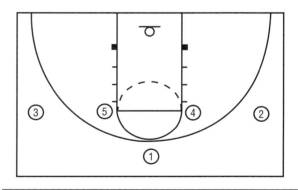

Figure 10.16 1-4 high set.

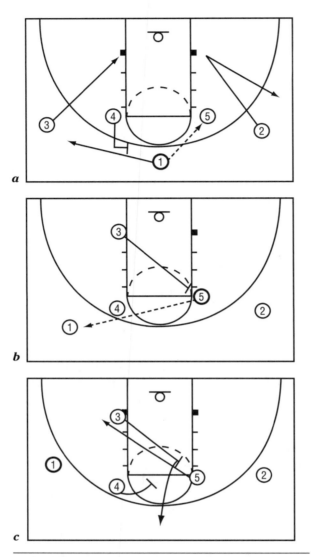

Figure 10.17 Post option. *(a)* 1 passes to 5; 2 and 3 make backdoor cuts; and 4 sets a flare screen for 1, *(b)* 3 back screens for 5, *(c)* 4 down screens for 3.

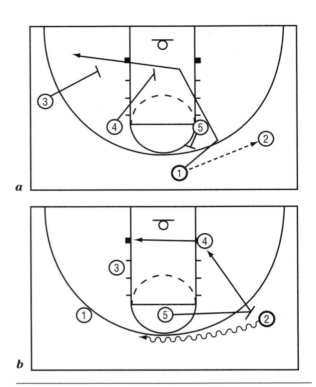

Figure 10.18 Two-man game. *(a)* 1 clears out, *(b)* 2 and 5 pick and roll.

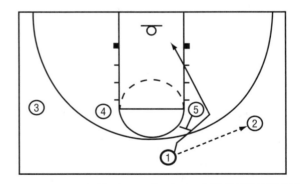

Figure 10.19 Point guard isolation.

strong players, we'll get into our two-man game (see figure 10.18, a and b). If our point guard has a mismatch or is a good scorer for us, we can isolate her out of the 1-4 set (see figure 10.19).

I have found our players have confidence running a set offense that complements their strengths and hides some of their weaknesses. We use a couple of set offenses in our offensive package.

Continuity Offense

In a continuity offense, a pattern is repeated over and over. The advantage here is that there's flow to the offense and you don't have to reset unless the flow breaks down. You can run a continuity offense in which all players run all positions eventually or a continuity offense designed to complement team and players' strengths. Our Baylor offense is an offense designed for all players to run all positions. It's a continuity offense in which a pattern is repeated over and over. Baylor starts with a perimeter entry pass, followed by a back screen and then a down screen. The ball changes sides of the floor, and the pattern is repeated (see figure 10.20, a-c). Keys to this offense are the ability of players to read the defense getting open after setting screens. The disadvantage of this offense is that you're not putting your best players in their best positions at all times. Also, your weaker players must handle the ball and have the same opportunities to score as your stronger players. To offset these disadvantages, you can run some quick hitters out of the offense that complement your better players.

Our Georgia offense is a continuity offense in which players do not run every position. This offense is designed as an inside-first offense, complemented by perimeter play. The pattern begins with a post-up on the block, a high–low post look, a point guard pop out, and then a cross screen for the post. The first three out of four options are inside oriented. The last option is a down screen for the wing. This pattern repeats itself but is designed to get the ball inside to your post players (see figure 10.21, a-e).

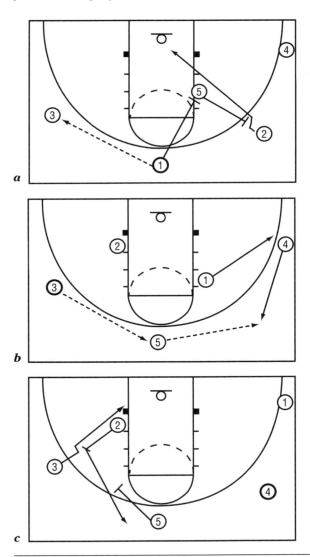

Figure 10.20 Baylor offense. *(a)* Back screen, *(b)* Down screen, *(c)* Ball moves to other side of court and play is repeated.

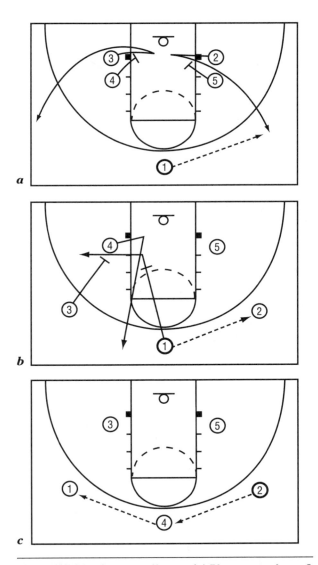

Figure 10.21 Georgia offense. *(a)* Players stack up; 2 and 3 pop out to wings, *(b)* 1 passes to 2 and executes a down screen for 4 while 3 sets a down screen for 1, *(c)* 2 looks to 5 and then passes to 4; 4 passes to 1.

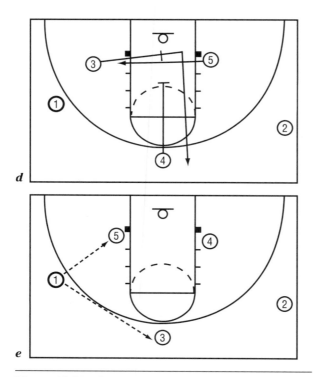

Figure 10.21 Georgia offense. *(d)* 3 screens across for 5; 4 down screens for 3, *(e)* 1 can pass to 5 on block or to 3 as she pops up.

Quick Hitters

When time is a factor and you require a go-to play, you need some quick hitters in your offensive play book. We run quick hitters for several reasons—we want to take advantage of a mismatch, we haven't scored out of our continuity or set offenses, we have a shooter with a hot hand, or it's the end of a quarter or the end of the game. Our quick hitters are designed for our players to get into quickly and execute quickly. In our offensive package, we have quick hitters for each position—post, wing, and point guard. I want to be prepared to take advantage of a mismatch or be able to go to a shooter with a hot hand. I also want to get the last shot in each quarter and at the end of the game if necessary. Some quick hitters have one option, and others have two. If there are two options, neither takes much time to run. If we have a dominant scoring point guard, we run a set called Double High, which gives our point guard a double screen and allows her to read post defense and make a play. If she's unable to get her shot off, she passes to the wing on her side of the court and sets a screen for the opposite wing. The low-post

player on the double screen slips the screen and posts on the ballside block. The top post player in the double screen screens for the point guard and also for the opposite wing. This play is designed for the point guard but has some secondary looks if the point guard doesn't get an open shot (see figure 10.22, a-c).

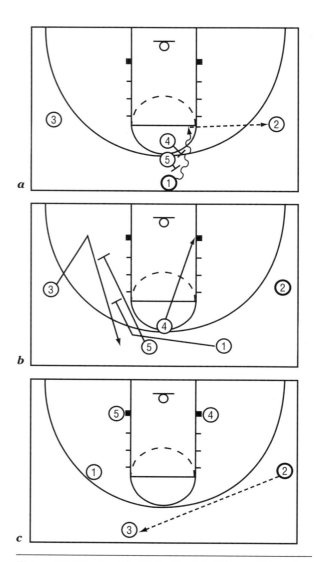

Figure 10.22 Double High. *(a)* 1 dribbles off 4 and 5's double screen; if 1 doesn't shoot, she passes to 2, *(b)* 4 slips screen; 5 and 1 set a double screen for 3, *(c)* 3 comes off the double screen; 2 passes to 3 for the shot.

We call "stack" and a player's name when we want to take advantage of a mismatch, either in the perimeter or on the post. This play is designed to isolate the player who has the mismatch in the lane area. Stack has only one option, so players must read the defense and make a play if they can't run the play (see figure 10.23, a-c).

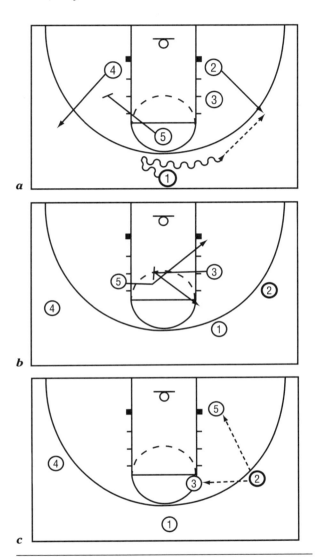

Figure 10.23   Stack. (*a*) Starting low, 4 pops out; 1 dribbles toward 4, reverses her dribble, and passes to 2, (*b*) 3 screens for 5, (*c*) 2 passes to 5 or to 3.

Motion Offense

A motion offense is a flexible offense that uses concepts such as player movement, correct floor spacing, passing, cutting, and setting screens. Instead of running set plays, players move and work together within a set of rules, which allows for greater flexibility and which

makes this a difficult offense to scout. A motion offense can be run against man-to-man, zone, or combination defenses. Once players have learned the basic concepts, special patterns or plays can be designed to take advantage of offensive strengths.

The motion offense can be run from almost any set, including the 3 out and 2 in, 4 out and 1 in, 5 out, and so on. If you have a highly talented team in which all five players can play any position, they can interchange or rotate into any of the five positions. If you have two dominant post players or outstanding perimeter players, you'll want to rotate your players in a way that exploits their strengths.

I have never run a true motion offense because a true motion requires a large time commitment to the teaching of offensive concepts and the reading of defenses. I've never been willing to commit this much time to this offensive scheme. Plus, I like having more control in offenses, channeling plays to my best scorers. However, if you have the time to teach it, the motion offense can be quite effective, particularly for a team of unusually athletic players.

ZONE OFFENSE

To attack a zone defense, you can use various alignments to break the defense down. You don't want to match up your offense to the alignment of the defense. If the defense sets up in an even front, such as a two-three, you want to set up in an odd guard front, such as a one-three-one. If the defense is aligned in an odd guard front, such as a one-three-one, you want your offensive set up in an even front, such as a two-one-two. This allows perimeter players to get into the gaps of the defense to create scoring opportunities for themselves or their teammates.

Once players have an initial offensive set, they need to understand zone principles if your zone offense is to be effective. Regardless of the zone you choose to run, certain principles, if applied correctly, help players get the most out of the offense.

Good Zone Principles

- Attack the defense—make the defense work.

- Be patient to allow for good shot selection.
- Make two defenders play one offensive player by getting into the defensive gaps.
- Drive the zone when called for.
- Make the extra pass.
- Reverse the ball to make the defense shift.
- Be an offensive threat—make the zone guard you.
- Skip pass when called for.
- Screen the defense when called for.
- Stretch the defense to open up gaps.
- Use pass fakes and shot fakes.
- Maintain good floor spacing.
- Balance the floor.
- Slash through gaps to rebound.

Breakdown Drills

As noted earlier in the chapter, breakdown drills allow players to practice running an effective offense. A breakdown drill works on one portion of the offense at a time.

Perimeter Drills

Our perimeter drills are closely aligned to our zone offenses. Initially, we work on perimeter shooting. We work on spot shooting from the baseline wing and the top of the key. These shots are available when we run overload offenses against a zone defense. We work on getting our shot off quickly, with a catch-and-score mentality. Next, we shoot these same shots but get into these shots from starting on one side of the floor and moving to the other side. This occurs when we ball reverse in some of our zone offenses or when we overload a side. Footwork is important. Players need to get their feet set and square their shoulders to the goal before shooting. Remind players not to shoot in a hurry.

Next we drill perimeter drives. We work on beating a baseline defender and pulling up for a jumper outside the lane. We drive from the wing into a gap for the same shot, as well as from the top of the key. To practice driving gaps, we set up defenders and allow players to drive the gap

between them and pull up for a jump shot. We set up our defense in a box set, 2-2, and perimeter players work at driving to shoot and driving to draw the two defenders and make the pass to an open teammate (see figure 10.24).

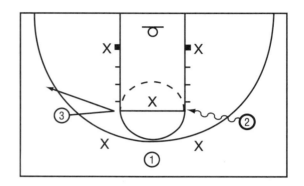

Figure 10.24 Driving the gaps.

To work on the skip pass and shot, we have shooters spot on the weak side and clear out to the weak side for a pass from a teammate (see figure 10.25). The skip pass needs to be a strong pass that doesn't float, or it can be easily picked off by the defense.

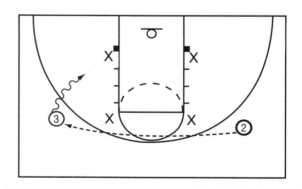

Figure 10.25 Skip pass and shot.

Depending on our offense, perimeter players work on screening the zone and popping or screening the zone and slipping inside the defense. In our high–low offense, perimeter players set a back screen on the top of the zone and then pop out for a three-point shot or for ball reversal (see figure 10.26, a and b).

In our UCLA offense, wing players clear to the other side of the court after making a down pass to the short corner player. As they clear

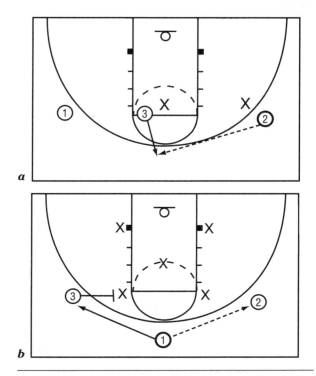

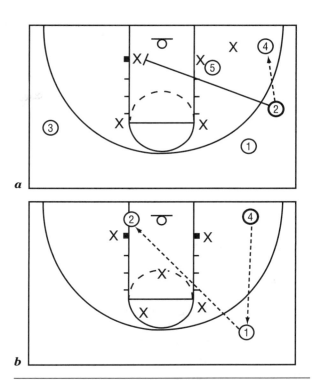

Figure 10.26 High–low offense. (a) Popping out for the three-point shot, (b) Back screen and ball reversal.

Figure 10.28 UCLA offense. (a) Post-up at the back of the zone, (b) 4 passes to 1; 1 passes to 2 who has posted up at the back of the zone.

out they run a cut to the weak side and post up on the inside of the back-line defender. We work on the give-and-go cut (see figure 10.27) and the post-up at the back of the zone (see figure 10.28, a and b).

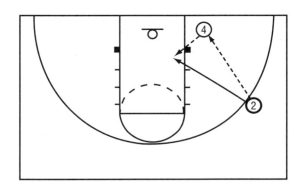

Figure 10.27 UCLA offense: Give-and-go cut.

Once again, offensive rebounding is an important skill for perimeter players to acquire. In a zone defense, defenders block out areas, not necessarily players. In a zone offense, you might have an overload, thus giving your team a

numerical advantage in that area for rebounding the ball. We teach offensive perimeter players to slash from the perimeter to the paint. They try to avoid contact as they pursue the ball. We drill offensive rebounding out of our three perimeter players against four defenders in a box defense. Once an offensive player has shot the ball, the other two offensive players try to slash through a defensive gap for the rebound. We encourage players to get to the paint before the ball gets through the net or touches the ground. In the case of a three-point shot, the ball will rebound longer, so pursuing the long rebound becomes the focus.

Post Drills

In zone defenses, perimeter players tend to play outside the defense. Post players tend to play inside or behind the defense. Our post zone drills are specific to our offenses. In our high–low zone offense, we're continually working the high–low game, trying to get the ball inside. Post players work on V-cuts, change of direction, and changes of speed (see figure 10.29). We emphasize allowing the zone defense

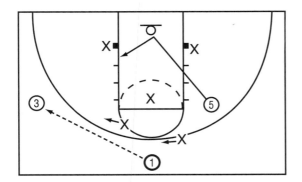

Figure 10.29 Post V-cut in high–low offense.

to shift and then make a hard flash in the gaps or behind the defense.

In our UCLA offense, our post players overload the floor in a short corner midpost set (see figure 10.30a). Post players work on moves and shots from both the short corner and the midpost. Midpost shots are faceup jump shots that usually involve no dribble (see figure 10.30b). Shots from the short corner include faceup jumpers and baseline drives (see figure 10.30c). When defense is added, post players drill the post-to-post pass and basket cut.

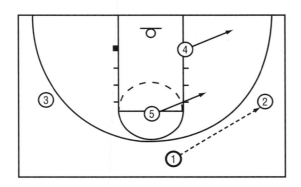

Figure 10.30a Overloading the corner.

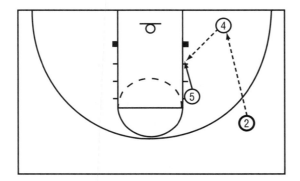

Figure 10.30b Midpost shot.

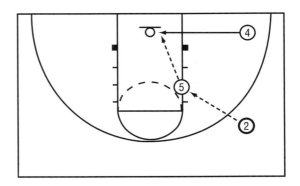

Figure 10.30c Baseline drive.

Our "Over" offense is a zone offense that requires one post player to screen the back of a zone while the other post player reads the screen and makes the appropriate cut. Post players drill on screening and opening up after they screen in case they are open for the shot. The post player using the screen works on reading the angle of her teammate's screen, cutting to the open area, and squaring to the goal for a short jump shot.

Building Up the Zone

Perimeter players and post players need to know how to complement each other in their zone offenses. With the ball in the hands of our perimeter players, we drill perimeter baseline drives and dish passes to the open post. We also drill drives from the wing or top of the key and the dump pass to a post inside. On ball reversals from a perimeter clear-out or a skip pass, we drill quick entries to the post as the defense begins to shift (see figure 10.31a). We also allow the low post to read the defensive shift and either flash or pin the weak side of the zone (see figure 10.31b).

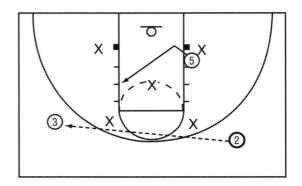

Figure 10.31a Skip pass ball reversal.

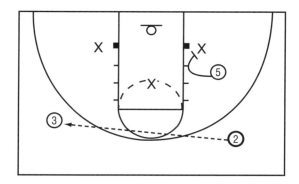

Figure 10.31b Pin the weak side of the zone.

With the ball in the hands of the low-post player, we drill a defensive trap or double team on that post and the pass out. Depending on where the defensive help comes from, the post player kicks the ball out to the perimeter player ball side or diagonally on the weak side. Wing players set their feet and shoot from the pass out.

As we work on our offenses together, posts and perimeter, we're constantly trying to give the offensive players different defensive looks. Sometimes the defense extends; other times they sag. We might have the defense shade a player or never guard a player with the ball. In doing this, players learn to both run plays and make plays, as well as work together, inside and outside.

Set Offenses

Similar to a man-to-man set offense, a zone set offense places players in positions in which they can be most successful. You can place weaker players in positions in which they are primarily passers and screeners or in which they are often away from the strong side of the offense. As I've mentioned, in zone offenses, you want to attack in a set that contrasts the defensive set—odd front versus even front or even front versus odd front. Our Over offense is designed to complement our strong inside scoring attack and to make the defense choose between a good outside shooter and a good inside player. The offense starts on one side of the floor and then swings to the other side. As the offense swings, the best outside shooter swings with the offense. The weak-side post player screens the middle of the zone defense for the stronger post player. The stronger post player reads the screen and the defense to make a play (see figure 10.32, a-c). The play is designed to go first to the post player who is screened for or second to the

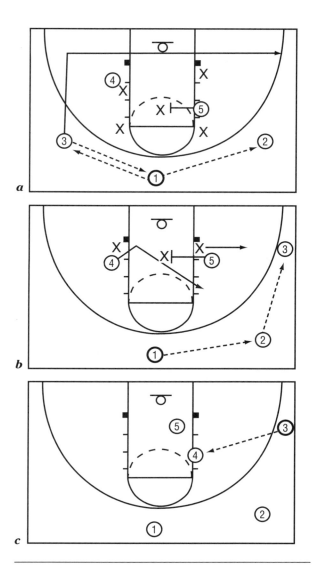

Figure 10.32 Over offense. (*a*) 1 passes to 3, 3 passes back to 1, and 1 then passes to 2; 3 clears to opposite side, (*b*) 1 passes to 2 and 2 passes to 3; 5 screens the zone; 4 reads the opening and cuts, (*c*) 3 passes to 4; 5 opens up after screening.

post that screens and opens up to the ball after the screen. If the defense sags to the inside, the best perimeter player has an outside shot.

Continuity Offenses

A zone continuity offense is similar to a man-to-man continuity zone. The zone pattern repeats itself over and over. You can place players within the framework of the offense to complement their strengths. For this offense to be successful, players must clearly understand their roles. We run a continuity offense to complement our players, to teach them to use the clock versus a zone defense, to stay in flow and not get in a hurry, and to make the defense work longer. We run a continuity offense called UCLA that implements zone principles such as good spacing, floor balance, basket cuts, screening, and ball reversal. UCLA also complements our inside game and our perimeter scorers. This offense begins with a diamond overload on the side of the short corner post player (see figure 10.33a). Any time the ball goes to either post player, the other post player makes a basket cut. The ballside wing player tries to make the back-line zone defender guard her. If the back-line defender guards the wing, the middle zone defender must choose which post to guard, short corner or midpost. The point guard is always a part of the overload set. Movement in the offense begins when the ballside wing player passes to the short corner and she clears out (see figure 10.33b). As the wing clears out, she looks first for a quick return pass and next for a pass as she pins or screens the backside of the defense. If she doesn't receive the ball, she pops out to the short corner position on the weak

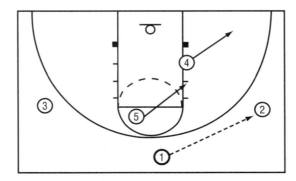

Figure 10.33a Diamond overload on short corner post side.

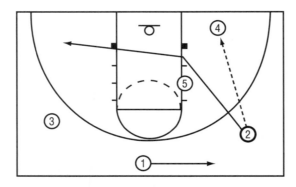

Figure 10.33b Wing passes to short corner and clears out.

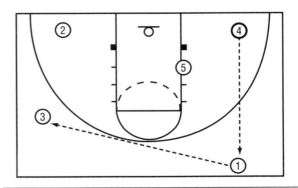

Figure 10.33c Short corner passes to point guard.

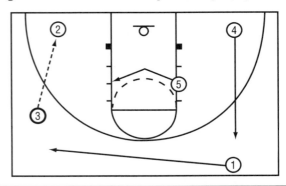

Figure 10.33d Midpost player reads the defense and flashes the gaps. Point guard slides to top of key.

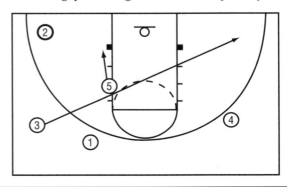

Figure 10.33e Pattern then shifts to the other side of the key and is continued.

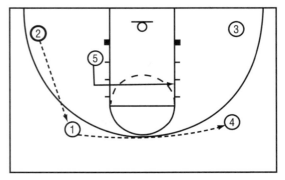

Figure 10.33f Wing and short corner positions continually interchange.

side. The short corner player passes the ball back up to the point guard and then slides up to the wing area (see figure 10.33c). The midpost player stays inside the paint and reads the shifts of the zone defense. She flashes to gaps in the defense as the ball changes sides of the floor. The point guard slides side to side at the top of the key, always becoming part of the overload (see figure 10.33d). The pattern is repeated on the other side of the floor (see figure 10.33e). Wing positions and short corner positions continually interchange (see figure 10.33f).

Go-To Play

When time is a factor and you need a go-to play, pull a quick hitter out of your play book. We run zone quick hitters to set up our go-to player, complement a shooter with a hot hand, or to get off a quick shot at the end of a quarter or the end of the game. Our zone quick hitters are designed to get into quickly and execute quickly. In most of our zone quick hitters, we try to make the defense shift from one side of the floor to the other. We want to get our shot off before the defensive can shift. In our zone package, we have quick hitters for each position—post, wing, and point guard. If our point guard has the hot hand and can shoot the three-point shot, we'll run Fade as a quick hitter against a zone. We want to pass the ball to either wing and make the defense shift. After the initial pass, the off-side wing screens the top of the zone and pops high (see figure 10.34a). The ballside wing skips the ball to the point guard for a three-pointer (see figure 10.34b). If the defender who is screened slips the screen, the player who pops after the screen is the open shooter. This play takes very little time to run and can be used to complement one or two three-point shooters.

To complement a strong perimeter shooter, we run a zone quick hitter called Clear. Again, we make the defense shift from one side to the other, and we screen the zone. If they take away our perimeter shot, we finish the play by reading the defense and making a play. The play starts in a 1-4 high set. Post players set up high to screen the top of the zone if possible. The point guard uses either post screen if possible, as she dribbles toward the best wing shooter. This dribble initiates a clear-out by that wing (see figure 10.35a). On the ball side, the post player and the point guard pick and roll. The

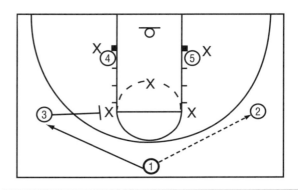

Figure 10.34a Off-side wing screens and pops high.

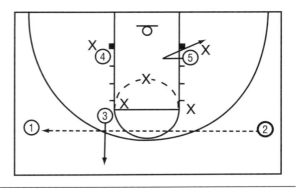

Figure 10.34b Ballside wing skips ball to point guard for the three-pointer.

weak-side action has the weak-side wing screening the back of the zone and the weak-side post player popping up high for ball reversal (see figure 10.35b). The ball is reversed from point to post to wing (see figure 10.35c). The options in Clear are a wing shot, a wing post-up after the screen, and a ball reversal post slashing down the lane. This is a quick hitter with three options. The offense reads the defense and takes the best shot available.

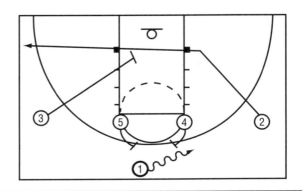

Figure 10.35a Point guard dribbles toward best wing shooter, prompting her to clear out.

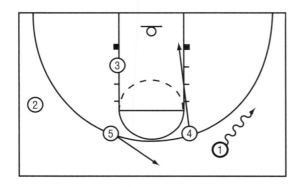

Figure 10.35b Weak-side wing screens back of zone. Weak-side post pops high.

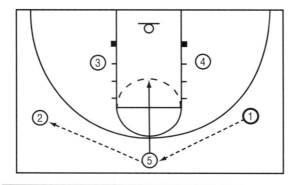

Figure 10.35c Ball is reversed from point to post to wing.

IMPROVING OFFENSIVE TEAMWORK

Whether you're running a man-to-man offense or a zone offense, teamwork is going to be the key for success. Players need to believe the team is stronger than the individual and that the team can achieve more together than each player can individually. The scorer might get her name in the press, but the offense won't work if all players don't do their part in passing, screening, and rebounding. Remind players you win as a team and lose as a team. It's much easier to defend a team with one star than to defend a team full of players who work together and don't care who gets the credit.

For the teamwork mindset to be accomplished, you need to take the lead. Recognize players in practice, in games, and in public when they do the little things that make an offense work. Remind players to acknowledge a good pass, an offensive rebound, or a great screen by their teammates.

I believe improving offensive teamwork goes hand in hand with players understanding their roles and happily playing their roles for the team. Not all players possess the same abilities. If every player wants to be the leading scorer on the team, selfishness sets in and like a cancer destroys your team. The game of basketball needs several players to fill roles offensively. A great passer can make an average post player look good because she knows how and when to set her teammate up for a score. An offensive rebounder can provide second and third shot opportunities. A great screener can take up space and make an otherwise hard shot easy for her teammate. What is an offense without a great floor leader? You want a player to be a coach on the floor with the ability to lead and direct the offense. There's no one offensive player who can fill all these roles. But without these roles being filled, the team can't achieve the level of success it's capable of achieving. Help your players find their niche on the team. Help them use their strengths and recognize their limitations.

Players need not only to accept their roles and play them as well as they can—they need to do this with enthusiasm and a positive attitude. Help your players recognize the importance of their role in the team's success. We live in an age in which role players are not fully recognized or rewarded. The leading scorer usually gets her name in the headlines, and the assist leader is an afterthought. Coaches and teammates should ensure that role players appreciate their value to the team.

SUMMARY

- There are many effective man-to-man offenses. Find and use the offenses that best suit your personnel.

- Use breakdown drills to teach the finer points of your offenses.

- Working on post or perimeter skills helps improve individual play, which eventually improves team play.

- You can use set offenses to complement your strongest players and minimize the weaknesses of your less talented players.

- Continuity offenses can provide a flow to your offensive scheme.

- Use quick hitters to take advantage of mismatches, talented players, and limited time sequences.

- Motion offenses are more flexile than set plays and operate within a basic set of rules.

- Recognize and reward role players. There is no "I" in "TEAM."

CHAPTER 11 PREPARING FOR SPECIAL OFFENSIVE SITUATIONS

The majority of your offense in a game comes from your transition game, man-to-man, or zone offenses. The remainder of your offense will come from plays in special situations such as inbounds plays and plays executed during the last few minutes of the game. You need to practice these special situations often so that your players can remain composed and handle the sometimes unusual circumstances with confidence. During a game is not the time to be doing or facing something for the first time. At Oak Ridge, we even practice diagramming plays using the dry erase board so players can learn to transfer a drawing on a board to movements on the court. Many times, a last-second inbounds play has been called to win a game or a press offense diagrammed to safely enter the ball. Our team had a painful reminder of the importance of preparing for special situations early in the 2004 season. We clung to a one-point lead with less than five seconds to go in the game. We had faced full-court defensive pressure all night, and now, for what seemed like the hundredth time, we had to safely inbounds the ball and secure it for a victory. Our standard "box" inbounds play had not been run correctly the past two times, so I decided to call a higher risk inbounds play, our "up" play. I had confidence in the player's ability to execute it. As I watched the play unfold, I painfully realized my sophomore guard did not remember what to do. As she stood at half court, instead of cutting to the baseline as

a decoy, her defender stood as well and suddenly recognized a long pass was about to be made. She wisely followed the flight of the ball, stole our inbounds pass, and was subsequently fouled. Luckily for us, she missed the free throws and we came away with the win, but this was a game we easily could have lost. This nightmare coaching moment reinforced my opinion that players need lots of repetitions on special situations so they don't freeze under pressure.

TIME AND SCORE SITUATIONS

How many times have you seen a team's poor execution down the stretch cost them a game? Both coaches and players need to have poise in the closing minutes of a game. Practicing special situations daily will help your team enter the last few minutes of a game with confidence.

To help players control the end of games, remind them to maintain their focus and stay sharp; stay with the offense and run their pattern for good shots; be prepared for the opponent to gamble if they are behind; work for the high-percentage shot, not the first available shot; maintain confidence when they are sent to the free-throw line—prove the other team made a mistake in whom they chose to foul—and keep screening, cutting, and rebounding—don't just stand around when they don't have the ball. As coach, it's your duty to let your players know when to foul and when to call a timeout.

Keeping a Lead

If you have the lead in the last few minutes of a game, your players should look for layups and free throws. Try to spread the court so players can drive to the basket or make basket cuts. Keep the ball in the hands of your best free-throw shooters. Make sure players are aggressively attacking the basket. Play to win, not to hold on. I have seen the tide turn quickly on a team who had a good lead but started to milk the clock early and became passive offensively. Suddenly, they're playing not to lose and begin to lose their confidence. Attack offensively, always looking for a high-percentage shot, ideally a layup or a free throw.

Playing Defense With the Lead

Strategy varies depending on how big a lead you have in the last two minutes. If only a three-point shot can beat you, play tight defense on your opponent and try to force her to drive to the basket. One way to prevent a three-point shot at the end of a game is to switch all screens aggressively. Or, if you have a foul to give, foul a dribbler before she can get a shot off. See Defending With the Lead in chapter 15 for more on the strategies to employ when your team is ahead near the end of a game.

Coming From Behind

If you're behind by two points with two minutes to go, be aggressive offensively. Look to drive the ball to the basket for a layup and perhaps a foul. The defense doesn't want to foul, so they might play soft, and an aggressive offensive play can produce a high-percentage shot. This might be a great time to run a quick hitter.

If you're behind by more than two points with two minutes to go, the defense will probably extend to prevent a three-point shot. The time left remaining, the score, and the bonus situation are critical factors in deciding what to do at this point. Before choosing your strategy,

consider how much time remains, how many timeouts you have and how many your opponent has, the foul situation, who is shooting well for your team at the free-throw line and who is shooting well at the line for your opponent, and how effective your defense has been. If there's time to get more than one offensive possession, go for a quick two-point play, especially if the defense is laying off. I've seen teams run off valuable seconds on the clock trying for the three-point shot when there was ample time to get a quick two-point basket and get the ball back again.

If a three-pointer is needed, the clock is the most important factor when you're deciding what to run. If there are three seconds left, there's probably only time for one good look at a three-point shot. If there's more than three seconds on the clock, you might be able to run an offensive set that gives you more than one three-point shot opportunity. Good defenses might take away your first option, so have a plan B.

Playing Defense When Behind

When you're behind, you need stops or turnovers, and you need them fast. Otherwise, you must resort to fouling and sending your opponent to the line. Strategies for defending when behind are described in chapter 15, Preparing for Special Defensive Situations.

LAST-SECOND PLAYS

I recommend practicing special situations with your team often during practice. Players need to feel confident they can execute in the final minutes of a game. They can gain this confidence if they have practiced trying to score under pressure, with little time on the clock.

Ideally, you want your best player on the court at the end of the game to run a play for a game-winning shot. However, things aren't always ideal. This being the case, you should have plays you can run that complement a couple of your best players at the end of the game. Have a quick hitter that can go to a post, wing, or a point guard. This way, you can go to a player who has the hot hand or is guarded by a weak defender. You might also need a play in which your best player is a decoy and your second-best player is the one you go to. Good coaches will often focus on your best player with the philosophy that someone other than her will have to beat them.

Half-Court Last-Second Play

To run some clock at the end of the game, we run a three-high set called Tennessee (see figures 11.1 and 11.2). This set is part of our man-to-man delay game. By using this set, we place our offensive players in positions to drive to the basket, post up, or perhaps get fouled and head to the

free-throw line. Our best three ball handlers and free-throw shooters make up the triangle. Our other two players position themselves in the corners. They are passers and backdoor cutters. The pattern in the triangle is continuity. The passing pattern is as follows. The 1 player has the ball. The 2 player screens down for the 3 player, slips the screen, and then replaces the 3 player at the free-throw line. The 3 player pops up to receive the pass, squares to the goal, and the pattern continues (see figure 11.1, a-c). If any of the three players in the triangle finds a gap to drive, she drives to the basket for a layup.

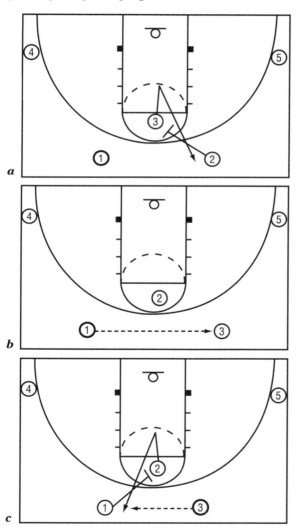

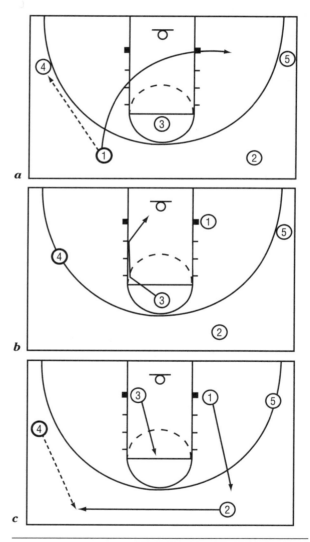

Figure 11.1 Tennessee. *(a)* Player 2 screens for player 3, replacing her at the free-throw line, *(b)* Player 3 pops up to receive the pass from player 1, *(c)* The pattern continues.

Figure 11.2 Tennessee post pass. *(a)* Player 1 passes to player 4, *(b)* Player 3, the high post, cuts to the basket following player 1. Player 4 passes to either player for the layup, *(c)* If neither is open for the layup, player 2 cuts across the court to receive the pass and reset the triangle.

If the triangle players throw to a corner player, the following action occurs. The 1 player passes to the 4 in the corner. The 1 makes a strong basket cut to the goal. The 3 at the high post cuts right after the 1 to the basket. The 4 can pass to either player for a layup. If neither player is open, the 2 comes hard across the court to receive the pass from the 4, and the triangle resets. The 4 and 5 players make a backdoor cut any time their defender turns her back on them (see figure 11.2, a-d). Out of this set, we get into our last-second plays.

Last-Second Plays Versus Man-to-Man Defense

Sometimes the simplest play is the most effective. If you have a dominant point guard, you can set up in a 1-4 low alignment (see figure 11.3). In this set, your point guard has ample room to go one on one and can overpower her defender, beat her off a quick step, or, if a double team comes, kick out to an open shooter. The 2 and 3 players on the baseline read their defense and pop out at the last second if needed for a perimeter shot. A variation of this play is called High Screen. In this set, your point guard and post player with extended range play a two-man game. The 4 player screens high for player 1 and pops, and the 1 makes the read (see figure 11.4a). The 2 and 3 read their defense and pop if necessary. The 1 can shoot, pass to the 4 who has popped, or kick to the 2 or the 3 for the perimeter shot (see figure 11.4b). Either play can be run within 10 seconds to give the offense a shot and a chance at an offensive rebound.

We can also run a number of our quick hitters to complement the player with the hot hand or

who has the biggest mismatch. For a post player, I would run Stack (see chapter 10) for a quick inside look, or else spread the floor in a 1-4 high set to isolate your best post player. In this set, the 1 player passes to the 5 post player, who will eventually get the last shot. The 4 sets a back screen for the 1 player; the 2 and 3 make quick, hard backdoor cuts. If the 2 player is not open, she comes back up to the wing area. If neither backdoor is open, the 5 passes to the 1. The 3, who is on the block, sets a back screen for the 5. The 1 passes to the 5 on the block. This play should start with about 15 seconds on the clock, which gives the offense time for a high-percentage shot and an offensive rebound.

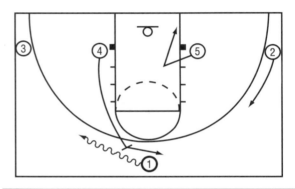

Figure 11.4a Player 4 screens high for player 1 and pops to the top of the key.

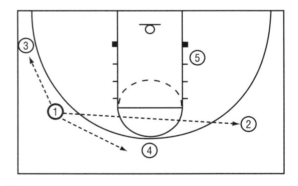

Figure 11.4b Player 1 can take the shot, pass to player 4, or pass to player 2 or 3 for the perimeter shot.

Last-Second Plays Versus a Zone Defense

To hold the ball versus a zone defense, we tweak our triangle offense. Players get into the same

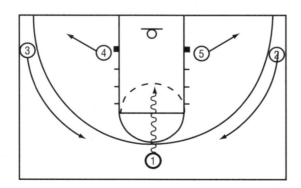

Figure 11.3 1-4 low alignment.

set, but now we spread the set and pass the ball. We shorten passes and step to meet the ball. Our last-second zone plays have already been discussed. For a last-second shot for a post player, we would run Over. For a wing shot, we would run Clear, with its many options. And if we wanted the point guard to shoot, we would run Fade. All of these plays start on one side of the floor and ball reverse. We start our zone plays with 15 seconds left, which gives us ample time to get our shot off and rebound a missed shot.

Last-Second Full-Court or Three-Quarter-Court Plays

The time remaining, the score, and the foul situation help determine which play to run either full court or three-quarter court. The ability or inability to run the baseline on the inbounds pass will also influence the decision on what play to run.

The play we choose depends on the clock. With two seconds or less, we teach catch and shoot. With three to five seconds, a player has time for one or two dribbles and a shot. With more than five seconds, we might want to get the ball to half court and call a timeout to set up a closer sideline inbounds play. With five seconds or more, a player has time to dribble or make a pass.

Along with knowing how much time remains, players need to know whether they need a two-point shot or a three-point shot. Some coaches call a quick timeout after their opponent has scored the go-ahead basket with less than 10 seconds to play. They want to make sure their team knows what play to run in the final 10 seconds. The disadvantage of calling a timeout is that you give the defense a chance to set up.

If the bonus is in effect, the defense often becomes afraid to foul, and a driving offensive play can be effective. I've seen many teams run what we call "Freight Train," a play designed for the best ball handler to drive the full length of the court for a layup or a last-second kick out (see figure 11.5). Often, the defense is retreating in a man-to-man style, but they are so afraid of fouling that they play soft, and the offensive player drives to the basket for a quick score.

If we have 10 seconds left at the end of the game, and we have timeouts remaining, we'll run

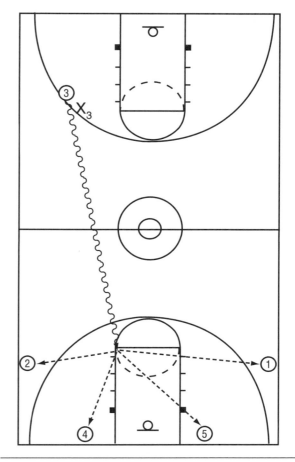

Figure 11.5 Freight Train.

Diamond to get the ball to half court and then call a timeout. In Diamond, our strongest passer passes the ball inbounds. She needs to take a good step back behind the baseline so she has room to step into her throw. This is usually our 5 player. The 3 player is a decoy. The 1, 2, and 4 players run picks; the picks are set to free up the 1 player for a sideline cut. As the 1 receives the pass, she immediately calls a timeout (see figure 11.6).

If we don't have a timeout, or if only a few seconds remain, we'll run our full-court play. Ladder is a play we can run for a two- or three-point shot or to draw a foul on our opponent. To score two or three points, this play requires two passes, so we need three seconds or more to run it. The 1 and 2 players line up as diagrammed (see figure 11.7). The 1 screens for the 2 to cut to the ball. As soon as the 1 screens, she cuts to the sideline for a pass from the 5. At the same time, the 3 and 4 players are aligned as

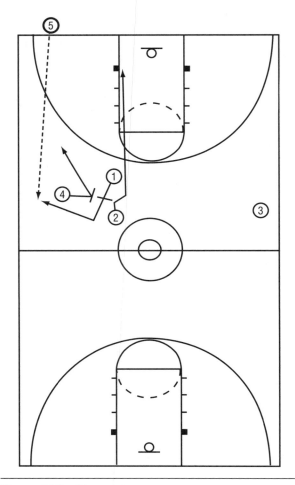

Figure 11.6 Diamond.

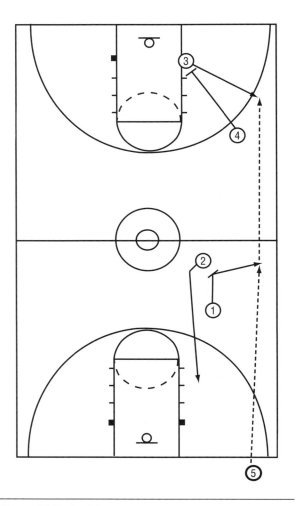

Figure 11.7 Ladder.

diagrammed. The 4 player down screens for the 3 to pop to the three-point line if a three-point shot is needed. The passing pattern is 5 to 1 to 3 for a three-point shot or 5 to 1 to 3 to 4 for a two-point shot.

Ladder Z is the play we run to try to draw a foul on the defense. For this play to work, the 5 player must have the baseline to run. The 3 and 4 execute the same as in Ladder. The 2 follows the 5's baseline run and is open to receive a pass if needed. The 1 player doesn't screen for 2 this time but sets up along the baseline to take a charge from 5's defender (see figure 11.8). If this is the play we want to run, we let the officials know so they'll be watching for the charge to occur. We don't want the officials to miss our players taking a charge on defense. It's important for the 1 player to set a legal screen to hold her ground and take a hit. Ladder can also be run from a three-quarter-court sideline play.

Lady Luck

It was our second game in the Nike Basketball Tournament of Champions last December. We had won our first game by one point, when our freshman, NaNa McClanahan made a free throw with two seconds left in the game. Once again we were involved in a nail biter. This time, we were down by two points with the length of the court to go and only two seconds to play. We needed a catch, shoot, and score play. These are the situations you have practiced many times over and now hope your players can execute. As a player, these are the moments you dream about.

Unusual for me, I decided to diagram a play instead of call a play the players had practiced. Both teams were in the bonus, and the other team's best player had four fouls. I decided to run a play to my post player, KeKe

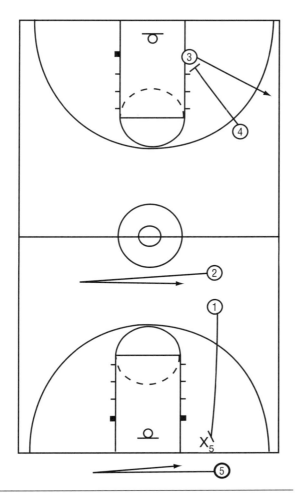

Figure 11.8 Ladder Z.

Stewart (who was guarded by the girl with four fouls) for a short jump shot or a foul. As the play unfolded, my passer out of bounds did not put enough air under her pass, and the pass appeared to be short, which meant KeKe had to extend out of the paint to the three-point line to catch the pass. Catch, shoot, and score is just what she did. She banked in a three-point shot for the win at the buzzer. That was the first three-point shot of her high school career.

INBOUNDS PLAYS

I always run my inbounds plays to score unless possession of the ball is more important than the score. There are times in a game when you have the lead and you want to keep the ball

out of your opponent's hands and run time off the clock. You want to shorten the game, so you milk the clock. Some of our inbounds plays under our own basket can be run versus a man-to-man defense or a zone defense. UCLA is an inbounds play we run against man or zone or junk defenses. This play is designed to go inside to our 5 player. The 1 player has the ball out of bounds. The 4 and 5 players line up in front of the ball on the block and elbow. The 3 and 2 players line up on the weak side at the block and elbow. Against a man defense, the 5 player pops to the short corner for the pass. At the same time, the 3 player pops to the three-point line, as the 4 and 2 players set a double screen (see figure 11.9a). After the 2 player screens, she pops to the left wing. The passes go from 5 to 3 to 2 (see figure 11.9b). After 2 has the ball, 1 and 4 screen for 5 to cut back into the lane for a short jump shot (see figure 11.9c). Versus a 2-3 zone defense, the play is adjusted. The 5 player pops to the short corner. The 4 and the 2 screen the top of the zone for 3 to receive her pass, and 2 still pops to the right wing. The 1 player now screens the outside of the 2-3 defense, and 4 screens the middle. The 5 player shoots in the pocket of the screeners. This play also works against a combination defense. If the defense is playing a diamond and one on player 5, for example, player 4 screens and opens up to the ball. If the defense overcompensates to guard 5, 4 becomes the open player. We tell our players to run UCLA and look for the "roll."

A simple yet effective inbounds play versus a man-to-man defense is our Box inbounds. Many teams run this play, which is a simple pick-the-picker play. We call "Box" and a name, so we can run this play to any player. Our players line up in the box set. Our scorer, player 5, is in front of the ball on the ballside block, and our best screener, player 4, is on the other block. The 3 player lines up on the ballside elbow and the 2 player on the opposite elbow. On the slap of the ball, the 5 player screens for the 3 player to go to the corner, the 2 player cuts to the ballside sideline, and the 4 player screens for the 5 player and opens to the ball (see figure 11.10a). The 5 player is open if the defense doesn't switch. If there is a defensive switch, the 4 player is open (see figure 11.10b). We practice all players in each spot so we can take advantage of our best scoring matchup.

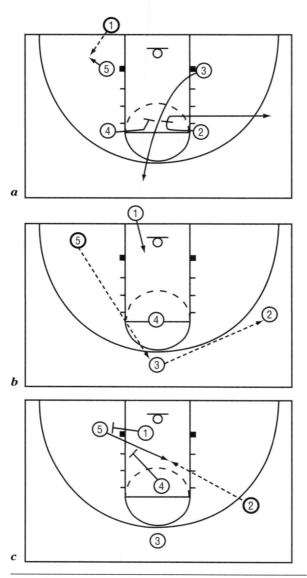

Figure 11.9 UCLA inbounds.

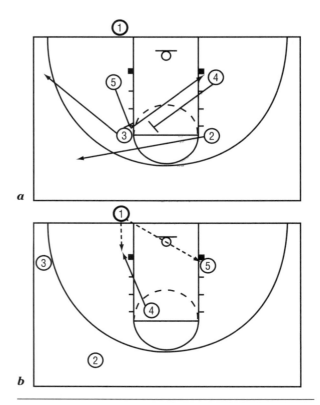

Figure 11.10 Box inbounds.

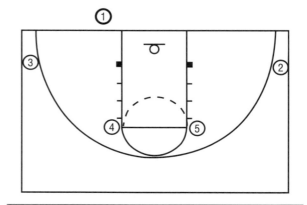

Figure 11.11a Spread set.

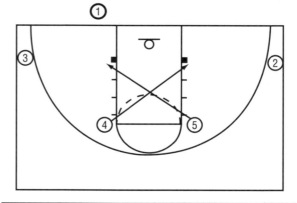

Figure 11.11b Spread elbows.

Besides UCLA, another zone inbounds play we run is our Spread set (see figure 11.11a). If a team is going to defend us in a zone, we want the defense to pick and choose who they will guard. In order to force this decision, we'll call "spread elbows." Our best perimeter shooters, players 2 and 3, line up along the baseline. Our post players, 5 and 4, line up at the free-throw line elbows. If the defense collapses, the 1 player throws wide for a perimeter shot. If the defense spreads out, the 5 and 4 players are "X cutting" into the paint for short jumpers (see figure 11.11b). The 4 and 5 can also make defensive reads. If the defense collapses to the baseline, the 4 and 5 can stay high at the elbow for a 15-footer.

We run another play similar to our Spread in which the defense must pick their poison. We call this our Four. In our Four inbounds, our 5, 2, 3, and 4 players line up shoulder to shoulder across the free-throw line. On 1's slap of the ball, 2 and 3 cut down the lane and then out to the perimeter, hoping to drag the defense with them (see figure 11.12a). The 5 and 4 players "X cut" to the open areas in the back of the zone (see figure 11.12b). The 1 player looks inside first and outside second. In both the Spread and the Four, if the ball is initially inbounded to a perimeter player, the opposite perimeter player rotates to the top of the key as the safety.

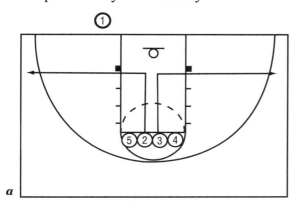

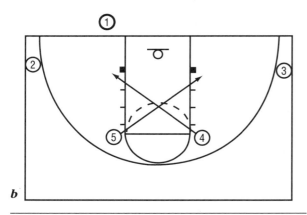

Figure 11.12 Four inbounds.

SIDELINE INBOUNDS PLAYS

My philosophy on sideline inbounds plays has changed over the years. I used to always run a sideline play to score, but now I want to make sure the ball is deep enough on my offensive

end to make the first pass a safe pass. Passes that initiate close to the half-court line are often too long, too soft, and easily picked off by the defense. So now we run plays to score only when the ball is not close to half court but near the three-point line. I believe this is a safe distance to enter the ball.

Most of our sideline inbounds plays have a couple of options. Against a man-to-man defense we run our Duke offense to look inside first and outside second. Duke starts in a box set with two out of bounds. The 3 player and the 1 player line up on the ballside block and elbow, and the 5 and 4 line up on the weak-side block and elbow. On the slap of the ball, 3 screens across for 5. If 5 is wide open, 2 throws to 5. If not, 1 and 4 set a double screen for 3 to come up the lane and pop out at the three-point line (see figure 11.13a). The 2 player throws to 3. If 3 has a good shot, she shoots. The finish of the play has 1 screening for 5 to cross the lane at the same time that 4 and 3 are executing a pick and roll. Shot options are 3 off the screen, 4 on the roll, and 5 coming across the lane (see figure 11.13b).

Against a very tight, aggressive man-to-man defense we run our 24 sideline play to take advantage of the defense overplaying us on offense. Again, our setup is in a box with our

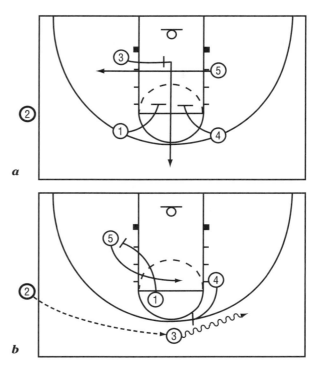

Figure 11.13 Duke inbounds.

scorer out of bounds. The 1 player screens down for 4 to receive the pass. At the same time, the 3 player screens down for 5 to entertain their defense (see figure 11.14a). After 4 receives the pass from 2, 1 sets a back screen for 2 cutting to the basket. If 2's defense is playing her tightly, you might get a backdoor layup. If 2 is not open on her backdoor cut, she continues on through the lane to the weak side of the floor. The 5 and 3 players set a stagger screen for the 2 player. Player 1 gets the ball out of 4's hands to reverse the ball. The 2 player comes off the stagger looking for the pass from the 1 player (see figure 11.14b). Our 24 Special is a variation of this play. The play starts out the same as 24 (see figure 11.15, a-b), but when the 1 player comes high to take the ball out of 4's hands, she fakes the exchange. The 4 player keeps the ball and drives to the basket for a layup (see figure 11.15c).

We take a play out of our quick hitter play book for our sideline zone inbounds play. We use our Clear play and a variation of this play to score from the sideline. On the sideline, Clear is called "20." Once again we use a box set. Our best perimeter shooter is out of bounds. Our post players line up on the blocks, the best scorer on the weak side. The 1 and 2 players

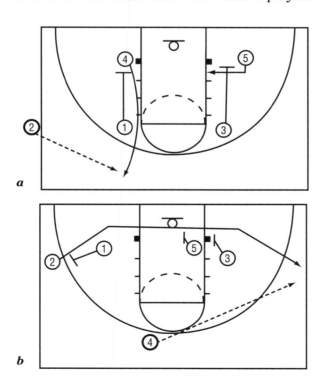

Figure 11.14 24 sideline play.

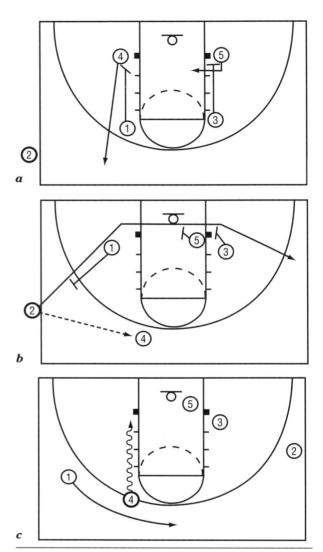

Figure 11.15 24 Special.

line up at the elbows, with the best scorer on the weak side. On the slap of the ball, the 1 player pops up to the three-point line, and 2 and 5 exchange to entertain the defense. The 3 player passes to the 1 player (see figure 11.16a). The 1 player then passes to 5. The 3 player clears to the weak side, and the 2 player screens the back of the zone for 3. 5 passes to 3 (see figure 11.16b), after which 2 posts up and 5 cuts down the lane. The 3 player has a shot or a pass to 2 or 5.

After running this play a couple of times, we run a variation of 20 Clear called 20 Back. This play sets up the same as 20 and starts the same way (see figure 11.17a). This time, however, 3 doesn't change sides of the court. She fakes her

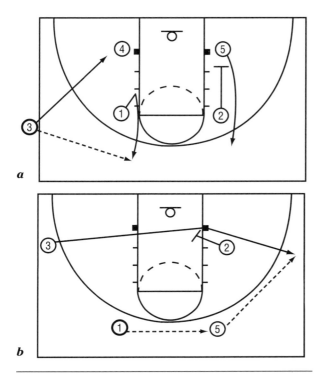

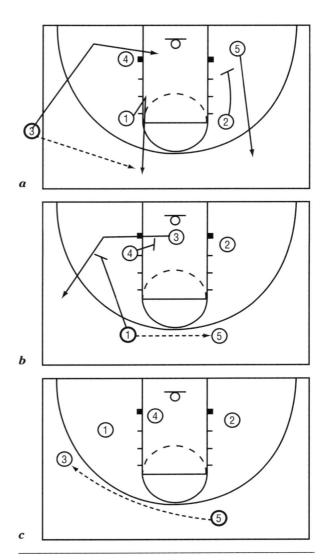

Figure 11.16 20 Clear.

Figure 11.17 20 Back.

clear out to the weak side and returns to the ball side. The 1 player passes to 5, and 1 and 4 screen the zone high and low for 3 to pop out (see figure 11.17b). 5 passes to 3 for the perimeter shot (see figure 11.17c).

You need to have a play you can run regardless of the defense you face. Some teams might junk your team at the end of a game, playing a combination defense. Some teams might trap. Have a play to run that gives you several options regardless of the defense. The key here is players making a defensive read and then running an effective option. To accommodate this, we practice making a play versus running a play.

Our Three-in-a-Row play is designed to read the defense and make an offensive play. The 1 player takes the ball out of bounds. She is a secondary shooter. The 5, 3, and 2 line up across from 1, as shown in the diagram. The 4 player lines up above the 2 player. The 5 player is our best inside scorer, the 3 is our best three-point shooter, and the 2 our best scorer off the dribble. The 4 can be an inside or outside player. On the slap of the ball, 3 and 5 screen for 2, who reads the screens to curl or flare (see figure 11.18a). After 3 screens, 4 screens 3 for a three-point look. After 5 screens 2, she

flashes back to the ballside elbow (see figure 11.18b). After 4 screens, she rolls to the weak-side block if only a two-point shot is needed, or to the weak-side wing if a perimeter shot is needed. The 1 player can pass to the 2, 3, or 5 player (see figure 11.18c). If the 3 player gets the ball, she can shoot or look to the 4 player. If the 2 player gets the ball, she can shoot, drive, or hit the 5 player cutting down the lane. If player 5 gets the ball at the elbow, she can shoot, pass to player 4 ducking in on the weak side, pass to player 2 slashing across the baseline, or kick out to player 3 for a three-point shot. Players read the defense and make an offensive play.

Any time a team traps, we want to get our heads inside. By this I mean we need to catch

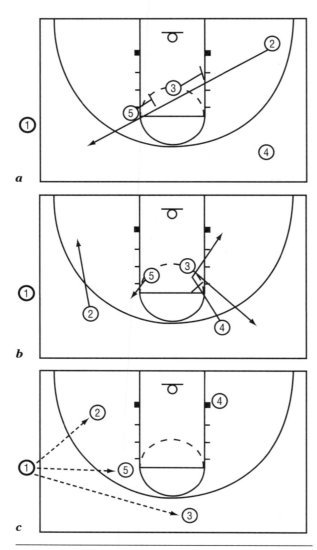

Figure 11.18 Three-in-a-Row play.

and immediately look inside for an open player. We need more than one option against a trap. Three in a Row gives us inside and outside options.

SUMMARY

- Players need to practice special situations daily to feel confident in their execution.
- Consider time remaining, score, foul situations, and timeouts when choosing your offense at the end of a game.
- Have a plan and a play for inbounding full court or half court.
- Make inbounds plays weapons for your team.

PART VI

COACHING DEFENSE

TEACHING DEFENSIVE POSITIONS AND SETS

As I have said, I believe every player can play defense. Some players might be more athletic or more talented than others, but all players can learn to play good, basic defense through proper technique, hard work, and determination. You've heard many coaches say it, and I believe it's true: Offense sells tickets, but defense and rebounding win championships. Despite the importance of solid defense to a team's success, it's generally the star offensive players who rake in the accolades. They're the ones who get the headlines the next day. Great defense goes unnoticed except by the coach.

A great defensive team can offset an average offensive team. Energy and effort are not always quick producers offensively, but on the defensive end they can turn a game around. There will be nights when a player's shot is off, but there should never be a night when her defense is off. A great defense can take an offensive team out of its comfort zone, disrupt its flow, speed an offense up, and wear offensive players down. Not every player on a team needs to be a great offensive player, but every team player needs to be a good defender. Great offensive teams will exploit weak defenders.

POSITION SKILLS

The game of basketball has changed a great deal over the last few years. Players today are not narrowly defined by their position. Many post players can step out on the perimeter, and many perimeter players are comfortable posting up. This provides coaches with challenging defensive matchups. When I scout a team, the first thing I do is decide on player matchups. Where can I gain an advantage? Where do I see the opponent gaining an advantage? It's not always easy to match post players with post players and guards with guards. The following are ideal or common attributes and skills of each defensive position.

Point Guard

The point guard is usually the floor leader offensively and has the same job defensively. She's the "safety" on offense, the first one to get back defensively. Being the first defender back defensively, she's usually in good position to call out the defense or give her teammates a defensive hand signal. If her opponents are a transition offensive team, the point guard is often the defensive player back to stop a two-on-one transition basket. To be able to fill this role, a point guard needs to be smart, quick in defensive transition, and great at communicating.

The point guard makes sure her teammates are in the right defensive alignments, either full or half court. She's the coach on the floor, just as she is on offense, and has the duty of communicating with the coaching staff during a game. She's the player who relays the coach's defensive change-ups to teammates.

The point guard is almost always one of a team's quicker players, but she usually has less height than her teammates, so she'll match up with a quick, small player on the opposing team. Because she's small and quick, the point guard needs to influence the ball in a half-court game. She also needs to be able to pressure the opposing team's point guard. Ideally, this pressure will influence her opponent's direction on the court, reduce easy scoring or passing opportunities, and set the tone for her team's defense in a half-court set. If she is the first line of defense in a half-court game, her intensity and pressure can set the tone for her teammates. Her intensity is exemplified by how hard and how long she can sustain excellent defensive pressure. Her defensive pressure must be great enough to make her opponent feel uncomfortable, perhaps slightly unnerved. I'm constantly asking my point guard, "Does your defense bother her?"

Wings

Perimeter players should match up defensively with their counterparts' size and athleticism. If the opposing team's best scorer on the perimeter is a wing player, your best perimeter defender will match with this player. To provide the best matchup, answer these questions regarding their perimeter scorer: Does she shoot off the dribble or off the pass? Can she create her own shot? Is she quick or slow? Can she post up? How active is she without the ball? What is her range? How strong is she? How hard does she go to the boards to rebound? Ask the same questions about the perimeter defender to be matched up on this offensive perimeter player. Can the defender defend a perimeter player who penetrates? Can she defend a perimeter player who can post up? Can she defend a player who works hard without the ball by constantly moving?

Answering these questions will help you match your wing players defensively. The opposing team's best scorer might be a three-point shooter who has deadly aim but can't create her own shot and is slow to get herself open. If this is the case, you might not need your best defender on her. A defender who can shadow her might be enough to contain her. You might want to save your best defender for a more mobile player.

If your opponent has good size on the perimeter and posts up that size, your defensive matchup needs to be able to defend a post-up perimeter player. Again, you would want to match big on big and small on small. Perhaps your opposition has a perimeter player who's not a scoring threat, in which case you could match your weakest perimeter defender on this player. Or this defender could be a help player on another offensive player. To make this work, the weak defender needs to be a smart player who knows when and how to help her teammates defensively.

If your opponent is strong on the perimeter, your perimeter defenders will need to adjust. Match your best defender to their best offensive player. This defender needs to focus on taking away the perimeter player's strengths, such as shooting off the dribble or shooting off a screen. Your weaker defender must play within her abilities. Give her the weakest perimeter matchup and, when possible, provide her some help from her teammates. Opposing teams will try to find a way to exploit a weak defender, perhaps by running plays that isolate your weak perimeter defender.

Perimeter players need to rebound. Match up contact players with contact players. A great defender who doesn't finish her defense with a block-out is a liability in a game. It's also important to try to match up players of strength and aggressiveness with similar players. Last season we had a physical perimeter player match up with a post player and a smaller, yet quicker, post player match up on the perimeter. As long as the matches work, you can interchange perimeter and post defenders.

Posts

Most teams will have one dominating inside player, usually playing the strong post. In finding a matchup for this player, ask these questions: Is the strong-post player a power or finesse player? Does she dribble or shoot off the pass? Is she big or small? Does she leap or stay on the floor? Does she have basically one move or many? Is she an aggressive rebounder? Another point to consider: Can your best offensive player, who is also your better post defender, guard the opponent's best inside scorer and stay out of foul trouble? Ideally, you want to match size with size, mobility with mobility, and strength with strength. If the opposing team has a post player who steps out on the perimeter, you need to match up on that player with a mobile post defender or perhaps with a bigger perimeter player. If the opposition has one weak inside player, you match your weakest inside player on her, and she also becomes a help player defensively. If the go-to player inside is strong and physical, you need to match accordingly. More than likely, one of your post defenders will need to be a contact player who doesn't mind the beating and banging of post defense. If that offensive player has a go-to move, your post defender needs to be smart to try to take that move away from her.

Post defenders need to be able to finish their defense with block-outs to rebound for their team. Usually, your leading defensive rebounder will come from a post position. A physical nature for post players is critical. It's hard to defend the paint if a player doesn't like contact.

TYPES OF DEFENSES

Perhaps you have a type of defense that has been your trademark. Perhaps you're known for your man-to-man defense, matchup zone defense, or aggressive trapping defense. If you can choose your players, you can choose your style of defense. But if you can't choose your players, I suggest you choose the defense that best fits your team's abilities and make that defense your primary defense. After choosing a primary defense, have a few backup defenses to use for change-ups or as weapons when needed.

Man-to-Man Defense

The most common defense is a traditional man-to-man defense. In this defense each player guards another player on the opposing team, positioning between the offensive player she is guarding and the basket (see figure 12.1). Players adjust in this defense as the ball moves around the court. Players defend in three defensive positions: on the ball, in a denial position, or in a help position (see figure 12.2). In a five-on-five defensive set, players assume one of the three defensive positions. They either guard the ball, guard one pass away from the ball (in a denial position), or guard two passes away (in a help-side position). Players adjust their position depending on their opponent's strengths and weaknesses.

Strengths of a Pressure Man-to-Man Defense
Man-to-man defenses allow you to match up player for player with your opponent.

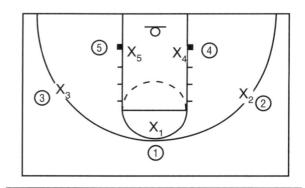

Figure 12.1 Man-to-man defense.

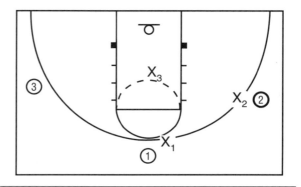

Figure 12.2 The three defensive positions of a man-to-man defense: on the ball (X2), in a denial position (X1), or in a help position (X3).

Matchups are designated by height, speed, and athleticism. In man defense, all players are accounted for offensively. Each offensive player has a defender assigned to her. Against a team with several good scorers, a man defense allows you to match up on these scorers. This may be an effective defense at the end of a game when you want all offensive players guarded and no player left open for a shot to win a game. Against an impatient offensive team, a man defense can make them work a little longer for a shot or force them to take an early shot in their offense.

Man-to-man defense can be played aggressively or soft, again depending on matchups and who has the advantage. If you have an aggressive, quick defender guarding your opponent's point guard, this pressure can cause a turnover, force her to play faster than she wants, force her away from her best scorers, or get into her head mentally and force her into mental mistakes. Similarly, you might have a great matchup in the post area. You might have a big, physical post player who through strength and aggressive post defense can neutralize an offensive post player.

Aggressive man defense can make offensive players uncomfortable. They might rush shots or make quick passes to avoid the pressure. Great defensive pressure causes teams to speed up.

Weaknesses of a Pressure Man-to-Man Defense Playing great pressure defense without the quickness and athleticism to do so can cause problems. A smart offensive point guard can burn a slower defender who is overplaying, leading to an easy score or an easy assist to a teammate. Overplaying defensively can also get players out of a help position. If a teammate closely guarded can beat her defender, the help defense might be too extended to recover in time, thus leading to another easy score or pass. This extended defense can also cause rebounding problems as players are beat, allowing numerical advantages for the offense. Conditioning can come into play with aggressive defense. A poorly conditioned team can incur several breakdowns if they play aggressive defense for an extended time.

Soft man-to-man defense can be a change-up, a base defense, or a complement to the aggressive man-to-man defense. As a base defense, a soft man defense might have an appearance of a zone. This defense can allow you to help inside on a strong post player or perhaps play off weak perimeter scorers. This defense can also cause an undisciplined offense (an offense that shoots the ball on their first open look) to take quick shots. Changing up from a pressure defense to a soft man defense might cause confusion for your opponent. They might think you have changed up to a zone defense and begin running their zone offenses. A soft man defense might be a way to hide a poor defender or protect a defender in foul trouble. Against a perimeter team that drives the ball, playing soft might allow a defender with better defensive positioning to stop an offensive player who likes to score off the dribble.

Soft man-to-man defenses won't work against good three-point shooting teams. Playing off these players allows them to do what they do best. If an offensive team is very patient, it can find a way to exploit soft defenders—either on cuts, post-ups, or perhaps off the glass.

Zone Defenses

Zone defense is different from man-to-man defense in that instead of guarding a particular player, each defender is responsible for guarding an area on the floor (a "zone") and any offensive player who comes into that area. Zone defenders move their position on the court in relation to where the ball moves. The most popular zone defenses are the 2-3, 1-3-1, 1-2-2, and 3-2 (see figures 12.3-12.6).

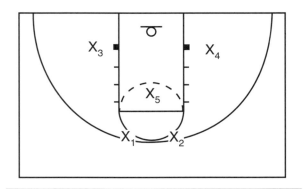

Figure 12.3 2-3 zone defense.

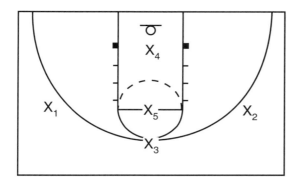

Figure 12.4 1-3-1 zone defense.

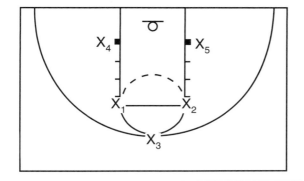

Figure 12.5 1-2-2 zone defense.

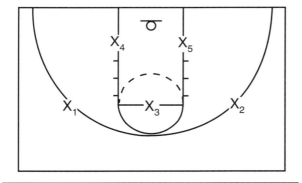

Figure 12.6 3-2 zone defense.

Strengths of a Zone Defense Your team might not have good, quick, athletic man-to-man defenders, making man matchups difficult. In such a case, guarding an area probably suits your talent better. Your opponent's offense might have a couple of players too quick or too strong to match up with individually. On the other hand, your team might have very tall and strong players who lack quickness. A zone can look big and intimidating to this type of personnel (too much space to cover or too many holes

to fill). With size, you might be able to "wall off" the lane area. Keeping your size close to the basket might also help with defensive rebounding. A sagging 2-3 zone defense, for example, might be played to protect the paint area.

A zone defense can be effective against weak perimeter shooters. Collapsing inside defensively, you give up the open perimeter shot. A poor shooting perimeter team might have a hard time getting the ball inside against a collapsing defense. Perimeter shots are open, but the lane is clogged up.

You might use a zone to protect a defensive player who's in foul trouble. Instead of allowing your opponent to attack your player in trouble, such as would occur in a man-to-man defense, a zone defense can hide the foul-plagued player.

Zone defenses are also used to disrupt a team offensively. Perhaps they practice their man-to-man offense quite a bit more than their zone offense. Maybe the majority of the teams in their league play man-to-man defense, and thus they have little game experience versus a zone defense. A team who is in a rhythm offensively might find they are out of sync against a zone defense. Similar to a soft man defense, a soft zone defense might cause a team to shoot quickly. An impatient offense might take their first open look, regardless if it's a good look or not. Some teams just plain don't like playing against zone defenses. In such cases, if you can take a team out of their comfort area, this might be a good enough reason to play a zone defense.

A zone might be effective when your team is in trouble. If a team beats your press, falling back into a zone might be the defense that saves an easy basket. Or perhaps your team needs a breather defensively—a quick change to a zone might give them that chance. However, this will depend on how soft or aggressive your zone defense is played.

A zone defense lends itself to trapping opportunities, which can be a weapon. A straight zone defensive look can easily be adjusted to trap a pass or a dribbler and then fall back to straight zone again on the next possession.

Zone Strengths

1. Defensive players aren't assigned a particular player to guard, thus avoiding potential matchup problems.

2. Zone defenses allow players to play close to the basket or out on the perimeter; big players can stay close to the goal.

3. Players in foul trouble can be protected in a zone defense.

4. Zone defenses can disrupt an opponent's offensive flow.

5. Changing from an aggressive man-to-man defense to a more passive zone defense might allow players a chance to catch their breath.

Going Against the Grain   For years our teams at Oak Ridge have played a very aggressive 2-3 zone defense. We have used our size, speed, and athleticism to extend our 2-3 zone defense. For all the reasons teams generally choose to play a zone, those reasons are the opposite for us. We don't want to play a soft zone but a very aggressive, in-your-face type of zone. We extend the top of the 2-3 to force the point guard to use her weak hand (usually left hand). The other top guard covers the high-post player (see figure 12.7). If there's no high-post player, she gets into the passing lane of the left wing. Forcing the offense left allows the back defenders to shift and overplay in their areas. Our philosophy is to apply great pressure on the perimeter and prevent good looks for inside passes. We want the offense to have to put the ball on the floor to beat us. I have not seen too many teams that have players put the ball on the floor and make great decisions. Watching from the stands, it's easy to see inside players who are open, but great pressure on the perimeter takes away this vision on the court. The reality is that if you have great athletes, all defenses correctly executed can be terrific weapons.

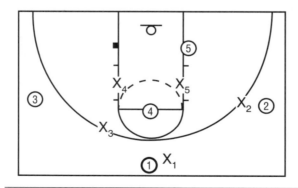

Figure 12.7   Oak Ridge zone defense.

Weaknesses of a Zone Defense   You have heard the phrase, "we shot them right out of their zone defense." Zone defenses can struggle against good shooting outside teams, especially teams that are patient to work to get the open perimeter shot. With the three-point shot in the game, zones are forced to stretch out farther and farther. If the zone really extends to shut down the three-point shot, they might be giving up an easy post feed on the inside.

Zone defenses rebound in areas without a specific player assignment. In a zone offense in which a side of the court is overloaded, rebounding becomes very tough for the defensive team. There's more than one player in their zone area, so it's likely one of those offensive players can get to the boards untouched. A slicing, slashing offensive team can get some easy offensive rebounds.

Zone defenses might give a great offensive player an edge. She might enter the game with the attitude, "nobody can guard me," which can be a big confidence boost for an already good offensive player. Along those same lines, the defense might be discouraged or disheartened if they feel they can guard opposing players man to man but the coaching staff believes only a zone defense will work. If this is the case, coaches need to sell a team on why they're "zoning" an opponent; they need to convince the team that they're playing zone defense as a weapon, not as a liability.

A team whose primary defense is zone might find it hard to play man to man when needed. At the end of a game, to shut down specific scorers, you might need to play tight man defense. If your players rarely play man, their confidence and execution might not be what's needed to win the game.

If you play a zone as your primary defense, and if it's a soft zone, it might not be effective if your team falls behind late in the game. A zone defense might not apply the type of pressure needed nor be able to speed up your opponent.

Finally, in transition zone defense, a weakness can be a player retreating back into her zone area instead of finding the ball and stopping an easy score. It's easier in man defense to switch players in transition than it is to switch zone areas.

Zone Weaknesses

1. A patient offensive team might get an open shot against a zone.

2. Rebounding can be more difficult out of a zone defense than from a man defense.

3. An opposing offensive player might gain confidence against a zone, believing the opposition has no one player to guard her.

4. A team that plays primarily zone defense might be uncomfortable playing man when a man defense becomes necessary (such as late in a close game).

5. In transition defense, switching zone areas to guard the player with the ball might become confusing and inefficient.

Combination Defenses

The majority of defenses played are either man-to-man defenses or zone defenses. A third category of defense is a combination defense, often called a "junk defense." In junk defenses, some players defend man to man while others defend in a zone. One of the most common junk defenses is a Box-and-One defense. In this defense, one player is guarded man to man while the other four players play a 2-2 defense in the form of a box. This box defends the lane area (see figure 12.8). If the perimeter area, instead of the lane, needs more help defensively, a Diamond-and-One defense might be employed. In this defense, one player is guarded man to man, and the other four defensive players form a diamond zone, which provides defensive help on the perimeter (see figure 12.9). A Triangle-and-Two defense has two players guarded man

to man and the other three players playing a triangle zone defense in the lane area (see figure 12.10).

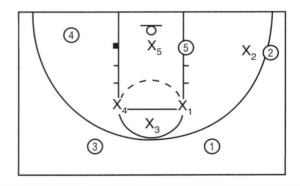

Figure 12.9 Diamond-and-One defense.

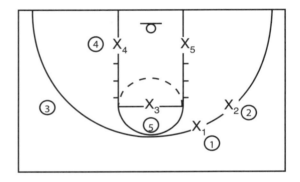

Figure 12.10 Triangle-and-Two defense.

Strengths of Combination Defenses Combination defenses can catch your opponent off guard. You might disrupt their offensive flow by surprising them with a defense they've had little experience playing against. They begin to lose confidence, and execution can be a struggle.

A junk defense might slow down a good offensive player or two and put scoring responsibilities on the other players. Suddenly, roles are changing right in the middle of a game, which some players might find quite disconcerting.

If you have scouted a team and seen that a junk defense is effective against them, it's certainly worth a try to see if that defense works again. Your opponent, having to relive this defense again, might mentally take themselves out of the game, thinking, "here we go again." If they didn't attack the junk well the first time, they might have little confidence a second time around. Finally, a junk defense at the end of a

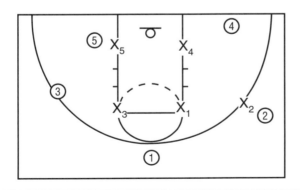

Figure 12.8 Box-and-One defense.

game can sometimes disrupt a structured team that runs its offense for only its better players to shoot.

Weaknesses of Combination Defenses Combination defenses are usually not a team's primary defense. Consequently, teams spend little time practicing junk defenses. Thus, your players might not execute them as well as you would like. Players might lack the confidence to play a defense they have practiced so little.

A team that is well prepared for combination defenses might be able to execute against the junk defense with success. A patient offensive team might still get a good offensive shot, even from the player or players being guarded man to man.

Another problem with junk defenses is they can lend themselves to poor defensive rebounding positioning. Players can get too focused in on the player or players being guarded man to man so they aren't as active in their zone defensive areas. Consequently, they're unprepared to block out once the shot has gone up. Also, because this defense has been practiced so little, players aren't as comfortable or as familiar with area block-out assignments.

SUMMARY

- All players need to be able to play defense.

- Player matchups in a man-to-man defense are predominantly decided based on size, speed, strength, and athleticism.

- Pressure man defense can cause a team to speed up, turn the ball over, and play outside of its comfort zone offensively.

- A soft man defense might be a good change-up to a pressure man-to-man defense.

- Without the right kind of athletes, overplaying defensively can give the offense easy scoring or passing opportunities.

- Zone defenses allow players to guard an area instead of a player and might be the best fit for your personnel or a particular game situation.

- Combination defenses can be useful in specific situations but rarely as a main defense.

CHAPTER 13 TEACHING DEFENSIVE SKILLS

Great team defense begins with great individual defense. Great individual defense begins with learning defensive skills and techniques. Individual defensive fundamentals are the foundation for team defensive success. Defensive skills aren't as complicated to learn as offensive skills, and players pick them up more quickly and easily. If they're willing to put forth the effort, most players can have some success with defense right away. None of this means that you should spend less time on defense than on offense. Many successful coaches stress defense because they know that a great defense can neutralize a good offense.

FOOTWORK

Defensive footwork needs to be drilled just as much as offensive footwork. Defensive positioning and the amount of distance a defensive player takes from the player she's defending depend largely on the abilities and skills of the two players. A super quick and experienced defender might move in closer on an opponent than an inexperienced defender with moderate quickness should dare do. When it comes to footwork, much depends on quickness, but even more depends on positioning. If you know where and how to move your feet, you'll have advantages over many opponents.

Proper defense and effective footwork begin with the stance. The defensive stance is neither natural nor comfortable, which is why many players struggle to defend in the correct stance. They are much more comfortable standing up than flexing their knees. In a defensive stance, a player's feet are slightly staggered and about shoulder-width apart. In a staggered stance, one foot is placed on the floor higher than the other foot. For balance, body weight should be equally distributed on both feet. Weight should be on the balls of the feet, not on the heels. Knees should be bent and thighs at a 45-degree angle to the floor. This allows defensive players a low body position, which makes for greater quickness, strength, and explosiveness (see figure 13.1).

A defender's upper body should be straight with the head up and centered directly over the shoulders. This posture helps maintain balance and provide court vision. Forearms should be flexed, and hands should be in front of the body, palms up. Active hands often bother a dribbler. But, in general, defenders shouldn't attempt to reach in with their hands to steal the ball because this can cause unbalance, which a skilled offensive player will take advantage of. Defenders want to pressure the ball while containing the dribbler.

Figure 13.1 Proper defensive stance.

Figure 13.2 Slide step.

Slide Step To move laterally when defending, a defensive player uses a slide step. Some coaches refer to the slide as a "step-and-catch" movement. To move to her left, a defender wants to push off with her right foot, step left with her left foot, and slide her right foot halfway to her left foot. This procedure is repeated to defend laterally. It's important that the defender not cross her feet or bring them too close together because these result in poor defensive balance (see figure 13.2).

Movement in a forward or backward direction is done in a similar sliding fashion. To move forward, the back foot pushes off, the front foot steps forward, and the rear foot slides up halfway to the front foot. To move backward, the front pushes off, the back foot takes a step, and the forward foot slides halfway to the back foot. Weight needs to be on the balls of the feet. These sliding steps are taken with quick, short

movements, and feet stay as close to the floor as possible.

Defensive positioning on a ball handler depends on both the defensive player's and the offensive player's strengths, weaknesses, and strategies. For example, a defender might overplay a dribbler's strong hand. If a player is right-handed, the defender might line up on the offensive player's right hand. If the offensive player is a poor ball handler, the defender can crowd her defensively. In a crowded defensive position, the defense guards her offensive player much closer than in a normal on-the-ball stance.

Drop Step The drop step is a defensive move used to counter an offensive player's change of direction. If an offensive player attacks a defender's high or top foot, the defender needs to execute a drop step to counter this move. This move is a defensive recovery to help the

Figure 13.3 Drop step.

defender avoid getting beat and giving up an easy score. The drop step is actually a reverse pivot. It is executed by pivoting on the back foot while performing a reverse pivot and swinging the opposite elbow and front foot in the direction taken by the offensive player (see figure 13.3). After the drop step is taken, the defensive player needs to regain proper defensive positioning.

Footwork Drills

Great defense starts with an attitude, a mindset that says, "Nobody scores on me or my team." Next, the heart must be engaged. Take pride in individual and team defense. Finally, engage your body. Defense is hard work; short cuts don't pay off. Nobody "scores" in footwork drills, but they transfer great footwork to the game, and literally nobody scores. Being in excellent condition can only improve individual and team defense. Great

defense expends energy, and well-conditioned teams can play great defense much longer than teams with poor conditioning.

Slide Drill

Purpose: To reinforce proper body positioning and defensive footwork

Procedure: Players line up in several lines across the court facing the coach. On the whistle, players slap the floor, yell out "defense!" and assume a defensive stance with feet parallel. A coach points to the right or to the left, and players execute the proper sliding technique. Players continue the slide in the same direction until the coach changes direction with another gesture.

Direction Drill

Purpose: To reinforce proper body positioning and defensive footwork

Procedure: This drill is the same as the Slide Drill except the coach adds forward and backward directions to her cues. When sliding in a retreat manner from a lateral slide, players execute the drop step.

Lane Slides

Purpose: To reinforce proper defensive slide technique and a low body defensive position

Procedure: Players line up inside the free-throw lane area with their outside foot placed against the free-throw lane line. On a coach's whistle, players slide from lane line to lane line. As each player's foot touches the lane line, so does each outside hand. This helps players stay low. Players count how many lines they can touch in 30 seconds.

Free-Throw Lane Drill

Purpose: To work on quick changes of direction and reinforce proper footwork

Drill: Players line up at the bottom corner of the free-throw lane line. At the whistle, players sprint to the top corner of the lane (called the elbow). When they touch the corner they quickly assume a defensive stance and slide to the next elbow. After touching the next elbow, players backpedal to the bottom corner. After touching the bottom corner (baseline), players use defensive slides to return to their original starting position. The area covered in this drill is the free-throw lane. The footwork pattern is forward sprint, slide, backpedal, and slide. This drill runs 30 seconds (see figure 13.4).

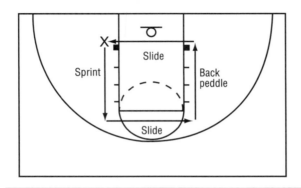

Figure 13.4 Free-Throw Lane Drill.

Quickness Drills

Basketball is becoming a game of speed. Players and coaches love the transition game. In a half-court set, you see more and more explosive moves offensively. To counteract these, a defensive player needs to increase her quickness. The following drills increase a player's quickness.

Line Hops Players stand on one side of a basketball court sideline. Keeping their feet together, they hop sideways over the line. Players count how many hops they can make in 30 seconds. The first set of hops is done sideways, and the second set is forward and back.

Cone Jumps Arrange 12-inch cones two feet apart in a straight line from the baseline to the half-court line. Players line up behind the baseline cone and jump the cones in three sets. The first set (to the half-court line) is with two feet together over each cone as rapidly as possible. The second set (back to the baseline) is done sideways, with the left foot leading. The third set (back to the half-court line) is done sideways with the right foot leading.

Rapid Fire Players spread out on the court and assume a defensive stance. On a coach's whistle, players move their feet up and down as fast as possible. For maximum benefit, players should lift their knees as high as they can. Increase the duration of this drill over time.

Directional Rapid Fire This drill starts the same as the Machine Gun. A coach adds turns by pointing in a direction as players are moving their feet up and down. If the coach points to the right, players execute a quarter turn to the right and then square up. If the coach points to the left, players execute a quarter turn to the left and then square up. Increase the duration of this drill over time.

Dot Drills Coaches can devise any number of dot drills by placing rubber dots on the gym floor. Dots 1, 2, 3, and 4 are 18 inches apart in the shape of a square. Dot 5 is in the center of the square (see figure 13.5). All drills are done first with both legs and then progress to single legs. All drills are done facing the same direction. Players are given a pattern to follow, and they follow the pattern with their jumps for 30 seconds, moving as quickly as they can.

Patterns

- 1, 2, 3, 4 = box
- 1, 4, 3, 2 = box reverse
- 1, 3, 4, 2 = criss-cross
- 2, 4, 3, 1 = criss-cross reversed
- 1, 5, 3, 4, 5, 2, 1 = figure-eight

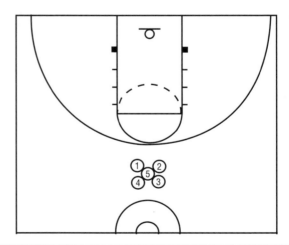

Figure 13.5 Dot Drill pattern.

Ladder Drills You can either use a real exercise ladder or draw one on the floor. There are many ladder drills that enhance a player's footwork, speed, and agility. Ladder drills can be run for a set time or a set number of trips down the ladder. The following list details a few popular ladder drills. They are also illustrated in figure 13.6.

- **Forward One In.** Moving as quickly as they can, players run through the ladder putting one foot in each square.
- **Forward Two In.** Moving as quickly as they can, players run through the ladder placing both feet in each square.

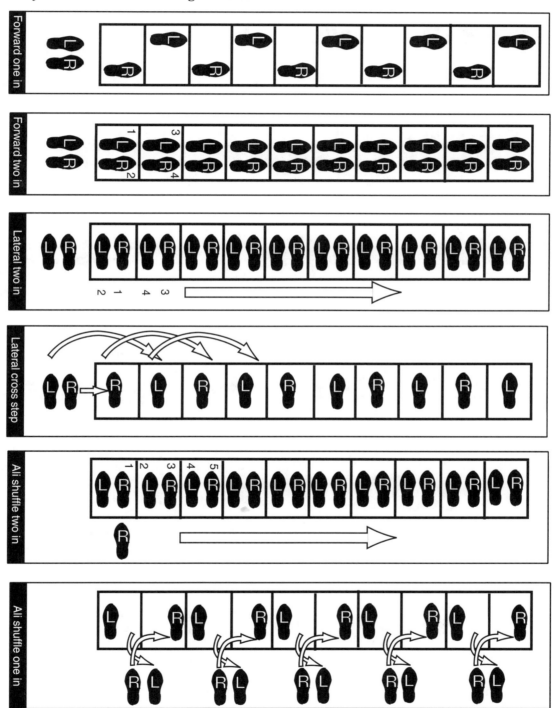

Figure 13.6 Ladder drills.

- **High Knee.** Moving as quickly as they can, players run through the ladder with high knees, putting one foot in each square.
- **Lateral Shuffle.** Moving as quickly as they can, players shuffle laterally through the ladder, placing two feet in each square.

ON-THE-BALL DEFENSE

On-the-ball defensive positioning might vary depending on the offensive and defensive players' strengths and weaknesses. If an offensive player is quicker than her defender, the defender will need to give a little ground and not guard too tightly. Giving an offensive player more space allows a slow defender to contain her offensive player and, we hope, prevent the defender from getting beat. If the offensive player is much more skilled right-handed than left-handed, the defender might stand in a way that overplays the left hand. Coaches might need to adjust a player's guarding position to allow her to best defend her offensive player. If the offensive player has just received the ball, the defender will need to defend the triple threat (a shot, pass, or dribble).

Defending in the Backcourt Sometimes a defensive player is asked to guard her player full court. When picking up a defender in the backcourt, it's important to contain the dribbler. The defender will need to judge the offensive player's speed and skills. The challenge is to contain the dribbler while influencing the dribble. Some coaches might force the dribbler to a side. Some might want the defender to turn the offensive player in the backcourt as many times as possible. Turning the offensive dribbler slows the beginning of an offensive transition game. To do this, the defender defends in a continuous retreating defensive slide, drop-stepping as the offensive player changes direction. To contain the offensive player, the defender doesn't need to try for a steal or lunge at the ball. These are gambles, and if the gamble doesn't pay off, the defender will likely lose her balance and become vulnerable to an offensive move.

On-the-Ball Defense in the Frontcourt In discussing on-the-ball defense in the frontcourt, we'll look here at defending the point guard position and the wing position. Post defense as well

as denial and help-side defense are discussed in the next chapter.

Defending the Point Guard The defender must initially defend the triple threat position. She should be close enough to stop a shot; her hands are active to deflect a pass; her body is influencing the direction of the dribble. She needs to be vocal when guarding the ball. Calling out the word "ball" over and over can give her energy and perhaps unnerve the offensive player. Most coaches want the point guard defender to force the point guard to one side of the court because this enhances total team defense. If the point guard is right-handed, the defender wants to force the guard to her left, forcing her to use her left hand. To influence the point guard in this direction, the defender starts in a defensive staggered stance, with her left foot slightly in front of her right foot. Knees are bent, hands are active, back is straight, weight is on the balls of the feet, and head is centered. The defender is about an arm's length away from the offensive player. As the offensive player starts her dribble, the defender retreats in a sliding defensive position discussed earlier. Once the dribbler has stopped dribbling, the defender steps into the offensive player to close the distance and calls out "dead!" This lets her teammates know the dribbler has killed her dribble. As the offensive player ends her dribble, the defender now has only the pass or the shot to defend. By stepping into the dribbler, she takes away an easy shot opportunity. As the offensive player looks to pass the ball, the defender mirrors the passing motions of the offensive passer in hopes to deflect the pass. If the offensive player shoots, the defender calls out "shot!" and then reverse pivots into the shooter to block her out. If the offensive player passes the ball, the defender jumps to the pass to assume a good off-the-ball defensive position.

The defender should not let the point guard attack the middle of the court. When this happens, most defenses break down. Over many years of coaching, I have changed how I defend a point guard. My point guard defenders were getting beat down the middle when they were trying to force the ball to a side. They were opening up defensively as they tried to channel the ball. To fix this, we now defend that position in a parallel stance. In a parallel stance, defenders have their feet directly across from each other, lined up toe to toe and heel to heel. I encourage the defense to force the dribbler east or west, sideline to sideline. We have given up much less middle penetration with this stance.

Defending the Wing   Once the ball is on the sideline, the defender wants to keep it there. This helps her teammates play good help defense. When defending a wing player receiving a pass, the defender needs to defend the triple threat position, just as the point guard defender did. Differences in defending the wing are keeping the defender on the side of the court without getting beat baseline and defending in a parallel stance, with the defender's top foot in place with the midline of the offensive player. By doing this, the defender will be slightly overplaying the baseline drive. The finish of the defense involves a good block-out, which requires contacting the offensive player to keep her from pursuing the rebound. Again, distance from the offensive player as well as positioning can be adjusted depending on the player's strengths and weaknesses.

INDIVIDUAL DEFENSIVE DRILLS

Total team defense is only as good as the sum of its parts—that is, the individuals that make up that defense. If you want your team to become a good defensive team, you'll need to teach your players to become good individual defenders. By breaking down your team defense into individual drills, you can start to build the foundation of your team defense. These drills are designed to work on one-on-one defense.

Defensive Zigzag Drill

Purpose: To improve defensive footwork.

Setup: Players form a line on the baseline, behind the lane line, and assume their defensive stance.

Procedure: Players slide in a defensive zigzag pattern, as illustrated in figure 13.7. With each turn, players must execute a drop step. Correct stance, form, and slides are reinforced. Players zigzag down and back.

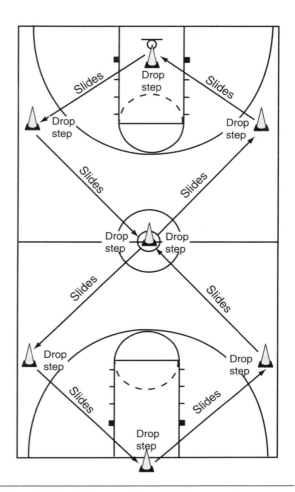

Figure 13.7   Defensive Zigzag Drill.

Offense and Defense Zigzag Drill

Purpose: To improve a defensive player's ability to guard an offensive player while dribbling a basketball. Specifically, to improve the defensive player's footwork technique.

Setup: Players form a line along the baseline and partner themselves off, one an offensive player and one a defensive player.

Procedure: In this drill, an offensive player dribbles the zigzag pattern. The defender guards the offensive player throughout the pattern. The defender has her head aligned with the dribbler's ball, not on the body of the offensive player. By doing this, the defender is in position to make the dribbler change directions. Technique is emphasized in this drill. The offensive player is dribbling at a slow speed, and the defense is not trying to steal the ball or turn the offensive dribbler. Each time the offensive player changes directions, the defender must drop step and aggressively slide step to catch up to the offensive player and defend again with the head and body out on the ball. Players exchange offense and defense once the baseline is reached.

One-on-One Live

Purpose: To improve a defender's footwork in an up-tempo and more gamelike condition.

Setup: Same as One-on-One Zigzag.

Procedure: The basketball court is divided vertically into thirds, and players play in the outside third of the court. Two players start at the baseline, one on offense with the ball and the other on defense guarding the offensive player. The defender starts with her hand on the ball for close positioning. When the coach says go, the drill begins. The offensive player tries to get to half court as fast as she can. The defender tries to turn the offensive player as many times as she can before she reaches half court. The defender must get her head and body out on the ball to turn the defender. Defenders adjust according to the quickness of the player they are guarding. Each time the defense gets beat, players stop, and the drill is reset at the place the defense got beat.

One-on-One Full Court

Purpose: To increase the intensity and duration of a player's defensive footwork.

Setup: Same as One-on-One Live.

Procedure: The drill starts out the same as One-on-One Live, but this time players don't stop at half court. Once the offensive player reaches half court, she will try to beat her defender baseline for a layup. The defender starts by trying to turn the offense in the backcourt. Once the dribbler reaches the frontcourt, the defender tries to keep her on a side (similar to wing defense) and overplay the baseline side of

the dribbler so as not to give up the baseline. Players switch offense and defense on the return trip down the court.

Roller Ball

Purpose: To have players engage in a very competitive one-on-one situation, both offensively and defensively.

Setup: Players line up in a single line behind the baseline. The first two players step onto the court. A coach rolls a ball down the floor slowly.

Procedure: On the coach's whistle, the players sprint to the ball. The first player to get to the ball is the offensive player, and the other player becomes the defender. Players play one on one at the far basket until one of them scores.

SUMMARY

- Individual defense must be practiced to reinforce execution of proper footwork, stance, and slides.

- Players need to defend on balance with their backs straight, heads up, and weight on the balls of their feet.

- The drop step is a defensive recovery move used to get the defender back into the proper defensive position.

- Drills can help improve the speed, quickness, and agility of a player's footwork.

- When defending a dribbler in the backcourt, turn her as many times as possible.

- When defending the ball in the frontcourt, begin by defending the triple threat position. Adjust defensive distance according to each player's strengths and weaknesses.

- Defend the middle of the court when guarding a point guard or a wing player.

- Be vocal as you defend.

- Finish your defense with a block-out.

- The best way to get better at defending one on one is to practice one-on-one defense.

CHAPTER 14 TEACHING TEAM DEFENSE

Once players understand individual defensive skills, you'll need to show them how they fit into your five-player team defensive system. Your team defensive system should be an extension of your defensive philosophy and should complement your players' skills and attributes.

As I've mentioned, playing good defense is a top priority for my basketball teams. I believe everybody can play defense—some players just choose not to. Defense is hard work. There's nothing easy about playing good defense. Not all players will be great defenders. Speed and athleticism can enhance a player's chance of becoming a good defender. But, unfortunately, the gifted athlete is often the lazy defender. Smart defenders can make up for lack of athleticism by knowing the strengths and weaknesses of the player they are guarding.

Each season you and your coaching staff need to put together your team's defensive priorities. Once these are developed, share them with your players, along with your expectations for them to adhere to these priorities. As our top priority, we remind our team they should never have an off night on defense. There should be no such thing. Players should never say, "I just had a bad night on defense."

Their defensive game should show up game in and game out.

Second, a good defensive plan disrupts your opponent's offense. You don't want other teams to comfortably "run their stuff." You want your team to take them out of patterns, make them go to a different option offensively, or make a weaker shooter take more shots. Third, your players should contest all shots. Tell them you want to see them getting their hands in the face of the shooter. Have them try to distract their offensive player or disrupt her concentration. Finally, your defense needs to eliminate your opponent's second shots. It's a good idea to practice defensive rebounding daily, with great emphasis on technique, contact, and an aggressive mindset. You can win the battle of the boards by having aggressive players and great technique, regardless of size. Don't overlook the value of communication as a critical component of a good defensive team. Quiet players struggle on defense. They don't call out screens, and their teammate gets beat. Defense is not meant to be played in hushed tones. Work every day on being a vocal defensive team. Stress these defensive priorities in your daily practices and reinforce in your pregame discussions.

Defense Keeps it Close

Our 2004 season only reinforced my philosophy that defense wins games and also keeps you in games when you're having a bad night offensively. In several games this season we shot 30 percent or worse from the field. Offensively, we were ugly to watch, whether you were a spectator or a coach. If it wasn't for our defense, we would have lost many of those games. Our defense provided us with two valuable things. First, we pressed and trapped whenever possible, which significantly increased the number of our opponents' turnovers. The increase in turnovers led to an increase in offensive possessions for us. So, although we shot a poor percentage, we took more shots than our opponents. Second, we were solid in our half-court defense. We took pride in trying to take away or minimize the best thing our opponent did in their half-court offense. More times than not, we were successful, and we won many games.

DEVELOPING YOUR DEFENSIVE SYSTEM

We use a numbering system to identify our defenses. All our half-court defenses are single digits. To vary a half-court defense, we might add a name or a word. For example, our man defense that helps in the paint is called "Five Cat." Our 1-3-1 defense that traps in the corners is called "3 Down."

We also use hand signals for trapping purposes. If we want to trap the dribbler out of our 2-3 defense, we call "2" and show a single fist. If we want to trap the first pass out of our 2-3 defense, we call "2" and show a double fist. Defenses are all visual cues, so they're easy to communicate to our players. One way we cue our defenses is during a free throw. Just before the free throw is shot, our players huddle, look to the bench, and receive their defensive signals.

Defensive Half-Court Signals

1 = 1-2-2
2 = 2-3
3 = 1-3-1
5 = man to man

Defensive Half-Court Trap Using Hand Signals

- Two fingers and one fist indicate trapping the point guard as she crosses half court done out of our 2-3 defense.
- Two fingers and a double fist mean trapping the first sideline pass after half court done out of our 2-3 defense.
- Three fingers and a thumb down traps a corner pass IF a pass is made to a corner offensive player out of our 1-3-1 defense.

Full- or three-quarter-court defenses are double digits. Similar to our half-court defenses, to vary a full-court defense, we add a name to the number or a hand signal. Our full-court 1-2-1-1 is called "11." We run four variations of this press cued via the front player in the press. We can deny players in the defense, play the pass back to the inbounds player stepping in, get up on the ball, or trap immediately. With a number and a hand gesture, the defense is communicated to all players.

Full-Court Defensive Signals

11 = 1-2-1-1 press
12 = 1-2-1-1 three-quarter press
13 = 1-2-2 three-quarter press
55 = full-court man

Wrists crossed = continuous 1-2-2 trapping (See our "Sharks" press described at the end of the chapter.)

MAN-TO-MAN DEFENSIVE POSITIONING

Great man-to-man defense starts with heart and hustle. Each defensive possession is a battle, and the team that wins the most battles wins the game. Every player must guard her player and the ball, so it's a team defense, not five individuals playing defense separately. In great man-to-man defense there is ball pressure, denial of passes, help defense, physical play, and great communication.

Man-to-man defensive positions are based on where the ball is and where their man is positioned in relation to the ball. If you divide the court in half, there is a ball side and a nonball side called the weak side or help side. Defenders adjust their positions depending on which side of the floor their offensive player is positioned. There are basically three defensive positions: on-the-ball defense, one-pass-away denial defense, and two-or-more-passes-away (or one-long-pass away) help-side defense. One pass away would be the distance a player would be from her teammate where an easy pass can be made. This happens when teammates are on the same side of the floor or the ball is in the middle of the court. Two passes away would be a greater distance where a skip pass across the court is needed from one side to the other, or two passes would need to be made, usually as the ball goes from one side of the court to the other. When working on defensive positioning, the three positions are referred to as "ball," "denial," or "help." These defensive positions can be taught in a simple three-on-three drill.

On-the-Ball Defense When playing good on-the-ball defense, players adjust their position-ing to try to negate their opponent's strengths and use their own strengths. The on-the-ball defender needs to be able to influence the offensive player while making sure she can also defend the shot, pass, and dribble. If their player shoots the ball, the defender needs to complete the defensive possession with a good block-out and pursuit of the rebound on a missed shot.

Review of On-the-Ball Defense Principles

- Defend the triple threat position.
- Pressure the ball without getting beat off the dribble.
- Channel the ball away from the middle of the court.
- Eliminate vision by mirroring the ball once the dribbled has ended.
- Pressure the pass.
- Contest the shot.
- Block out after the shot.

Off-the-Ball Defense—Denial The defender whose offensive player is one pass away should position herself between the player and the ball. The defender should be one step off the ball line. Her chest should face the offensive player, and her back foot should be positioned so that it cuts the offensive player in half in line with her

Figure 14.1 Denial defense stance.

midline. Using peripheral vision, a defender in this position can see both her player and the ball. In addition, the defender should be slightly up the ball line, toward the ball. By playing up the line, the defender is in a good help position should her teammate get beat off the dribble. The defender should have her top leg, top arm, and top hand in the passing lane, denying the pass to her player. The palm of the top hand should be facing the ball in a ready position to deflect the pass (see figure 14.1).

If the wing successfully denies the pass in her denial position, the offensive player is forced to go backdoor, in which case the defender will receive help from her teammates positioned in help-side defense. Denying the pass also allows the defense to dictate some of their opponent's offensive decisions. If the offensive player cuts to receive a pass, the wing defender continues to slide in her defensive positioning, working hard to take away any pass. The wing defender constantly adjusts in relation to her defender and the ball as her offensive player continues to move.

Off-the-Ball Defense—Help Side   Players are in help-side defense if the player they are guarding is two or more passes away (or one long pass, such as a skip pass, away). Players continue to guard their player and the ball, but they're closer to the ball in a defensive position, ready to help a teammate who gets beat defensively. Players adjust their help-side defense depending on the position of the ball and their player. If the ball is above the free-throw line, help players should have both feet in the paint, one step off the ball line (see figure 14.2).

Players stand in an open stance from which they can see the ball and, using their peripheral vision, the player they're guarding. If the ball goes below the free-throw line, the help player slides closer to the ball, with both feet to the middle of the lane. This help-side positioning looks almost like a zone away from the ball and puts defenders in a better position to help prevent inside passing and dribble penetration.

DEFENSIVE ROTATION

If your team plays aggressive man-to-man defense, there will be times when players get beat. If the point guard gets beat down the middle of the lane, the perimeter wing players are there to help on the drive. That is why these players are up the line instead of hugging their players. These players would open up from their denial position, slide to the middle to help stop the drive, and then recover back to their player. Low-post defenders do not want to help up on the drive. This would make them vulnerable to a dump pass over their heads to their player. Post players can help in, but they should not try to help up (see figure 14.3). If a wing defender is beat on middle penetration, the point guard defender can open up from her denial position, slide to help stop the drive, and then recover back to her player. If a wing player drives the baseline and beats her defender, help comes from the opposite wing player. We use this help player instead of the post player. Some coaches teach the ballside post player to help. We don't

Figure 14.2   Adjusting help-side defense to cover the ball.

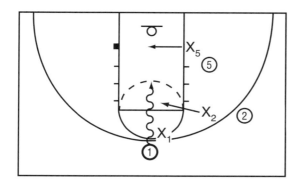

Figure 14.3 Defending a point guard drive.

want the wing to dump pass to the ballside post player, so we don't help from this position. When the weak-side wing player helps, the point guard needs to slide down and help out on the wing player. This slide is called "rotation." All players rotate to the ball. The weak-side wing helps the ballside wing, and then the point guard helps the helper, the weak-side wing.

Post help and rotation can come from different areas. If a pass is made from the wing to the ballside post, the wing can double down to help. Another form of help can come from the weak-side post player. If the weak-side post player slides over to help, the weak-side wing defender slides, or rotates, low to help the helper and defend the weak-side post player (see figure 14.4). Coaches will have their own rules for help and recovery. Player rotation is necessary for good team defense, but there are different ways to give help and rotate.

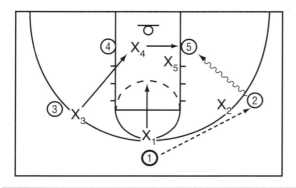

Figure 14.4 Post help and rotation.

Man-to-Man Team Defensive Drills

Several aspects of team defense can be practiced in drills using the same set, a four-on-four

shell set. In this set, you have three perimeter players on offense and one low-post player (see figure 14.5). Defenders match up four on four and work on positioning, dribble penetration, cutters, rotation, and defensive block-outs.

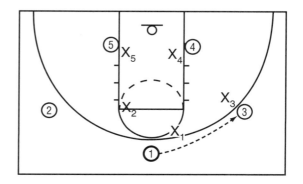

Figure 14.5 Four-on-four shell set.

Positioning

Purpose: In this drill players are familiarized with correct defensive positioning.

Setup: Offensive players position at the point, left and right wings, and low post. Each defender matches up with an offensive player.

Procedure: The ball starts with the point guard. All players call out their position, "ball," "denial," or "help." Before a pass is made, coaches critique proper defensive positioning. The point guard defends the triple threat position, wings are in denial, and post defense is in denial (see figure 14.6a). The point guard makes a pass to the right wing. The defense allows the pass to be made and then jumps to the ball on the pass. The point guard defense is now in denial, right wing is on the ball, low post is in denial on the high side, and the left wing is in help-side denial (see figure 14.6b). When playing help-side defense, one good way to see your player and the ball is to have the help defender point one index finger at her player and her other index finger at the ball. This helps keep her body in an open position. Continue to pass the ball, hold the ball, and pass again, making defensive adjustments.

Once players are familiar with positioning, play the four on four live, having defenders try to steal the ball.

Offensive rules: No dribbles allowed. No screening allowed. Make cuts to get open.

Defensive rules: Call out positions. If the ball is stolen, return the ball to the offense and rotate positions.

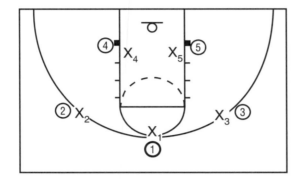

Figure 14.6a Positioning drill (shell set). X1 = ball; X2 = denial; X3 = denial.

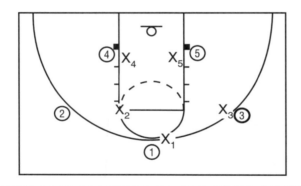

Figure 14.6b Positioning drill (shell set). X3 = ball; X1 = denial; X2 = help.

Dribble Penetration

Purpose: The focus of this drill is to defend penetration one on one, give help on penetration when needed, and recover.

Setup: Players set up as they did for the Positioning Drill.

Procedure: The ball starts with the point guard. All defenders assume correct defensive positioning. The offensive perimeter players try to beat their defenders one on one and draw help defense from another defender. Perimeter

defenders help in their areas and recover to their player. The post defender helps only if needed. Offensive players continue to penetrate and kick to an open player or pass inside to the post (see figure 14.7). Players rotate offense and defense after the defense makes three defensive penetration stops.

Offensive rules: Penetrate and kick to the open player. Pass to the post when open and relocate on the perimeter.

Defensive rules: Defend one on one. Help on penetration when needed. Recover back to your own player after helping defensively.

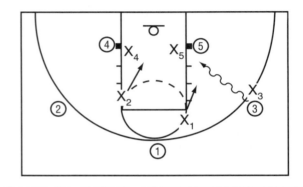

Figure 14.7 Dribble Penetration Drill (shell set).

Cutters

Purpose: This drill works on ballside and help-side positioning, defending weak-side cuts from the post and perimeter, and being physical in the lane.

Setup: Players set up in the same way they did for the previous two drills.

Procedure: The ball starts with the point guard. As passes are made, defenders do not attempt to steal the ball. The point guard passes to the right wing. All players jump to the ball and assume correct defensive positioning. The right wing then skips the ball to the left wing. All players jump to the ball on the pass. Now the right wing and low-post offensive players are on the weak side. On the "wing" command, the weak-side offensive wing (the right wing) cuts to the lane to receive the pass. The right-wing defender steps up in the lane, chests the cutter with her forearm and body, and forces the cutter out of the lane (see figure 14.8). On the second command, "post," the weak-side post player cuts to the lane to receive the pass. The low-post defender steps up in the lane, chests the cutter with her forearm and body, and forces the cutter out of the lane. The right-post cutter returns to the weak side. The low post stays on the ballside block. Coaches critique the defenders' technique. Then the ball is skipped to the right wing, and the cutting action begins. Players rotate after the defense has successfully cut the cutter four times.

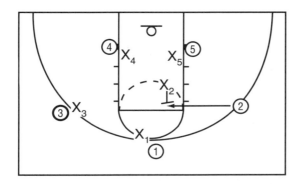

Figure 14.8 Cutters Drill (shell set).

Rotation

Purpose: This drill works on understanding and practicing defensive rotation and on rotation and recovery.

Setup: Players set up as they did for the previous drills.

Procedure: The ball starts with the point guard. As passes are made, defenders do not attempt to steal the ball. The point guard passes to the right wing. All players jump to the ball and assume correct defensive positioning. The right wing drives the right baseline, and the right wing defender allows herself to get beat. The low-post player slides up the lane line. All players rotate. The weak-side wing defender stops the penetration outside the lane. The ballside post

defender stays with her player as she slides up the lane line. The point guard sinks and rotates to the off-side wing player. The right wing that got beat matches up with the point guard. Once the penetration is stopped and all players are matched up, the drill begins again with a pass to the left wing. The offensive post player slides over to the left block. Players rotate after the defense has successfully rotated and rematched four times.

Five-on-Five Transition

Purpose: This drill works on defensive transition, defensive matching, and defensive positioning.

Setup: Five offensive players line up across the baseline. Five defenders line up across the free-throw line.

Procedure: Play begins when a coach passes the ball to any offensive player. The offense must get the ball to the middle of the court and try for a layup. If a layup is not an option, the ball is passed to a perimeter player, who brings the ball into the wing area and kills her dribble. As the defense drops and works on defensive transition, players must match up defensively with someone other than the player directly across from them at the beginning of the drill. Defenders retreat and rematch. As defenders retreat, they must stop a layup, match up, and assume correct defensive positioning once the ball has been passed to the wing player that kills her dribble. Score is kept by the defense. The defense gets two points for stopping a layup and one point for assuming correct positioning after the wing pass. Their score automatically goes to zero if one defender fails to call out the player's name she is guarding. Play to five points and then switch offense and defense players.

Five-on-Five Circle the Wagons

Purpose: This drill works on defensive communication, defensive block-outs and rebounding, and physical toughness.

Setup: Five offensive players spread around the three-point line. Five defensive players circle up inside the lane and match with each offensive player.

Procedure: On the whistle, defenders run in a circle, changing their matchups. This part is what we call "circling the wagons." Defenders call out the players they are matching with throughout the circling. When a coach throws up a shot, the offensive players crash the boards, and defenders must block out (see figure 14.9). Defenders must make contact on initial block-outs. If the offense gets the ball, they try to score. If the defense gets the ball, they make a safe outlet pass. The defense must make four stops and four safe outlets before they switch offense and defense.

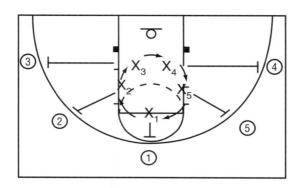

Figure 14.9 Five-on-Five Circle the Wagons.

Three-on-Two Take a Charge

Purpose: This drill works on proper technique for taking a charge and defensive blocking out.

Setup: Defenders play a tandem defense in the lane, one high and one low.

Procedure: Offensively, players start with the ball in the middle of the floor at half court. The offense attacks the tandem in a three-player set—one point guard and two wings. The point guard takes a few dribbles and passes to one of the wings. The wing who receives the pass drives in for a layup. The other wing slashes in for an offensive board. The point guard stops after her pass and is no longer in the drill. The

bottom defender defends the wing driving in for the layup and tries to take a charge on the drive. The top defender must block out the wing slashing from the weak side. She wants her block-out to occur outside the lane (see figure 14.10). Defenders then switch high and low positions and change defensive jobs. It's important for the offensive player driving to drive straight at the goal for a layup and not avoid the charge. Coaches critique both defenders.

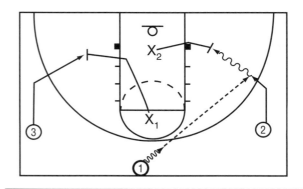

Figure 14.10 Three-on-Two Take a Charge.

Breakdown Drills

When we practice our team defensive drills, all players defend on the perimeter and in the post. Players need to know how to defend inside and outside. Besides practicing team defensive drills, we also incorporate position defensive drills. In these drills, players get extra repetitions defending an area of the floor they will defend the most in a game.

The following drills are specifically geared for post players to improve individual defense and position defense.

Three Out, One In

Purpose: Post players work on playing good post defense in the paint.

Setup: Four offensive players are placed on the court in the following positions: one at the point position, one on the left wing, one on the right wing, and one player just outside the lane near the block as a post player. One post defender matches up on the post on the block.

Procedure: Perimeter offensive players pass the ball randomly from player to player. The offensive post player works hard, posting and flashing to receive a pass. The defensive post player works hard to defend the entry pass to her player from various passing angles (see figure 14.11).

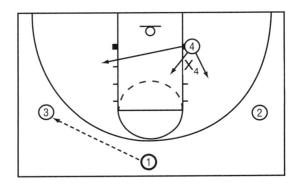

Figure 14.11 Three Out, One In.

Variation: The drill is done in the same way except the offensive post player never moves. Post defense plays ballside defense, then assumes help-side defensive positioning. The post defender works on ballside and help-side positioning.

Two-on-Two Inside

Purpose: Play good post defense on the low-post ball side and help side.

Setup: Three offensive perimeter players place themselves at the point and both wings. Two offensive post players post up on each block. Two post defenders match up on each post (see figure 14.12a).

Procedure: The three perimeter players pass the ball, hold the ball, and pass again. Post defenders continually adjust to ballside defense, then help-side defense. Defensive players must jump to the ball on the pass (see figure 14.12b).

Variation: Defend a ballside post-up, weak-side post, and weak-side post flash. Run the drill in the same way as described, but once the pass

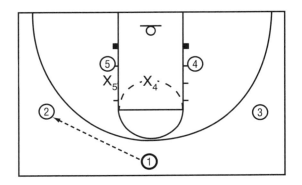

Figure 14.12a Setup for the Two-on-Two Inside.

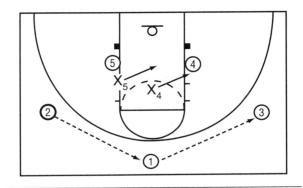

Figure 14.12b Two-on-Two Inside.

is made to a wing, a coach calls "flash!" and the weak-side post player flashes to the lane. The weak-side post defender must "cut the cutter," as described earlier in the chapter (in the Cutters Drill).

Penetration Recognition

Purpose: Post defense practices when and how to help on perimeter penetration.

Setup: Offensive wing players have the ball.

Procedure: They start on the wing and drive to the basket for a layup. The offensive post player posts up, sees the wing driving, and slides up the lane for a pass. There is no defense on the wing, but there is defense on the post player.

As the wing drives, the post defender fakes help on the drive and slides into the lane to defend her player on a dish pass (see figure 14.13).

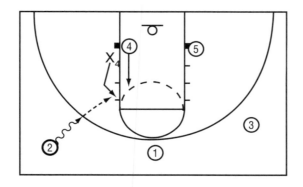

Figure 14.13 Penetration Recognition.

Defending One on One

All players need to be able to defend, one on one, regardless if that is outside the lane or inside the lane. The following drills are designed to help perimeter and post players defend one on one.

Perimeter and Post

Purpose: This drill is done by all players so they can defend all types of offensive movements, including a give-and-go cut, a post-up, weak-side positioning, and a weak-side flash.

Setup: Two offensive players are needed: a point guard and a wing.

Procedure: Only one defender is needed (on the point guard). The point guard passes to the wing and runs a give-and-go cut (see figure 14.14a) with a jump-to-the-ball manuver (see figure 14.14b). She then posts up ball side for two seconds (see figure 14.14c) and cuts away

to the weak-side wing in a three count (see figure 14.14d). Finally, she flashes back to the lane to receive the pass. The point guard's defender must defend all offensive plays, including the give-and-go cut (figure 14.14a) with a jump-to-

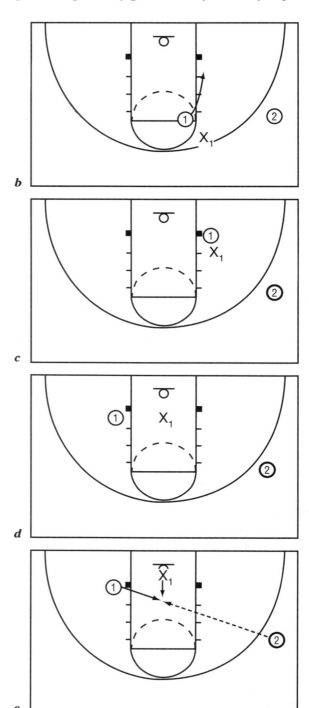

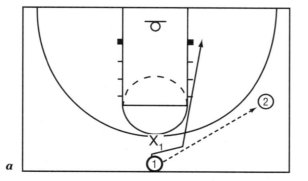

Figure 14.14 Perimeter and Post. *(a)* Give-and-go cut, *(b)* Jump-to-the-ball maneuver, *(c)* Ballside post-up with post defense, *(d)* Weak-side positioning, *(e)* Cut-the-cutter defensive motion.

the-ball maneuver (figure 14.14b); the ballside post-up with good post defense position (figure 14.14c). On the weak side, she's in a three-quarter denial stance between her player and the ball (figure 14.14d) and makes a weak-side flash to the basket using a cut-the-cutter defensive move (figure 14.14e). Players rotate spots continuously.

By practicing this drill, players learn to defend against the various offensive moves that a perimeter player makes without the ball. This drill should be done at a speed in which the defender can learn to make the correct adjustments.

Wing Denial

Purpose: Wing player correctly denies and opens up on the perimeter.

Setup: Offensive players are a point guard and one wing. The only defender is on the wing.

Procedure: The offensive wing player makes V-cuts from the three-point line to the block to get open. The wing defender slides back and forth with the offensive player in a denial position (see figure 14.15). The wing defender tries to deflect passes made to her player. If the offensive wing gets open and receives a pass safely, she holds the ball while the wing defender assumes good on-the-ball perimeter defense.

In the second part of this drill, the offensive wing player cuts into the lane, puts her head under the basket, and pops back out to the wing. To defend the offensive player when she steps into the lane, the wing defender executes a reverse pivot and opens up to the ball. For a brief

moment, the defender loses sight of her player but not the ball. As the offensive wing player pops back out to the wing, the wing defender executes a forward pivot and reassumes a denial position.

Variation: This variation offers another way to practice defensive help and recovery. As the wing defense is denying her player, she's not only on the line but must be up the line. Every few seconds the point guard drives into the lane. When this occurs, the wing defender must open up to the ball, slide toward the ball to help stop penetration, and recover back to her player in a denial position once the ball has been stopped.

Perimeter Two on Two

Purpose: Quickly shifting from ballside defense to denial defense and back again.

Setup: Two offensive players are needed: one at the point position and one on the wing. Defenders match up.

Procedure: The point defender pressures the ball as she plays good on-the-ball defense. As the point guard passes to the wing, the point defender must jump to the pass and assume a denial defensive position. The wing defender begins the drill in a denial stance. She allows the pass to her player. Once the pass is made, she assumes correct defensive positioning (see figure 14.16).

The first few times through the drill the offense plays passively, allowing the defense to work on positioning. Then the offense plays live and tries to score in one of these ways: a point guard penetration layup, a point guard give-and-go layup, a wing penetration layup, or

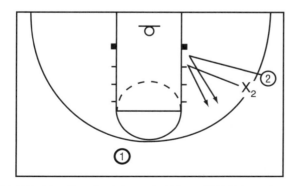

Figure 14.15 Wing Denial.

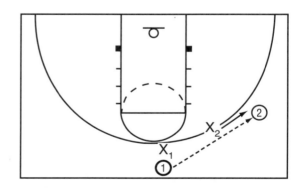

Figure 14.16 Perimeter Two on Two.

a wing backdoor. If layups are given up defensively off the dribble, coaches need to correct positioning.

Defending Penetration

Purpose: To work on the correct method of closing out on a player, defending a drive, and finishing the defense with a block-out.

Setup: Players form three defensive lines under the basket. Three offensive players start out on the perimeter in three spots: at the top of the key and both wings.

Procedure: The first three players in line step out on the court, each with a basketball. One at a time, they roll the ball out to the offensive player in front of them. The offensive player drives to the basket with a three dribble limit. The defensive player who rolls the ball out defends by running out to the player she's defending, using a choppy step the last three steps as she approaches her player; assuming a good on-the-ball defensive stance, knowing her player is going to drive; defending the drive; and finishing her defense with a block-out (see figure 14.17).

The wing offensive players try to beat their defenders baseline. The top-of-the-key offensive players try to beat their defender down the middle of the lane. Defenders must defend each player and position in the correct way. Players stay on defense three times and then replace the offensive player. The offensive player goes to the end of the defensive line.

Variation: Offensive players can shoot or drive. Defensive players must be able to defend the

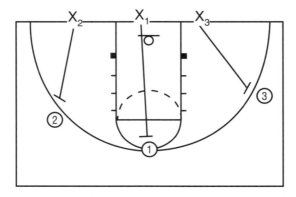

Figure 14.17 Defending Penetration.

three-point shot, the drive, and the pull-up jump shot.

HALF-COURT TRAPPING OUT OF MAN-TO-MAN DEFENSE

Trapping out of your man-to-man defense can be a great change-up and very disruptive to your opponent. Trapping can cause the offense to turn the ball over, force strong players to give up the ball, disrupt a team's offensive pattern or flow, force weaker players to handle or shoot the ball, and help the defense control the tempo of the game.

Trapping the Point Guard

To set up this trap, the point guard's defender must make the point guard dribble to a side of the floor once she crosses the half-court line.

The first defender (X1) plays on the dribbler's left side as she crosses midcourt. This overplay forces the ball handler to her right, where the second defender (X2) is ready to trap her. When the dribbler is within six feet of X2, X2 runs toward her under control in a defensive stance to trap with X1. As X2 leaves her player to trap the dribbler, she yells "go," which signals the trap to her teammates and triggers the defensive rotation. The "go!" yell and running hard toward the dribbler might unnerve the dribbler and force her to pick up her dribble prematurely, contributing to her offensive troubles.

After X1 and X2 have contained the dribbler in an area, they begin to close in together to trap the dribbler. Defenders in the trap need to stay low and balanced. The trap should form a V, with defenders overlapping their foot closest to the basket. This closes the gap, and active hands take away court vision to the basket. If the dribbler continues her dribble, the trappers try to maintain their trap by sliding together to keep the dribbler within the trap.

If the offensive player picks up her dribble, the defenders close the trap even tighter, keeping their feet and hands active, cutting off the passing lanes and blocking court vision. Trappers need to resist the temptation to try to steal the ball, which could lead to off-balance defense or even a foul. Their hands should mirror the movement of the ball as the offensive player attempts to pass out of the trap.

If the trappers do a good job of hemming up the dribbler, their defensive teammates have time to rotate defensively. Steals can result from a hurried pass out of the trap. The defense can also force the offensive dribbler into a violation, such as a five-second call, travel, double-dribble, or a charge.

On X2's command of "go," X3, X4, and X5 begin their defensive rotation. X4 leaves her player to intercept the pass to X2's player. X5 rotates over to take the ballside post, and X3 anticipates the weak-side wing cutting to the ball for a pass and denies her that pass.

The only player left unguarded is the farthest player from the ball. Ideally, the trappers have put enough pressure on the offensive player that she can't see the open player or make a good pass to her. If the trap gets broken, either by a dribble or a pass, defensive players must scramble to help and recover defensively until every offensive player is guarded. Defensive players must rematch aggressively on the offensive players, communicating well among themselves.

Trapping the Wing

To trap a wing player, the defense must invite the pass to the wing. X1 forces the ball to the right side of the court. X2 allows the pass to be made to her player. On release of the ball, X1 follows the pass down to the wing. There is no audible signal, just the point guard's hand signal earlier to alert teammates trapping on the wing that the pass is about to occur. X2 adjusts her defensive position to defend on the baseline side. X1 and X2 contain the dribbler on the wing. They close the trap, staying low and balanced, forming a V, interlocking the back foot, and applying trapping principles (as described earlier in the chapter).

The defenders begin their rotation as the pass is made from the point to the wing. The ballside post player stays on her player, and the weak-side post defender cheats to the ball side. The weak-side wing defender rotates up to deny a return pass to the point guard. As in the previous drill, this rotation leaves the offensive

player farthest from the trap unguarded. Ideally, great trapping won't allow the unguarded player to be seen by the dribbler. If the trap gets broken, defensive players must scramble to help recover defensively until every offensive player is guarded.

Trapping the Post

There are several ways in which a defense can trap a post player. Defenders can trap from the other post position, from the ballside perimeter player, or from the weak-side perimeter player. We call our post trap "Five Cat." "Five" means we're in our man defense, and "cat" cues in our help in the post area. We designate a player to be our "cat" player. This player, X2, is usually a smart, quick defender who does not guard one of the better perimeter scorers. Her job is to double down on the designated post player. Her help comes from the top. She tries to smother a post player, taking away her turn to the middle of the lane or a dribble to the middle of the lane. We run this defense when we need help on a very good offensive low-post player. The post defender, X5, who is receiving the help, defends her player in a particular way. When her player is on the ballside block, she defends on the baseline side, inviting the pass from the wing or the point.

When the pass is made into the post, X5 and X2 trap the post, closing their V. Ideally, the offensive post player has no room to turn, either to shoot or pass. Her best option is to throw the ball back out to the ballside perimeter.

As the pass is made to the low post and the trap is set, all other players begin their rotation and positioning. The ballside wing player doesn't allow a pass back to her player. If the cat's player is on the ball side or on top, players rotate to take away the pass out. X3 stays on her player. X1 rotates to the top to take away the pass to the point guard. X4 and X5 stay with their players. The open player is on the weak-side perimeter, which is why it's important that the trap defenders do not let the post player turn to the middle (because she'll see the open player).

The surprise element of the trap might cause the offensive post player to turn the ball over. If the post player makes a safe pass out, the defense must scramble to help and recover and then rematch defensively. The cat player might end up matched with her same player or with another offensive perimeter player.

The cat defense can be played on any low-post player, can be changed to different players during the game, or can be used on and off during the course of the game.

ZONE DEFENSE

Zone defenses are named according to the configuration of the zone starting with players closest to the centerline. For example, in a 3-2 zone, three players form the front line near the free-throw line and two players are closer to the basket. Zone defenses are characterized by having an odd front line or an even one.

The choice of which zone to use depends on the individual abilities of the defensive players and the capability of the opponents. Each zone has certain strengths and weaknesses, depending on the configuration of players. A zone is strong at the point where it has the greatest concentration of players and weak at the point where fewer players are positioned.

2-3 Zone Defense The 2-3 zone's greatest advantage is in protecting the lane area and allowing your big players to play close to the basket. The 2-3 is considered one of the better rebounding zone defenses. Its weakness is that it can be beaten by good perimeter shooting because there are open areas at the top of the key, wings, and high post.

The 2-3 zone has two defenders on top and three closer to the baseline. Each defender has a certain area, or zone, to guard. Defenders must also help outside of their zones when a teammate needs it. The X1 and X2 zone areas include the top of the key, wing areas, and the high post. X3 and X4 must defend the baseline areas and help on the wing when needed. X5 covers the middle of the lane, the low-post or block area, and the high post as needed (see figure 14.18).

We call our basic 2-3 defense "Two." We play this defense very aggressively to take away easy perimeter shots. Our X2 picks up the ball handler three strides above the three-point line. If the offensive player is right-handed, X2 forces her to her left. X1 covers the high post if

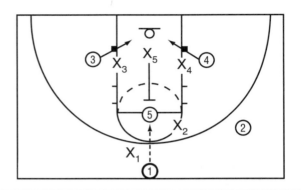

Figure 14.18 2-3 zone defense.

an offensive player is there; if not, she defends the left wing. X4 has the low post if there's no baseline player. If there is a baseline player, X4 defends her. X5 fronts a low-post player on the block if the ball goes to the corner. X5 should not front a post player who steps off the lane because this pulls her too far out from the basket. X5 also has high-post coverage if a high-post player receives a pass and squares up to the goal. In this situation, X3 and X4 must sink quickly to defend the block areas. Players help out of their zone when their teammate can't get to their area in time. For example, on a skip pass to the wing, the back-line player, X3 or X4, might help out on the offensive player until X1 or X2 can get there.

Against teams who try to exploit our extended 2-3 defense, we also run a "Two Low" in which we pack the defense in the paint and vigorously defend the inside play of our opponent. This defense is also effective against teams who successfully penetrate gaps in the zone.

1-2-2 Zone Defense We frequently use our 1-2-2 zone defense to counter a strong outside shooting team. The top player in the zone defends the top of the key, while the next two defenders cover the wings and the bottom two defenders control the paint (see figure 14.19). The slides of the 1-2-2 zone can be run in different ways. If you want to keep the back of the zone home and protect the paint, the wing players cover the wings and the baseline. They end up chasing defensively if the offense overloads a side (see figure 14.20a). If you bring your back-line player out to the baseline to defend, the other back-line player slides across the lane to help on the ballside block, and your perimeter players sink to help inside (see figure 14.20b).

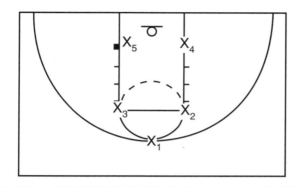

Figure 14.19 1-2-2 zone defense.

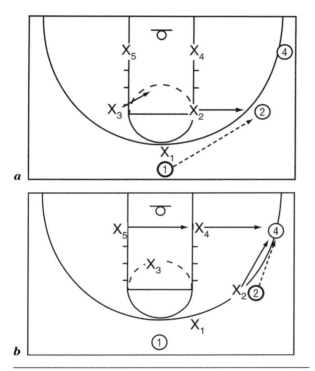

Figure 14.20 1-2-2 defensive slides.

The weak points of the 1-2-2 zone are the high-post area and the middle of the lane. In playing this defense, the usual zone principles apply: defend players in your area, help and recover out of your area if a teammate needs help, pressure the dribble and the pass, don't allow penetration into the lane, and communicate with each other.

1-3-1 Zone Defense In the basic setup (see figure 14.21a), X2 is on the ball when the ball is at the wing. X4 fronts ballside low post and X3 covers the backdoor while X1 covers the

ballside elbow and X5 covers the middle of the paint (see figure 14.21b). When the ball goes to the corner, X4 covers the corner and X5 fronts the low post while X3 covers the backdoor and X1 sinks to the free-throw area. X2 splits the distance between the wing player and the ballside elbow (see figure 14.21c).

The 1-3-1 zone is strong at the free-throw line and the wing positions, but weak in the corners and at the top of the key. This zone isn't a strong rebounding defense, but the perimeter setup has the advantage of applying pressure outside the three-point line.

In games we run our 1-3-1 defense as a trapping defense called "Three Down." In this defense we apply great pressure on the point

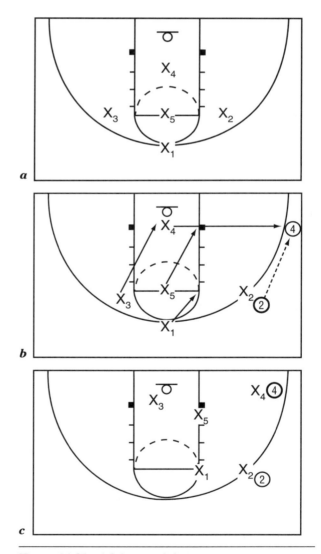

Figure 14.21 1-3-1 zone slides.

and on the offensive wing players. We invite the pass to the corner. When the ball goes to the corner, X4 and X2 trap.

X5 fronts the ballside low post. X1 splits the high-post and wing areas, trying to pick off a pass to any player in those areas. X3 has backdoor responsibilities, but if the trap is good, she can cheat to the top of the key, anticipating a pass to that area. If the offense passes out of the trap, we assume our 1-3-1 set, pressure up high, and wait to trap again if the ball is passed to the corner (see figure 14.22).

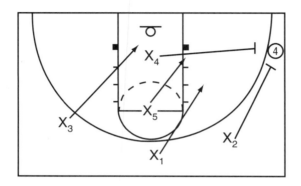

Figure 14.22 1-3-1 Three Down trap.

Matchup Zone Defense A good matchup zone defense acts a lot like a good man-to-man defense. Sometimes matchup defenses are called "combination" defenses because they combine elements of man-to-man on-the-ball defense and zone defense away from the ball. The on-the-ball defenders play solid man to man, and the zone defenders away from the ball resemble help-side man defense. The matchup zone also resembles a switching man to man because defenders switch freely with one another to keep big defensive players at home, close to the paint, and quick guards on the perimeter.

A good matchup might confuse your opponents as they try to figure out what defense you're actually playing. In addition, your defense might influence or even dictate the offense's basic set and get them out of their comfortable sets. You can create your own matchup rules, as long as players know and understand their coverage. In most matchup defenses, there's pressure on the ball, the low post is fronted, passing lanes are denied, and help is given on any inside penetration.

2-1-2 Matchup Versus a 1-3-1 Offensive Set
X1 defends player 1. X2 guards player 2, and X3 picks up player 3. X4 and X5 have easy and natural matches (see figure 14.23).

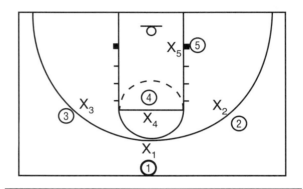

Figure 14.23 2-1-2 matchup versus 1-3-1 offense.

2-1-2 Matchup Versus a 3-2 Offensive Set
The coverage pattern is identical to that of the 1-3-1 set except X4 drops down to the low block to defend player 4 (see figure 14.24).

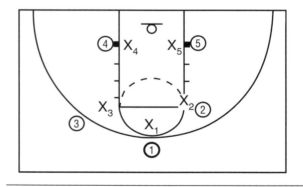

Figure 14.24 2-1-2 matchup versus 3-2 offense.

ZONE HALF-COURT TRAPS

Many zones lend themselves to half-court trapping. The 1-3-1 zone, with its extended perimeter play, easily lends itself to trapping. Our Three Down defense is one of our trapping defenses already discussed. In addition, we run a "33" half-court trap out of a 1-3-1 set.

We run our 33 when we want to trap but want to keep our big player at home.

In this defense, we want size, or athleticism, on the point of the zone, X3. We place a quick and aggressive defender at the free-throw line, X2. The back point of the defense is our big post defender, X5. The wings are usually our point guard, X1, and a perimeter player, X4 (see figure 14.25). Our X5 defense is simple: Defend the paint and stay at home. We want this player to intimidate, defend, and rebound. Our X3 provides great ball pressure and channels the ball to a side. X3 traps soft at the wing and covers the high post when the ball goes baseline. X1 and X4 trap soft on the wing side, trap hard on the corner side, and cover backdoor when the ball is on the weak side. X2 and X3 work in tandem, one on the ball and one at the high post. These two must be aggressive, smart, and willing to work. Our 33 is designed to speed teams up and force them to take quick perimeter shots, usually from the baseline. In this defense, we want to channel the ball to the baseline, where we can execute a good hard trap, anticipate the pass out, and create an easy scoring opportunity for ourselves.

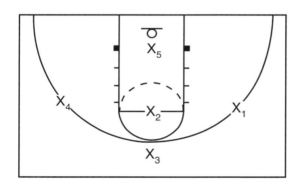

Figure 14.25 Setup for the 33 half-court zone trap.

Out of a 2-3 zone defense, you can trap the point guard, wing, or post player. At Oak Ridge we run all three half-court traps out of our 2-3 defense.

Single Fist To disrupt the point guard, we run our 2-3 "Single Fist." In this defense, our top two defenders, X1 and X2, wait until the point guard crosses the half-court line. As soon as she crosses over, they rush the point guard and work together to trap her (using the trapping principles described previously in this chapter). Ideally, this is a surprise trap for the point guard and causes her to turn the ball over, commit an offensive foul, or make a quick pass before her

teammates are ready. As X1 and X2 trap, the other three defenders are anticipating a quick and early pass into the offense. X3 and X4 cheat the pass to the wings in their area. X5 cheats the pass to a high post. The open player, the low post, is the player farthest from the ball. If the point guard is forced to make an early pass, X3, X4, and X5 are all in position to intercept (see figure 14.26). If a safe pass out is made by the point guard, or if the point guard dribbles out of the trap, defenders return to their 2-3 defensive positions. The trap occurs only one time per possession.

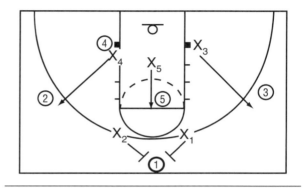

Figure 14.26 2-3 Single Fist trap.

Double Fist If we want to trap either wing, we run our 2-3 "Double Fist." In this defense, we invite a pass to the wing. We don't put great pressure on the point but do protect the high-post area. Once the pass is in the air to the wing, all defenders are moving. The back of the 2-3, X4 or X3, and the top of the 2-3, X1 or X2 (whichever player is ball side) are the trappers. X3 and X1 execute the trap. X2 must take away the pass back to the point guard, whom she guards man to man. Often the trapped wing's first reaction is to throw the ball right back from where it came, to player 1. X5 takes the closest player out of the trap ball side. This might be a baseline player or a low-post player. X4 takes the high post if X5 has a low post. If there's only one player ball side, X5 takes that player. X4 might have two players on the weak side. She splits the difference between the two players, edging toward the player closest to the ball. As happens with all traps, the offensive player farthest from the ball will be the open player. All defenders out of the trap are in position to steal a pass to an offensive player (see figure 14.27). If a safe pass is made out of the trap or the wing dribbles out of the trap, all defenders return to their 2-3 positions. The trap occurs only one time per possession.

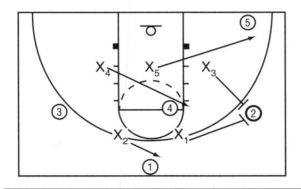

Figure 14.27 2-3 Double Fist trap.

Two Cat Our "Two Cat" trap is similar to our Five Cat. If we need help on a post player but can't afford to totally sink off perimeter players, we run our Two Cat. With our X5 and either X1 or X2 players, we double team the post player on the block once she has the ball. We trap with whatever guard is on the off side. Similar to the Five Cat, the guard who doubles the post jams her so she can't turn to the middle. X5 takes away the baseline turn. Ballside defenders, X4 and X1, deny passes out. As in all traps, the open player is on the weak side (see figure 14.28). If the post player successfully passes out of the trap, the cat guard must return to her original 2-3 position. This defense can be used on one post player in particular or on any post player on the block. This trap can occur more than once during an offensive possession.

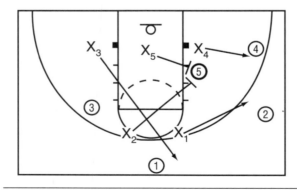

Figure 14.28 2-3 Two Cat trap.

FULL-COURT DEFENSES

If your team has practiced individual defensive skills and team defensive skills and principles, you're ready to implement a full-court defense. Every team needs a full-court defense, either zone or man, for those games in which you're trailing in the last few minutes and you need to force a turnover.

There are other times when a full-court defense can benefit your team. A full-court defense can influence the tempo of a game, take advantage of superior speed and quickness, force an opponent to play baseline to baseline, and take advantage of a team that doesn't handle the ball well.

There are many ways to run a full-court man-to-man defense. You might simply apply some soft pressure in the backcourt to disrupt a team's flow. If you want to force a turnover, a more aggressive run-and-jump man-to-man full-court defense can be employed. In a dead ball situation, you might pick up full court, denying all inbounds passes. In another variation, allow the ball to be inbounded and then trap the first pass, denying the pass back to the inbounder; all defenders rotate to the ball, leaving open only the offensive player farthest away. The best full-court man defense is the one that complements the players you have. Full-court defense takes a great commitment from all players. One weak defender can cause this defense to break down, giving the opponent an easy score.

ZONE PRESSES

Zone pressure defenses are sometimes played by teams with one weak defensive player, who is placed in the area in which she can do least damage (which area this is depends on the zone defense being used). The purpose of the zone press is to double team the ball handler, zone the rest of the opposition, and play the angles to intercept passes. Two defenders cover the passing lanes to two opponents closest to the ball handler. The remaining defender covers the passing lanes to two opponents but must play closer to the player who's in a more dangerous scoring position. By double teaming the ball handler and closing the passing lanes, the defense hopes the opponent is forced to use high passes that are more easily intercepted. If a weaker defensive player is part of your press, you need to hide her in one of the less aggressive positions, X2, X3, or X5. Perhaps she is best placed at the back of the press or in one of the front-wing areas.

1-2-1-1 Zone Press and Variations

For 25 years at Oak Ridge, we have run a 1-2-1-1 zone press with many variations. Figure 14.29 illustrates the initial setup for running this zone press.

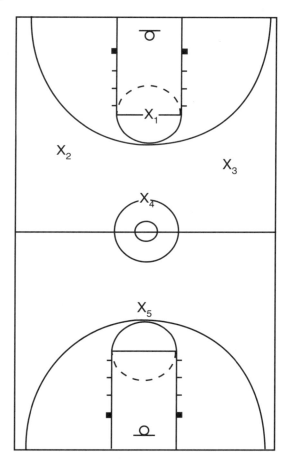

Figure 14.29   Player placement in a 1-2-1-1 zone press.

Characteristics of Each Position in a 1-2-1-1 Press

Note: If we need to hide a player defensively, we'll never play her in the X1 or X4 position.

X1: Intimidator—a hard worker who puts constant pressure on the ball

X2: Good trapper

X3: A quick player who anticipates well

X4: The team's best athlete and best defender

X5: Strong rebounder who excels in 2-on-1 play

The first thing we do in teaching the press is clarify our press rules:

1. Match up initially with whomever is in your area to prevent a long entry pass.
2. Allow the entry pass to be made at the free-throw line and below.
3. Use constant ball pressure; don't let the opponent "see."
4. Trap the ball handler on the first dribble.
5. Trap in these three situations: at the free-throw line extended, at the half-court line and sideline, for any dead ball across the half-court line near the sideline.
6. Keep the ball out of the middle of the floor.
7. Reset when opponents swing the ball and the ball remains in the backcourt.
8. Break through the passing lanes—be aggressive.
9. Never allow the press to be broken the same way three times in a row.
10. Never give up a layup.
11. Stay in the press until the defensive leader calls the half-court defense.

We call our 1-2-1-1 full-court press "11." We teach the press by calling out first and second traps and explaining defensive coverage in those traps. On the initial entry pass, X1 always pressures the ball. Trapping begins only when the offensive team starts to dribble, a pass is held, or a defensive call initiates immediate trapping.

First Trap and Coverage   X1 and X2 trap. X2 has sideline responsibilities and X1 the curl. X3 defends the pass to the middle of the court. X4 defends any sideline pass. X5 has long diagonal pass and basket coverage (see figure 14.30).

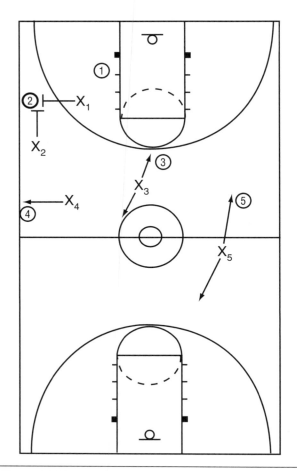

Figure 14.30 First trap and coverage.

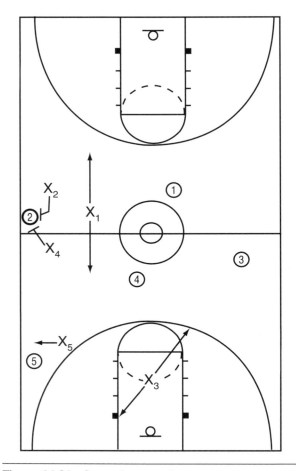

Figure 14.31 Second trap and coverage.

Second Trap and Coverage X2 and X4 trap. X1 defends the pass to the middle of the court. X5 has any sideline pass. X3 has basket coverage (see figure 14.31).

Any time the press gets beaten to the middle and the offense starts to dribble down the middle of the court, X4's job is to defend the ball one on one. She tries to slow the dribbler down until her teammates are in position to either reset the press or get into a half-court defense.

We vary our press by cuing in change-ups. Some of these change-ups involve only the front players in the press. All change-ups are one and out. If a turnover doesn't result, players assume their regular 1-2-1-1 positions. Following are some examples of our 11 change-ups:

1. 11 deny = X1, X2, and X3 deny passes in.

2. 11 clap = X1 and X2 trap immediately; X3 takes away pass to the out-of-bounds player stepping inbounds.

3. 11 pass back = X1 fakes pressure on the passer and plays the pass back to the player out of bounds stepping back inbounds.

1-2-1-1 Three-Quarter-Court Press Our 12 press is our 11 press backed up to a three-quarter court press. If a team's press offense floods the backcourt, such as a 1-4 press offense, we back our 11 press up, and it becomes our 12. In this press, we are not as aggressive. We squeeze the middle of the court and back up our defensive set. We primarily defend cutters in the middle of the court. This is an excellent press to use at the end of a quarter just to keep the ball in front of your defense and make your opponent use some clock.

The following drills simulate the defensive requirements of the 1-2-1-1 press.

Three-Man Front of the Press

- Player 2 is positioned between the baseline and free-throw line.
- Player 1 inbounds the ball to player 2. X2 and X4 close in to trap. X2 has sideline coverage, and X4 has the curl coverage. X1 covers the short middle.
- Player 2 passes the ball back to player 1. Defensive players reset.
- Player 2 passes the ball to player 3. All defenders shift. X4 follows the ball and continues to pressure the ball and stop the curl. X1 has sideline coverage. X2 covers the short middle.
- Players defend three times and rotate out.

Variation: Out of this set, we also can work on our player-deny defense, clap defense, and pass-back defense.

One on One Sideline

- Player 1 starts on the baseline; X1 starts at the free-throw line.
- Player 1 tries to beat X1 up the sideline.
- X1 works on the angle of pursuit to cut off the sideline.
- The defense cuts off the sideline two times and rotates out.

Two on One Contain

- Two defenders, X1 and X2, try to contain one dribbler, player 1.
- X1 and X2 work on trapping technique.
- X1 defends the sideline and X2 defends the curl.
- Trappers make two defensive stops and rotate out.

Angles of Pursuit

- Front of the press, X4, works on angles to pressure each pass (see figure 14.32, a-c).
- Player 1 passes to player 2.
- Player 2 passes back to player 1.
- Player 1 passes to player 3.

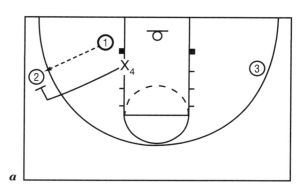

a

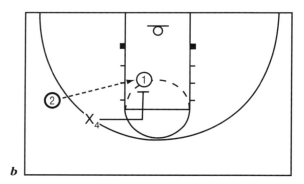

b

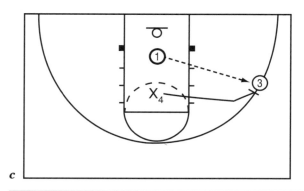

c

Figure 14.32 Angles of pursuit.

Break Through the Ball

- Five offensive players position on the court as shown in figure 14.33.
- X3 mirrors the ball from player 1 to player 2 to player 3.
- X3 breaks through the ball line and tries to deflect passes to player 4 and player 5.

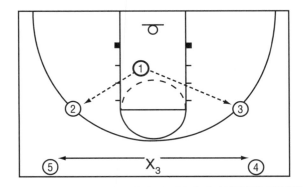

Figure 14.33 Break Through the Ball.

Two on One

This is a drill specific for the player who plays the back of the press.

- Offensive players 1 and 2 have beaten the traps and are attacking the basket.
- Playing the back of the press, X1 defends two on one against the offensive players.

Defensive Partners

- At least five offensive players form a circle.
- X1 and X2 work together on each pass.
- One defender pressures the pass, and one defender tries to deflect or steal the pass.
- One defender is up on the ball, and the other plays center court.
- Defenders exchange jobs on each pass.
- Offensive players can't pass to a player directly next to them.

- The defense is working on applying ball pressure and anticipating passes.

2-2-1 Zone Press

The 2-2-1 press is a great complement to the 1-2-1-1. In our 1-2-1-1 press, we have our quicker players up front and try to force the offense into mistakes early in the backcourt. In the 2-2-1 press, we place our size up front, apply softer pressure, and force the offense into mistakes farther down the floor, closer to the half-court line.

We call our 2-2-1 zone press "22." In it there are three rows of defenders. X5 and X4 are our post players. Their job is to pressure the ball, keep the ball out of the middle, force a high, lofty pass, or trap near the half-court line. X2 and X3 are our wing defenders. Their job is to intercept a pass, trap with X4 or X5, or defend the basket. We put our point guard, X1, deep.

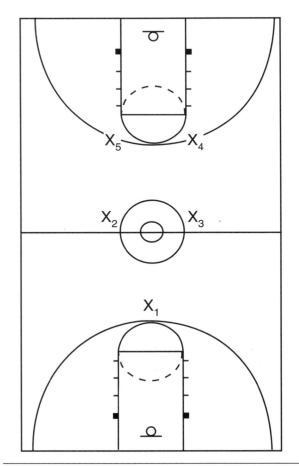

Figure 14.34 2-2-1 zone press.

She is our quickest player and makes the best defensive reads. She guards the basket or defends the sideline pass out of sideline traps (see figure 14.34).

First Trap Coverage X5 and X2 trap. X4 takes away the middle pass. X1 has the first pass sideline. X3 has the basket (see figure 14.35).

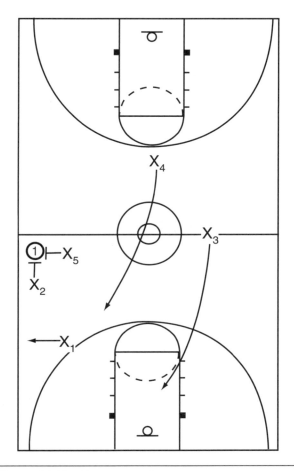

Figure 14.35 First trap and coverage.

Second Trap and Coverage If the first trap fails and the ball is advanced up the sideline, a second trap is executed: X2 and X1 trap. X5 has middle pass coverage. X3 has the first pass sideline. X4 has basket coverage (see figure 14.36).

When teams try to flood the half-court line with offensive players to beat the 1-2-1-1 press, the 2-2-1 is a good change-up. The 2-2-1 press is stronger at the half-court line than the 1-2-1-1 because its initial set has two players at half court.

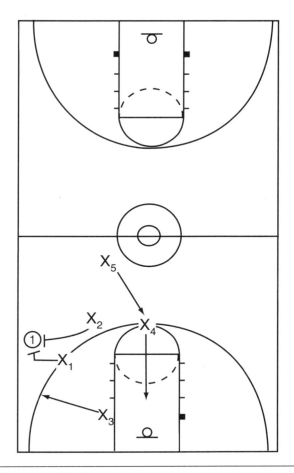

Figure 14.36 Second trap and coverage.

Sharks

Sharks is a half-court or three-quarter-court 1-2-2 press. We run this press to force the action, speed teams up, take teams out of set patterns, and create turnovers.

The basic alignment of Sharks is a 1-2-2 set. There is no set position for players in this defense. Positions are filled in defensive transition in the following order: (1) the first two defenders back guard the basket and align on the blocks, (2) the next two defenders back defend the elbow areas, and (3) the last player back plays the top of the 1-2-2 (see figure 14.37). She finds the ball and begins the defensive pressure. The alignment just mentioned is a deep setup, more of a half-court trap. Sharks can also be extended and run as a three-quarter-court trap.

The defense begins like a 1-2-2 trap. However, in Sharks, the trapping is continuous. Each time

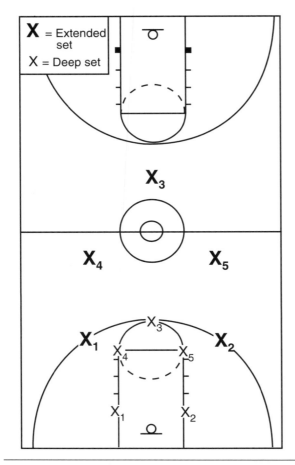

Figure 14.37 Sharks press.

the ball is out of the middle of the court and on a side, a trap occurs. Sharks can be used as a surprise element at any time during a game or when a team is very disciplined offensively and perhaps would struggle when required to scramble as they tried to attack Sharks.

Coverage

- Two players are always in the trap.
- Two players are the interceptors.
- One player defends the basket.

Because the trapping is continuous, all players eventually rotate to all defensive spots. All players must learn all spots.

Shark Rules

- All players learn all positions.
- Do not retreat defensively to a favorite position; fill positions in the correct order.
- Defend the basket first, then find the ball.

- Force the ball to a side.
- Keep the ball out of the middle of the court.
- Trappers move as one and close in together.
- Interceptors will have two people to guard.
- Don't continually chase the ball; sit out one pass in order to trap effectively.
- Front the low post.
- The closest player to the basket guards the basket.

With its continuous trapping, Sharks is a challenging defense to run. We find that we get our best results when we put it on a couple of times and then take it off. If you have success early, your players get excited, adrenalin flows, and your Sharks press becomes a man eater.

Be Careful What You Ask For

We wanted the opportunity to play the best, and that is exactly what we got. Oregon City High School was number 1 in the *USA Today* Prep Basketball Poll. Our school, Oak Ridge High School, was number 2. We both headed to Florida to compete in a pre-Christmas tournament. Number 1 in the nation versus number 2—as you'd expect, there was a lot of hype, and we were excited to have a chance to prove ourselves. If we won, we'd almost surely take over the number 1 ranking.

Just minutes into the game, our excitement and joy turned into frustration and doubt. They were bigger, stronger, and more physical than we were. More than anything, their defense was relentless and unnerving. We struggled to get anything going offensively. We got down by 20 points early, battled back to get within 10, but we could never mount a real threat.

We lost the game and our number 2 ranking, but we came away with a prize. The defense Oregon City used to dismantle us was coming back to Oak Ridge with us and, with a few new wrinkles, would become part of our defensive arsenal. The result is our Sharks defense, which we run with great excitement and defensive pride.

IMPROVING DEFENSIVE TEAMWORK

If your team has worked on individual defensive skills and team defensive concepts, you have laid a good foundation for good defensive teamwork. Now it's time to address the intangibles. Plainly and simply put, defense is hard work. Great defensive teams take pride in working harder than their opponents. Our team believes we can stop or contain any good offensive player as long as we all buy into great defense. As long as you, the coach, emphasize, recognize, and reward great defense, your players will have a good lead to follow.

I tell my players from day one that the best defensive player on the team will start. I don't say the best offensive player will start. All players can play defense, and if they choose not to play defense, they don't play. Of course, some are better than others, but everyone can get the job done.

Becoming a Defensive Stopper

When Stefanie Holbrook was a freshman at Oak Ridge High School, she started on the varsity squad. She was an outstanding three-point shooter. By her senior year, she held all of our three-point shooting records. Unfortunately, her defense was way behind her offense. At first, Stefanie was discouraged. She felt I was asking her to do something defensively she wasn't capable of doing. She continued to go to the gym and practice her shot, and I continued to preach defense to her. I knew she wanted to play college ball, and I told her she needed to be more of a sell than just a three-point shooter. By her junior year, Stefanie really began to buy into the importance of playing both ends of the court. In her senior season, she was one of my best defenders. She wasn't the most athletic player or the quickest player, but now she understood how to defend. She became much more physical, and she played smart, studying her opponents' habits to gain an advantage. She became a player I could ill afford to lose defensively.

Stefanie is a shining example of a player who chose to defend and found ways to complement her strengths and minimize her weaknesses. Players willing to work on the defensive end, no matter how hard it is, will help to build and sell defensive teamwork.

Let's face it—if you're going to expect players to work hard at defense, they will want to reap some benefits. Our players like to press—they love to play Sharks. They want to force turnovers and score easy baskets. They believe they're in better condition than their opponents and can wear them down. They love to run, so if they press successfully, they get to do what they love best: run the ball on their opponent. Remember our saying painted on the wall: "We have more fun because we press and run." I recently had a player's parent say to me, "She's just not your kind of player." When I asked what that meant, his response was, "You expect them to play aggressive defensively and constantly talk on defense." Amen.

SUMMARY

- Your defensive system needs to reflect your defensive philosophy.

- Visual cues can help communicate your defenses to your players, especially in a loud gym.

- To play good man-to-man defense, players need to understand the basic principles of on-the-ball defense, one-pass-away denial defense, and two-passes-away help defense; they also need to know how to rotate and recover defensively.

- To help achieve good team defense, break your drills down into post and perimeter defensive drills.

- Trapping out of a man or zone defense can disrupt your opponent's offensive flow.

- Zone defenses have advantages and disadvantages. Your player personnel should influence your decision to implement a zone defense.

- Matchup defenses can disrupt and frustrate offenses and offensive players.

- Players usually reflect their coach. If defense is a priority for you, preach it, teach it, and reward it.

CHAPTER 15

PREPARING FOR SPECIAL DEFENSIVE SITUATIONS

During a game, special defensive situations can occur that your team needs to be prepared for. Such situations might require you to alter or adjust your basic defense. Your players need to feel comfortable in making adjustments and see them as potential weapons. Take time in your practices to work on special situations. How ready your team is for them can be the factor that makes a difference in big games.

DEFENDING INBOUNDS PLAYS

Some coaches enter the game with a defensive strategy, and that plan does not change. Other coaches like to play a chess match, modifying defenses according to the situations presented. Some coaches always play zone on inbounds plays, and others swear by man to man. We like to be somewhat unpredictable in defending inbounds plays.

I used to believe in zoning all inbounds plays under the opponent's basket. Our team got beat too often in our man defense by teams who ran inbounds plays with effective screens. But, now, with the three-point shot, offensive strategy has changed. Teams tend to really spread a zone out and make it hard for the defense to take away the three-point shot and defend the inside post play. To counter this, we've become unpredict-

able in our defense. Our goal defensively is to disrupt the pattern or play, speed up a shooter, and take away the opponent's best option.

If we zone inbounds plays, we have a couple of different looks out of our 2-3 zone defense. In our basic 2 defense, the back line, players 3, 4, and 5 stay at home and wall off the lane. We don't want a post player to get an easy two points on a cut, pin, or lob. Nor do we want the outside of the 2-3 to cover the corner pass and weaken our interior defense. To keep our back line home, players 1 and 2 have corner, wing, and top of the key coverage, depending on where the offense lines up. If the initial pass is a corner pass, players 1 and 2 defend. If the ball is next passed up to the top of the key and then returned to the corner, then players 3 and 4 become corner defenders, just as in our regular 2 defense. So, the way it goes is first pass, top of the zone, second pass, back of the zone.

Trapping inbounds plays is another effective defensive strategy. A trap can cause your opponent to rush a shot or a pass or to create a turnover. We sometimes run our Two Double Fist trapping defense when a team automatically throws to the corner. This corner pass plays right into the defensive strategy of our Double Fist, allowing us an opportunity for a hard corner trap and a tough pass out of the trap.

You can zone the inbounds play yet pressure the passer out of bounds. If we want to pressure the ball out of our 2-3 zone, we run our Two Turn defense. In this defense, the 3 or 4 player, whomever is in front of the out-of-bounds player, turns and faces this player. Her job is to pressure the pass and if possible deflect it, or at least block the out-of-bound player's vision. The two remaining back-line defenders must wall off the paint by themselves. The top two guards' coverage is the same.

By scouting a team, you can learn which defense is the most effective against your opponent's inbounds plays. For example, if I know a team likes to run their inbounds plays out of a spread set, and I have good player-to-player matchups, I might choose to play straight man-to-man defense. If I know a team runs a screening set that we can defend and our line-up has good size at each position, we defend in our 50 defense, in which we switch all screens. This switching can be effective if it's a surprise tactic or if you have good size in all positions. If this defense catches the inbounds player by surprise, you might get a five-second call. In addition, the offense might not recognize the switches and thus not take advantage of any mismatches. Again, I believe it's important to be defensively sound when defending inbounds plays, but being unpredictable can be a good weapon.

DEFENDING LAST-SECOND PLAYS

When defending last-second plays, you have to ask yourself, "Do we let a team run a play at the end of the game and defend it the best we can? Or do we force the team to make a play to get the win?" How you answer this question should help determine your defensive strategy. Perhaps your opponent has not yet solved the defense you have played. You might decide to stick with that defense and not consider a defensive change-up. Your defensive decision might be affected by what players your opponent has left in the game who can score. If the only scorers left in the game are post players, you might choose to play a packed-in zone to invite a perimeter shot. If your opponent has only one scorer in the game, you might choose to run a combination defense on her.

Unless there's an obvious defense to play, your best strategy is probably to make your opponent work hard for their last shot. Even if you don't have the ball at the end of a game, you will want to direct or try to control what occurs. Don't give your opponent a chance to run a special play they have practiced or allow them to set up their best scorer. Make them scramble to get a shot off. Try to force a secondary scorer to take the last shot.

Pressing or trapping a team at the end of the game can cause your opponent to scramble. We like to run our 1-3-1 trap or our 1-2-2 trap at the end of a game. We want to disrupt a set play or an offensive pattern, and we want to speed up our opponent. Even in our trapping, we're well aware of who and where the go-to players are on the court and try to shadow them in our traps.

Listed below are other end-of-the-game factors to consider when deciding on your defense. One of these factors is the free-throw situation: Does your team have fouls to give? The clock and the score will also influence your defensive decision.

- Time remaining
- Score
- Opponent's effectiveness versus zone or man defense
- Scorers left in the game
- Foul situation

DEFENDING SCREENS

There are several different ways to teach your players to defend screens. You might have a screening package put together and change your strategy depending on your opponent, a specific player, the game situation, or player matchups. Or you might defend screens in a particular way no matter who you're playing. Regardless of your screening philosophy, players need lots of repetitions on defending screens.

On-the-Ball Screens

The most common ways to defend on-the-ball screens are to help and recover, to switch, to slide through, and to trap.

Help and Recover

Advantage—the defense gets help on the ball, the potential shooter.

Disadvantage—on a quick offensive slip of the screen, the help player can get beat.

- Player 1 passes to 2 and sets a screen on X2.
- X2 makes sure she doesn't get beat baseline as she anticipates the screen.
- X1 calls the screen and helps on player 2 as 2 uses the screen.
- X1 aligns toe to toe with player 2, forcing her to drive high or wide.
- X2 chases over the screen and recovers to player 2 as quickly as she can.
- X1's help is aggressive and quick as she recovers aggressively to her player (player 1).

Switch

Advantage—the screen becomes fairly ineffective.

Disadvantage—it can create a mismatch.

- Player 2 might drive baseline as the switch begins.
- The offensive action starts out the same— Player 1 passes to 2 and sets a screen on X2.
- As player 1 screens, X1 calls the screen and then immediately calls for the switch.
- X1 and X2 switch players.

Slide Through

Advantage—the player must shoot quickly right on top of the screen.

Disadvantage—a good shooter will get an open look on top of the screen.

- Player 1 has the ball and is looking to dribble to the right; player 2 sets a screen on X2.
- As player 1 uses the screen, X2 calls the screen, steps back, and allows X1 to slide behind the screen but in front of her (see figure 15.1b).
- X2 must hear and see the screen coming and step back to allow X1 to slide through and avoid the screen.

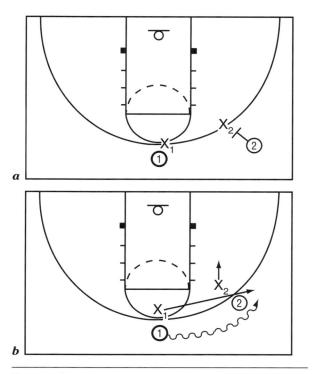

Figure 15.1 Slide through.

Trap

Advantage—can disrupt a play or the player with the ball and might cause a turnover.

Disadvantage—a team prepared for the trap can slip the screen to the basket for a pass and a score.

- Player 1 passes to player 2.
- X2 must force player 2 to use the screen.
- X1 calls the screen and positions herself to trap player 2 with X2 (see figure 15.2).

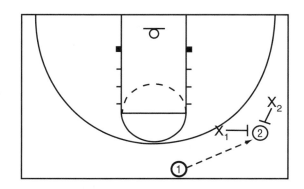

Figure 15.2 Trap.

Off-the-Ball Screens

The most common off-the-ball screens are cross screens, down screens, back screens, and staggered or double screens. You might have a basic way of defending all off-the-ball screens, such as switching or sliding through. The following are the most common off-the-ball screens that teams set and effective ways to defend them.

Cross Screens

- If the offense goes low off the screen, use the slide-through method.
- If the offense goes over the top, have defenders switch or chase (see figure 15.3, a and b).
- If the offense flares, defenders stay on their player.

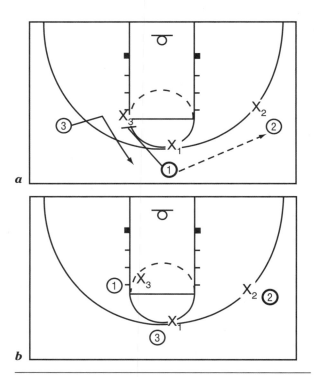

a

b

Figure 15.3 Cross screen switch.

Down Screens

- The defender being screened can slide over the top of the screen to stay with her player (see figure 15.4a).
- The player defending the screener must leave a gap for her teammate to fight over the screen (see figure 15.4b).

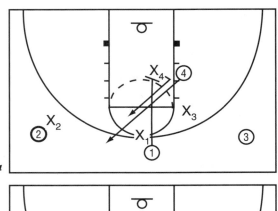

a

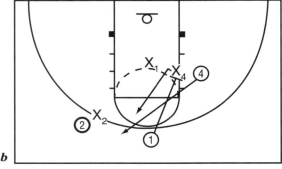

b

Figure 15.4 Defending down screens.

- The player defending the screener always defends the basket.

Back Screens

- The defense can use the slide-through method.
- Because this screen usually leads to a basket cut, the defense can switch all back screens.

Staggered or Double Screens

- The defender uses the "tuck and trail" method.

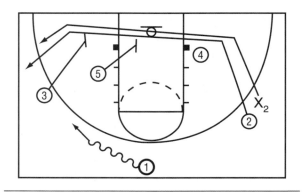

Figure 15.5 Defending staggered screens.

- The defender follows the footsteps of her player, chasing closely behind.
- After clearing the last screen, the defender sprints to close the gap on her player, up and on the line (see figure 15.5).

POST-TO-POST SCREENING

Again, you might have a standard philosophy on what you do in the lane with post-to-post screens. If screens are off-the-ball screens, you might choose to implement your off-the-ball screening rules. In our system, we switch all post-to-post screens if they are block to block. We don't want our opponent to get a quick and easy inside score. If the screens are off the ball, and if the offensive players are not similar, such as post and wing screening, we implement our defensive slide-through rules. The following are some points to remember when defending screens.

- Communicate that the screen is about to be set.
- Use proper man-to-man defensive positions to try to avoid the screen.
- If help is required, help and recover quickly.
- Defenders should see the ball and their player at all times.
- The player guarding the ball must put pressure on the ball if a pass is about to be made.

DEFENDING WITH THE LEAD

When your team has the lead in the last two minutes of a game, you need a plan for defending your opponent in a way that most likely ensures a victory. This strategy can vary depending on how big a lead you have. If only a three-point shot can beat you, play tight defense on the perimeter and force your opponent to drive. Make a player take a shot inside the three-point arc. During this drive, don't let a teammate leave her player to help you defend as your player

goes for the hoop. If she helps, her player could get open for a three-pointer.

To stop a three-point shot at the end of a game, you can switch all screens aggressively. If you have a foul to give, you might foul a dribbler before she can get a shot off. I once watched a team foul five times in the last 30 seconds, and this strategy was quite effective. The team committing the fouls was up by three and was not in a bonus free-throw situation. With each foul, the game was shortened by seconds. The team with the ball never managed to get a good shot off at the end of the game.

Defensive trapping and pressing are other strategies to use in stopping a team run an offensive set at the end of a game. Trapping and pressing can be especially effective if you have not trapped earlier in the game, allowing you to catch your opponent by surprise. Trapping might also be a good weapon when your opponent calls a timeout to set up a three-point play. This defensive change might make your opponent scramble to make a play against your trapping defense instead of being able to run a set play.

DEFENDING WHEN BEHIND

When your team is behind, your defense needs to make stops and create turnovers. Often the team with the lead will spread the court to eat some clock and make the defense have to work harder. This might be a time to gamble and try a press or a trap as a surprise element. As time clicks under a minute, you'll likely need to foul the weakest free-throw shooter on their team. If this player doesn't touch the ball, then at least try to avoid fouling their best free-throw shooter. Of course, an opposing player will try to get the ball in her hands, and if this happens, you have no other recourse but to foul and cross your fingers that she misses at the line.

SUMMARY

- Decide if you want to defend inbounds plays with your basic defense or change up defensively.

- Decide if you want your opponent to run a play or make a play at the end of a game. Your decision will affect your choice of defense.

- Make sure your players are aware of the strategy you want to use in defending on- and off-the-ball screens.

- Practice your defensive strategy for both when leading at the end of a game and when trailing at the end of a game.

PART V

COACHING GAMES

CHAPTER 16 PREPARING FOR GAMES

There is no substitute for good preparation. As coaches, we must prepare ourselves and our teams so that we have the confidence that if we play hard, smart, and together, we have a chance for successful outcomes. Most of a team's preparation is done on the practice floor. It's during practice that you work on what your team does best and on strategies to counteract what your opponent does best. At most practices, your focus will be on strengthening the weaknesses of your team. If you're weak in rebounding, you'll likely incorporate rebounding drills into your daily practice schedule. If you're weak on the free-throw line, you'll spend extra time there. As you get closer to game day, however, your focus during practice might switch to strategies that exploit the weaknesses and minimize the strengths of your opponent.

PREGAME PRACTICE

What you learn from scouting your opponent should directly influence your practice sessions leading up to the game. If they don't, then why bother to scout? The number of days you have to prepare for your opponent also affects your practice plans.

At Oak Ridge, we have a routine we follow for every upcoming game. Two days before a game we have an extremely competitive and hard workout. One day before the game, we scale down on the length of practice and on conditioning.

The day before we play an opponent, our practice routine is fairly consistent. We begin by discussing our opponent's scouting report. We start out discussing their personnel and then talk through their offenses and defenses. We emphasize the things they do best and conclude our talk with what we need to do to win the game. We like to practice against male athletes the day before a game, which is especially effective if we don't have great depth. This way our top players get quality practice minutes, and the male athletes present a fresh and competitive challenge. We have to be at the top of our execution and fundamentals to be competitive with the boys.

Our on-the-court work begins with full-court offenses and defenses. If we believe we can run on our opponent, we discuss that advantage and try to determine how our opponent will most likely defend our transition game. We work on that aspect of the game. Next, we work on our presses and traps. We usually do this out of special situations, such as a made free throw or an out-of-bounds play. After the score, we jump into our presses and traps. The boys simulate our opponent's press offense, which makes for a very competitive atmosphere.

Next we address our half-court work. We begin with our half-court defensive package for our opponent. Each male player tries to simulate the opponent he represents. In our man-to-man work, we assign matches, and the boys run the opponent's offense. If we play zone, the boys simulate our opponent's zone offense. We practice all offensive options we know about our opponents. We want our players to be as familiar as possible with our opponent's offenses and player tendencies.

We then have the boys play defense while we work on our offensive package. We want our players to leave practice with confidence, knowing we have a good game plan to attack our opponent offensively. We often finish our practice with a full-court controlled scrimmage.

In our closing minutes of practice, we huddle up and review our opponent's tendencies and our plan for success. It's important to be honest with players. I don't want to build an opposing team up if they aren't that strong. I want my players to believe what I say, so there's no point in altering the truth. If our opponent is weak, I tell my players that, and then our focus for the game becomes more on our team and less on our opponent. We discuss the importance of improvement with every game and how this game can help us get better. If our opponent is extremely competitive, we talk about the importance of execution and the keys to winning. Regardless, we remind our players that from game to game you never stay the same. A game takes a team in either a positive or negative direction. We finish practice on a positive note.

SCOUTING

Scouting is critical in preparing your team for your next opponent. There are many ways to scout your opponent—videotape is now the most popular—but I like to be there in person. When you see a team in person, you not only scout the Xs and Os of the game, but you get a sense of some of the intangibles, such as player attitudes, demeanor, and conditioning level. I especially want to see our district opponents in person because those games are the most important to our team.

If I can scout a team in person, I study the players to try to gain every possible advantage. When watching a post player, for example, I look for her favorite move. Does she put the ball on the floor? When double-teamed, does she pass the ball out well? The answers to these questions help us prepare one part of our defensive plan.

A scouting calendar can help you keep organized. On the calendar, you might want to include both scrimmages and games. Our calendar includes the months of October through March. We want to scout a team near the time that we play them. If you scout a team in early December and don't play them until late January, you might be surprised to discover the team has significantly changed over eight weeks.

Send each of your opponents a copy of your game schedule and request theirs in return. I get better results when I send ours in advance. Once you have all of your opponent's schedules, plug them into your calendar (see figure 16.1). You don't need to put down each game, but look at a two-week window. See if you can possibly scout a team within two weeks of playing that team. This works out for us for most of our opponents. Also, there could be teams you want to scout more than once. As you get closer to tournament time, you might want several scouting opportunities on your biggest rival.

After plugging in your opponents' games, devise your plan. Who will scout what games? If a game can't be scouted by you or one of your assistants, can you find a qualified person to scout for you? If scouting in person isn't possible, can you arrange for a tape exchange? If that isn't an option either, resort to the Internet, which can be very helpful in a pinch. You probably won't be able to download game footage (although those days are coming fast), but you can get access to rosters, articles, and other possibly helpful information.

Scouting your opponent really gives you an inside track on the tendencies of your opposition, coach, and players. You can learn a lot about coaches by watching them in action. Are they hot headed or low keyed? Do they sub freely or play their better players the majority of the time? Do they change up defensively or maintain the same defense throughout the game? How much strategy is involved in their coaching? Answers to these types of questions help a lot in preparing your team.

When studying opponent's tendencies, you can look at individual players, offensive and defensive schemes, and the team's overall style

Wildcat Basketball Schedule

	OPPONENT	DATE	DAY	PLACE	TEAMS
(Scrimmage)	Cookeville	Nov. 16	Tuesday	Home	GV, BV
(Scrimmage)	Morristown West	Nov. 18	Thursday	Home	GV (6:00)
	Fulton	Nov. 18	Thursday	Home	BV (7:30)
	Land-Air Tip-Off Classic, Greeneville, TN				
		Nov. 22-27	*Mon-Sat*		*BV*
	Cookeville Thanksgiving Classic, Cookeville, TN				
(Tape)		*Nov. 26*	*Friday*	*Away*	*GV (3:30 EST) vs Upperman*
		Nov. 27	*Saturday*	*Away*	*GV (4:30 EST) vs Cookeville*
(Watch)	Campbell County	Nov. 30	Tuesday	Home	GJV, GV, BV
(Watch)	Clinton	Dec. 3	Friday	Away	GJV, GV, BV
(Watch)	Powell	Dec. 6	Monday	Home	BJV, GV, BV
(Tape)	Cleveland	Dec. 7	Tuesday	Away	GV, BV
(Tape)	Bradley County	Dec. 10	Friday	Home	GV, BV
(Watch)	Maryville	Dec. 13	Monday	Away	BJV, GV, BV
(Watch)	Farragut	Dec. 14	Tuesday	Home	BJV, GV, BV
	2nd Annual Rotary Hoops Classic, Oak Ridge				
		Dec. 17	*Friday*	*Home*	*GV (7:30), BV (9:00)*
		Dec. 18	*Saturday*	*Home*	*GV (5:30), BV (7:00)*
	Gulfshores Shootout, Naples, FL				
(Tape)		*Dec. 26-30*	*Sun-Thurs*	*Away*	*BV*
		Dec. 30-Jan 3	*Thurs-Sat*	*Away*	*GV*

Figure 16.1 Sample schedule and scouting calendar.

of play. Most of this information can be charted on a scouting report (see figure 16.2).

An opponent scouting report can provide a thorough glimpse into your opponent, including strengths, weaknesses, tendencies, and more. Ideally, the report provides some insights into what you must do to win the game.

Our Scouting Report

We try to get the following information for our scouting report:

- Opponent's starters
- Our best matchups versus their starters and bench
- Individual player strengths and weaknesses
- Player depth and at what positions

- Jump-ball plays
- Defenses used each quarter
- Overall defensive plan
- Overall offensive style—half court, run and gun, set plays, continuity
- Go-to offensive players—when and how
- Inbounds plays
- Delay-game attempts
- Keys to their offense
- Keys to their defense
- Strengths we must combat
- Weaknesses we can take advantage of
- The bottom line—what we can do to exploit their weaknesses and win the game

Opponent Scouting Report

Date _____ *_____ vs. _____

STARTERS
Our matchup   #   Position   Strengths/Weaknesses

_____   _____   _____   _____
_____   _____   _____   _____
_____   _____   _____   _____
_____   _____   _____   _____
_____   _____   _____   _____

BENCH

_____   pos. _____   _____   # _____   pos. _____   _____
_____   pos. _____   _____   # _____   pos. _____   _____

Jump ball alignment
court diagram

Defenses
Q1 _____
Q2 _____
Q3 _____
Q4 _____

Defensive Summary

_____

Offensive Summary

_____

Half-court sets
court diagrams

Go-to player(s) _____

Inbounds
court diagrams

Delay game
court diagram

Keys offensively _____
Keys defensively _____

Strengths _____
Weaknesses _____

In order for us to win: _____

_____

Figure 16.2 Sample opponent scouting report.

If I or an assistant scouts the game, we might not fill out our scouting report as we sit and watch. Coaches all have their own way of scouting. I prefer a notepad and take lots of notes throughout the game. I complete our scouting form after the game to help me organize my notes and thoughts. Once I transfer my notes to the scouting report, I get copies made and share them with my coaching staff. The official scouting report is then placed in the opponent's file, ready to use when needed.

I also fill out another form on my opponent if we have played them once and will play them again. The night we play a team, or early the next day, I fill out an opponent summary form (see figure 16.3). I find it very helpful to write down my thoughts as close to the completion of the game as possible. Sometimes I want to remember something that worked quite well, something that was not beneficial, or perhaps just a feeling about the game. Maybe it was a matchup that didn't work, or perhaps a player was sick during the game. Of course I'll have the opportunity to watch the replay of the game, but that might not jog my memory and remind me of certain things I can recall immediately after a game concludes.

Another simple form I use is called an opponent game score form (see figure 16.4). On this form, I simply keep up with scores and scorers of opponents. I have found this handy as I prepare to play a team. Perhaps a player is averaging 20 points per game, but I notice she has not played in the last three games. The information on my scoring form alerts me to find out if she's hurt or being disciplined. As another example, I might discover on my scoring form that a player averaging less than 10 points a game has had several big scoring games in a row just before our game with them. Most game scores and box scores are easily found in a newspaper or on the Internet.

Opponent Summary

Date _____ Opponent _____

STARTERS

Point guard _____

Wing _____

Wing _____

Post _____

Post _____

Opponent's Offense   Our Offense

Opponent's Offense   Our Offense

Strengths/Positives

Weaknesses/Negatives

Figure 16.3 Opponent summary form.

Opponent Game Score

Opponent _____

Date   Final score   Record scorers (Big three-point scorers are circled)

_____   _____   _____   _____

_____   _____   _____   _____

_____   _____   _____   _____

_____   _____   _____   _____

_____   _____   _____   _____

_____   _____   _____   _____

_____   _____   _____   _____

_____   _____   _____   _____

Figure 16.4   Opponent game score form.

Scouting Can Make the Difference

We had won one game with a last-second free throw and the next game with a shot at the buzzer. Now we were in the finals of our bracket in the prestigious Nike Tournament of Champions in Phoenix, Arizona. This was December 2004. We stood tall with one 6-foot player and the rest at 5 feet 8 inches and under. Our opponent loomed extremely large with three players at 6 foot plus. We felt like David up against Goliath. We were excited and quite motivated, but I could see doubts in our players' faces. During our pregame talk, it was my job to convince them we could win. We had beaten bigger teams before. We had never let size make us feel we couldn't win. I believed we could win, so we spent our pregame talk time discussing the opposing team's strengths and how to take them away. We were quite specific on what needed to be done to shut down their scorers.

We ended up losing the game. Our opponent had better talent, was much more physical than we were, and played well down the stretch. To our players' credit, they battled and never lost faith. I praised them for sticking to and accomplishing our primary goal: to limit the points of their best player. We held her way below her scoring average. Her teammates managed to pick up the scoring slack. I had done the best I could to scout this team, but because they were from out of state, we didn't have as much as usual to go on. Mainly, we knew they had size and dangerous scorers, whom we battled pretty well. What we didn't know hurt us—and that was the role of their support players. The frustration of losing that game after shutting down their top scorer reinforced my belief that scouting is a critical component for preparation. Had I had a chance to see this team play a couple of times, we might have been better prepared to win.

PLAYER PREGAME ROUTINE

Each player has her own routine on the day of a game, just as most of the coaches do. I don't interfere too much with our players' personal game-day routines, but I do give them some guidelines.

- Eat a good pregame meal.
- Get some rest—at home, in the locker room, or on the bus.
- Once in the locker room, limit conversation to talks about the upcoming game.
- Leave problems outside the locker room door.
- Visualize your role for the team and the game.
- Stretch to warm up your muscles.
- Get mentally prepared for the game.

At Oak Ridge, we have an open campus that allows students an opportunity to go out for lunch. Many players eat lunch together. They go to the same restaurant each game day and order the same meal. Some players are creatures of habit, and others are superstitious—but if eating the same meal at the same restaurant gives them confidence, I'm all for it. When school is out, most players head home to relax. Many eat another small meal. They arrive at the gym one hour before game time. If there's no game before our game (such as a junior varsity game) players put their uniforms on immediately and shoot for 20 minutes or so. If the court is not available, players report to the locker room and begin their stretching and mental preparations. Once in the locker room, players may listen to music, talk with their teammates, or sit quietly. I have found no two players prepare in the same way. I don't force them to prepare a certain way—only encourage them to get themselves ready to play.

Locker Room Talk

Thirty minutes before the tip-off, our coaching staff meets to discuss any last-minute details. Then we report to the team room to meet with our players. The first thing we do is circle up and join hands in unity. Then we have a moment of silence in which players prepare themselves mentally for the game and visualize their role.

Next, we discuss our opponent. Players are seated facing a dry erase board. On the board is our entire game plan. We review matchups, offenses and defenses, and keys for winning. This talk takes about 10 minutes. The last thing our players hear is a review of the keys for winning.

Game Motivation

As a coach, you know your team better than anyone else. You know there are some games your players have a hard time getting up for. For these games, we try to change our goals to help challenge players and encourage them to produce and achieve good results. In tournament games, rival games, and when the crowd is huge, motivation is built in. Players are sky high and maybe a little uptight. You might need to relax them a little bit. If you want players to perform to the best of their ability, you need to have a feel for your team and their level of motivation prior to each contest.

Enjoy the Journey

In 1997 we were playing for the Tennessee state championship. We were 36 and 0 and had a chance at a state title, a national ranking, and a bit of history if we could finish off a perfect season. I remember thinking, I wish we had lost a game along the way. How fair would it be to lose only one game all season and have it be your last? My entire pregame talk was about enjoying the journey, the fellowship of each other, and the joy of the game. I wanted them to feel good about what they had already accomplished. I knew they were excited, prepared, and ready for their final opponent. They didn't need any more fuel. They needed to relax and have confidence, knowing they were well prepared. We finished the season 37 and 0 with a state title, a number three national ranking, and the bit of history our team desired.

SUMMARY

- Scouting your opponent is key to good game preparation.
- Scouting provides insights into your opponent's tendencies.
- You can scout in a variety of ways. There's no good excuse for not scouting your opponent.
- Pregame practices fine-tune your players for their opponent. Working on your opponent's offensive and defensive tendencies can give your players confidence when they enter the game.
- Help your players with their pregame routines.
- As their coach, you need to know how and when to motivate your players before a game. Do you need to fire them up or help them relax?

HANDLING GAME SITUATIONS

Getting a team ready to play takes much more than solid fundamentals and well-planned Xs and Os. No matter how much time you spend on preparation on the front end, you'll have many decisions left to make right up until game time—and then some more during the game. Your main priority is having your team physically and mentally prepared to play. During the pregame warm-up you can often get a sense of how ready your players are. Do they look lose or tight? Distracted or focused? If anything about your team looks wrong to you, try to address the problem and loosen your players up before the game starts.

BEFORE THE GAME

As a coach, you do not want to feel you have not done all you can to prepare for a game. I tell my players, regardless of our opponent and their strengths or weaknesses, preparation is a vital part of success. You want to be able to look into a mirror, player and coach alike, and feel you have done all you can to get yourself ready to play or coach at the highest level.

Pregame Warm-Up and Introductions

Players should warm up at the same tempo and with the same focus they'll have during the game. A half-hearted warm-up doesn't get a player ready. We address three areas regarding our pregame warm-ups:

- **Image.** As soon as we take the court many eyes are on us, from players and coaches alike. We want to portray a positive image in the way we look and the way we act. That is why our uniforms are tucked in and worn properly and why we warm up at gamelike speed.

- **Attitude.** Our attitude needs to be upbeat, positive, and team oriented. We're focused and not wandering through the crowd with our eyes. With the right attitude, we go through our warm-ups crisp and sharp with an emphasis on mental focus and efficiency.

- **Enthusiasm.** We don't wait until the jump ball to get up for a game. Enthusiasm is contagious. I don't want our players to be overly hyped up before a game, but enthusiasm is a positive component that gets players ready to be the best they can be.

You probably have a set procedure that you and your players follow for your pregame introductions. When we're playing at home, our players are accustomed to our routine. After warm-ups are completed, we line up on the sideline in front of our bench for the playing of the national anthem. When the anthem is finished, I give players confirmation on their matchups,

Warm-ups are an important part of pregame preparations.

in case a change has occurred in the opposing lineup or uniform numbers. Next, players gather behind the bench area and wait for their names to be called. As players are introduced numerically, they sprint through a "run through" to the half-court area. Our run through is a swinging door with a wildcat drawn on it. As each player is introduced, players clap and greet each other. The nonstarters are the last players to sprint onto the floor. The players then have their final huddle at half court and quickly report to our bench.

If we're on the road, starters sit side by side in a particular order. The point guard sits in the middle, with her post players on her left and wings on her right. Nonstarters stand and encircle the starting five. We talk as the opponent is introduced, reminding players about each opposing starter. When it's our turn to be introduced, nonstarters form two lines out from our bench and clap hands as the starters race through their lines to the midcourt area.

Starting Five

As I've said previously, the players who accomplish the most in practice are rewarded with an opportunity to start. There are exceptions to this rule. If a player has practiced hard but continues to struggle in games, I might bring this player off the bench in hopes of jump-starting her. In such a situation, I'll let the player know in private before the game. I don't want to surprise her or discourage her. Another possible exception is a player who has played so well off the bench and clearly outplayed the regular. This player might be rewarded with a start. Again, I'll let the usual starter know beforehand. A final exception concerns matchups. I might have decided to start a very big lineup to counter an opponent with great size. If this is the direction I've decided to take, the players affected are always informed beforehand so that there are no surprises.

The five players who will start generally play together the day before a game. If there are six to eight players in the mix of possible starters, all of them will get opportunities to play together the day before a game. On game day, starters are listed on the board in the team room, with their opponent matchups. Illness, injury, and discipline can always affect the lineup on game day. During our pregame talk, the starters sit side by side so I can see their faces at the same time. Much of what we discuss during this meeting is directed at them as a group.

Bench Players

For a couple of reasons, we have players sit together by position (point, wing, or post) on the bench. This way they can talk about what's happening in the game in reference to their specific position. This seating arrangement also allows all players to sit next to their position coach. In our games, the posts sit to my left, my assistant coach to my right, and the perimeter players to her right.

Bench players need to keep their heads in the game. Substituting is often quick and unpredictable. Players need to be tuned into the offensive and defensive strategies the team is executing throughout the course of the game. Bench players also need to feel like they are a part of what's going on in the game. Often, I talk with my post players on the bench to help them stay tuned in. When I get ready to sub a player, I let that player who is subbing in know what I expect from her in the game. I might say something as general as "provide some energy" or as specific as "take away the post player's drop step to the baseline."

Matchups

If man-to-man is your primary defense, player matchups are critical to the success of your team. As mentioned earlier, when I scout an opponent, matchups are the first part of the scouting report I address. Player matchups quickly make me either anxious or calm.

The three key players I try to match up with first are the opponent's best perimeter scorer, best post player, and primary ball handler (usually their point guard). This is why, in our system, the best defender always starts. If the perimeter player is their leading scorer, our best defender matches on her. (In my 25 years of coaching, we've very rarely had a big post player as our best defender.) We put our second-best defender on the other team's best inside scorer. If their best scorer is the post player, I try to determine if I have a good post defender matchup. If my matchup is not a good one, I try

to see if I can get help from a perimeter player on the inside. A perimeter player guarding a weak scorer can help off her player and give help to the inside player.

When matching on the opponent's ball handler, consider that player's strengths. Is she a scorer or a playmaker? Does she drive or spot up? Great teams usually have a point guard who is an impact player. Defensively, we want to minimize what the point guard can do for her team. If the best thing she does is shoot the ball, then we might pick her up full court and try to tire her out as we make her work baseline to baseline. If the best thing she does is drive to the basket, we will play off her and work extremely hard to contain her.

Tough Matchup

In 2005, Karmen Smith, my best perimeter defender and often best post defender, will more than likely be my best ball handler and leading perimeter scorer. She will assume the job of point guard for the first time in her career, which will add leadership duties to her role. As a coach, I have to decide how big her role should be. What's fair to Karmen and best for the team? I have rarely had my leading scorer be my best defender. Of course, we'll try hard to prepare another teammate to take on the job of top defender. It's easy to say that Karmen's plate is full and give her a lesser opponent to guard, but will this be best for the team? With the season months away, only time will tell. This is why it's important to be flexible—you need to decide what's in the best interest of not only the player but also the team. Sometimes you need to go with your gut feeling. Talk with players up front to let them know if there will be big changes in their role. I'm usually pleasantly surprised how players handle a new role if it doesn't come as a surprise to them.

As you work to find matchups on your opponent, your opponent is doing the same thing. Each coach wants to exploit matchups in his or her favor. If there's a definite size matchup in your favor, can you find a way in your offense to post that player up? As the game progresses and your opponent gets a player in foul trouble, yet still plays her, can you run an offense to attack that player and get another foul? Be flexible with your coaching to take advantage of all matchups in your favor.

Taking Away Your Opponent's Strengths

Are most of your opponent's strengths in their individual players or do they do something particularly well as a team? Once you have answered this question, you can devise your defensive strategy. If their strength is a three-point shooting guard, have a defender crowd her shot to invite her to drive. If their strength is a physical post player, put your most physical post defender on her. Playing good team defense might be more important than playing great individual defense. If a defensive matchup is not working, consider trying another defense. The key is to get the job done defensively.

Figure It Out and Take It Away

In December 2003 we played in the Greene County Bank Ladies Basketball Classic in Greeneville, Tennessee. We were preparing to play the host school, Greeneville, and my assistant coach and I were scouting them the night before. It became apparent early on why Greeneville was having so much success. At least part of it was because of the number of transition baskets they made. As we prepared to play them the next night, our number one focus was to take away the best thing Greeneville did: score in transition. To accomplish this goal, we knew we had to limit our turnovers, crash the boards, and play great transition defense. We managed to take away their main weapon and won the game in a great battle. I was happy to have an important lesson reinforced for my players—if you can key your defense on what the opponent does best, you force them to try to beat you with their lesser weapons.

Although you probably can't stop a great offensive player entirely, you'll want to do your best to slow her down. Defensively, you're trying to take away what your opponent does best. You want to take away their best weapon. Sometimes the strength of the team is the team itself. If this is the case, you may not be able to zero in your defense on any one player. Now you may be preaching great team defense and remind your team you can not afford to have a weak link defensively.

DURING THE GAME

When I enter a game, I have a very thorough and comprehensive game plan. I know what we want to accomplish on both ends of the floor and the strategies I think will be most effective to accomplish those goals. However, you won't catch me going down with a sinking ship. If I thought before the game that our opponent could be pressed, but then we can't press them, I'm going to drop the press, at least temporarily. As coach, the adjustments you make during a game, major or minor, can have significant influence on the outcome. You often need to adjust your system to fit the circumstances that occur during a game.

I recommend staying flexible during a game. Don't be so bullheaded that you sacrifice a win for the cause. Maybe you're a strict man-to-man coach, but in the course of a game, an opponent's offensive player is scoring on each possession and on every defender you put on her. In this case, you need to dump your man defense and look at other options—fast!

As part of your game plan, you and your staff will have guidelines on how you want to play certain situations. For instance, how long do you hold out a player in foul trouble? The game, not necessarily your guidelines, may dictate the answer to that question.

Sometimes, games just don't go the way we planned them. No matter what we try, it doesn't seem to work. I don't think the answer is to scratch your entire game plan. If your gut reaction is to scrap the whole plan, you have to ask yourself if you were truly prepared. In most cases, I think you need to continue to chip away at what's working well and try to adjust what's not working. To try to change everything in the middle of a game is extremely hard on players. They're not physically or mentally prepared to do this. Plus, they might think you're panicking. Make adjustments as best you can, and when the game's over, decide what went wrong and why.

Substitutions

There are many reasons why a coach needs to substitute during a game. A player might be getting tired or might be in foul trouble, or a matchup might not be working. Coaches should inform players what they expect when players sub in and out for each other in a game. In our program, the player who is subbing in will get instructions from one of the coaches, usually her position coach. The player then grabs a hand towel and reports to the scorer's table. When she's signaled in by the officials, she quickly heads to the player she's subbing in for, hands her the towel, and exchanges a brief but positive word. Players should have a positive exchange. If the player subbing out is unhappy, she shouldn't take it out on the player subbing in. We treat this as selfish behavior if this occurs, and it's immediately addressed. The player subbing out hustles to the bench and sits down next to her position coach. There are many reasons for subbing a player out. If she's unhappy about being subbed out, she can sit down, place her towel under her chair, nod yes or no to the assistant offering a water bottle, and then calmly ask her position coach why she was subbed out. Sometimes she'll get an immediate answer, and sometimes she won't. Players should understand that a coach might not always be able to address their issues immediately. In some cases, the coach might be unhappy with the player and choose to wait until emotions simmer down to talk with her. At some point in the game, at half time or immediately following the game, that player will have a chance to discuss her feelings with a coach.

Timeouts

Coaches have differing philosophies on using their timeouts. For obvious reasons, we try to save most of our timeouts for the end of the game. We want to make sure we have the opportunity to stop the clock and set up strategy in the final minutes. However, in some circumstances a timeout is needed and you're forced to call one earlier than you would like.

You should consider calling a timeout for the following reasons:

- To fix your team's execution
- To review a last-second play
- To review a special defensive segment
- To freeze your opponent at the free-throw line
- To gain some control when the opponent is having its way
- To give your players a breather and a chance to regroup

When in Rome

This past summer I had a chance to coach a Sports Festival team with USA Basketball in Colorado Springs. Our games were played using international rules. The timeout rule is quite different internationally than in the United States. Internationally, only the head coach can call a timeout, not a player. The head coach has to submit a timeout to the scorer's table. The timeout is awarded only on a dead ball or following an opponent's made basket. It might seem like a small rule change, but what a difference it can make! For example, your opponent makes an offensive run and you desperately need a timeout—no luck. You want to set up strategy at the end of a game and you need a timeout to do so—no luck. Your player is falling out of bounds and wants to call a timeout—no luck—and she has just turned the ball over. Under high school federation rules, you get that timeout immediately. Under international rules, lots of time can elapse before any timeout is awarded. Now your opponent's run is over, and you must decide if you want to rescind the timeout you requested at the scorer's table.

This experience really made me appreciate the timeout rule we have in the states. As a coach, I like to have control of what's happening. I felt that the international rule really took away a weapon I count on: strategies with timeouts. If the opportunity arises again to coach international basketball, I'll have a better plan of attack to deal with and handle the international rules.

In our games, either players or coaches can call a timeout. Players are instructed how and where to call a timeout. When possible, we try to call a timeout right in front of our bench. This allows us the opportunity to run a sideline inbounds play if we so choose. Players hustle off the court as soon as a timeout is granted. During the timeout, players sit according to position—point guard in the middle, posts to her left, and wings to her right. The bench players form a close circle around the seated players. Instructions are short and clearly stated and then restated just before players take the court. I don't like to overload players with too much information.

Half-Time Procedures

In our games, half time is 10 minutes long. As the buzzer sounds, our players hustle off the floor into the locker room. Here they have a few minutes to get a drink, use the rest room, and discuss the game among themselves.

During this time, our student assistants are downloading our first-half statistics. The coaches each get a copy of the stats sometime during the half time. Coaches meet and discuss the first half. Initially, we usually address fouls, rebounding, and turnovers. Next we evaluate our game plan and any changes we feel are necessary to implement in the second half.

When we enter the locker room, all player conversations stop, and player's eyes are on the coaches. To get their attention quickly, I usually begin my talk with something positive. Next I express what we need to get done in the second half. My points are few and concise. I repeat those points just prior to leaving the locker room. I don't want to overload our players. We just want to let them know what we feel are the keys for success in the second half. When four minutes remain in half time, a student assistant knocks on our team room door. We strive to be back on the court at the three-minute mark. Players hustle onto the court and begin their layup drill. I want them to shoot prior to the second half beginning. Just as in pregame warm-ups, players need to be focused and shoot at game tempo to best prepare for the start of the second half.

Free Throws

We use free-throw situations as a time to cue in our defenses. When we're shooting free throws, before the shots are taken, our players briefly huddle at the free-throw line, join hands, and fix their eyes and ears on the bench. Quickly, a defensive call is signaled in. They repeat the call in their huddle and then assume their free-throw spots. Officials often warn our players not to huddle, explaining it slows down the play. Sometimes they threaten us with a delay-of-game technical foul. However, in all my years of coaching, we've never received a technical for our quick huddles. I believe these huddles are great opportunities to communicate and build morale.

Inbounds

We have a set procedure for running our inbounds play. We want our out-of-bounds player to slowly get to her spot. As she's doing this, she looks to the bench to get her offensive call from my assistant. By slowly walking to her spot, this gives my assistant time to survey the defense and make a good out-of-bounds call.

Coach and Player Conduct

You'll want to cover as many possible game scenarios with your players prior to the opening tip. We have a team meeting to address situations that might occur in the game and to discuss how we want our players to respond or handle each of them. Many of these situations are then addressed in practice situations. Giving players a handout to review and to familiarize them with special situations can be helpful (see figure 17.1). You want to make sure they have a clear understanding of your expectations and procedures.

Winning the officials over can go a long way in making the game run smoothly. I think good relations with the officials start with the coach. They begin when we have our initial meeting on the court before the game starts. During this meeting, I make a point to say something positive to the officials and to let them know we're pleased to have them working our game. We tell our players to treat all officials with respect

LADY WILDCAT GAME SITUATIONS

1. Team room attitude
   —mentally (your role/opponent game plan)
   —physically (stretch)

2. Officials
   a. Win the officials over—be courteous
   b. No negative comments or facial expressions
   c. Hand the official the ball
   d. Retrieve loose balls

3. Pregame warm-up
   a. Game tempo
   b. Image, attitude, ENTHUSIASM

4. Pregame introductions
   a. AWAY—Starters seated by position
      HOME—All come through run through
   b. AWAY—Nonstarters form 2 lines

5. Bench
   a. Sit by positions
   b. Active and supportive of teammates—HEAD IN THE GAME

6. Substitutions
   a. Get instructions from coach
   b. Report to the "X" with a towel
   c. Wait until official waves you in
   d. Have a POSITIVE exchange with teammate you are subbing for
   e. Know the OFFENSE and DEFENSE we are in
   f. Hustle off the floor
   g. Sit by your position coach

7. Timeouts
   a. Know how and where to call a timeout
   b. Hustle off and back onto the floor
   c. Five on the court coming off, sit by positions

   d. Players on the bench, stand
   e. Towel and water

8. Free throws
   a. QUICK huddle at free-throw line
   b. Receive instructions from Coach Prudden

9. Inbounds
   a. Player out of bounds, SLOW to spot
   b. Recognize opponent in ZONE or MAN defense
   c. Receive play from Coach Tisdale

10. Half-time procedures
    a. Hustle off court
    b. Restroom/water
    c. ATTENTIVE when coaches are talking
    d. Coach Tisdale check in second half starters
    e. Three line layups/jumpers

11. Postgame procedures
    a. Shake hands
    b. Hustle off court
    c. NO changing until coaches have finished talking
    d. Be attentive

12. Media relations
    a. Be positive
    b. Be humble and gracious
    c. Don't criticize teammates, coaches, or opponents

13. School policies
    a. Be aware of ALL athletic and school policies
    b. Be in school the appropriate amount of time to be able to play

14. SPORTSMANSHIP

Figure 17.1 Sample handout of possible game situations.

and to go out of their way to be of help to an official during the game. For example, if a ball gets kicked during a game, our players know to run after it and return it to the official. When a player receives a call she doesn't like, she does not express her feelings audibly or in any other way. No facial gestures or inappropriate body language. If this does occur, she's removed from the game and her actions immediately addressed. In all my years of coaching, I have received only three technical fouls. Some would criticize me, suggesting I should have gotten more to "stand up for my team." I disagree. If I expect my players to treat officials with respect, I need to be an example they can follow.

Conduct in a game is where character counts. As a coach, we must walk the talk, backing up our words with our actions. A coach's conduct in game circumstances must be beyond reproach. As coach, you represent your family, your team, your school, and your community. You are the focal point during the game, the leader. Players get their cues from you on how to behave and how to respond to situations. Once you lose your cool, composure, or temper, they will find it easier to do the same. In addition, your behavior can influence the crowd. An unruly crowd is not a good atmosphere for athletic events.

When I am unhappy with an official, I usually let him or her know it. But I don't rant and rave and make a scene. I find a way to catch an ear and calmly express my concerns. I don't want my behavior in any way to take away from the hard work my players are showing on the court. Yet, if I believe my comments can help my players, I want to catch the official's ear.

I have the same expectations for myself, my staff, and my players. Poor behavior is not tolerated. Once players know you mean business, and they see your leadership in action, they will conform to the behavior you expect. I try to find ways to praise a player who makes a positive decision when there appears to be chaos all around her. Don't take for granted good decisions players make in the heat of the battle. Just as it's hard for you at times to do the right thing, it's often hard for your players. Let players know you appreciate the good decisions they make.

AFTER THE GAME

Postgame procedures are similar to half-time procedures. Players hustle off the court and take a few minutes to themselves. Student assistants hurry to download final statistics. The coaching staff gathers for a few minutes to discuss the game. When the coaches enter the locker room, talk subsides and players become attentive. I try to keep my comments brief. If we have won, I point out what we did well as a team and recognize individual accomplishments. If we have our stats, I point out positive stats, either team or individual. If we have lost the game, my comments are still brief but with generally more negative emotion. I might point out an area or two we were deficient in and then conclude by acknowledging we obviously have work to get done and that we'll do that in our next practice. I want to be honest and yet leave our players with the hope that we'll get better, though it will take work and a team effort. No individual ever gets blamed for a loss. I remind players that we win together and lose together. We don't point fingers. We learn from what went wrong and find ways to fix it. We end each postgame with a team huddle, joining together as a sign of unity.

We have all experienced the thrill of winning and the agony of defeat. Players need to know how to handle both and keep things in perspective. If we win or lose, we shake hands with the other team at the end of the game. This might seem like a little thing, but I have been a part of many games in which the losing team just walks off the court. I have also been in games when a team has beaten us in an upset and their players pile on each other at half court in celebration. I have had my players stand there waiting, for what seems like eternity, for the opportunity to shake their hands. As painful as it is to stand there and watch the celebration, I believe it's the right thing to do.

If we win the game, we handle our on-the-court behavior with class. We don't taunt our opponent or pour salt on their wound. We shake hands quickly and head to our locker room. In the locker room, I want our players to have the freedom to celebrate after a win. I want them to be happy for themselves and their teammates. What a joy it is as a coach to walk into a locker room full of smiles. I remind players it's their hard work and good team play that have put those smiles on their faces. There are times after a win when all faces are not smiles. Perhaps not every player had a good game or not every player got to play. To address this, I remind players the work really gets done in practice and that all players have contributed. I encourage all players to feel good about the team's success and their part in it. The win is simply the fruit of their labor.

After the win, the local newspaper or live radio show will often ask to speak with a player or two. These players are encouraged to participate. We usually remind the chosen players that they are positive ambassadors of our program and that comments need to stay focused on what we did well that night. There should be no negative comments about our opponents.

When we lose a game, we take some time to recover. As hard as we work in practice, losing is tough on players and coaches alike. In addition, there's the extra burden you feel that you have let down your family along with all who were in attendance that night. As coaches, we're sensitive to this for our players. We want players to keep losses in perspective. Did we lose because our effort was poor or because the other team played better? We quickly try and decipher the main reason we lost and discuss it briefly. Next, we follow up with a verbal decision to correct these problems; we assure players a plan will be implemented. Finally, we address the things we did well.

Proud Moments

The hardest locker rooms to enter are the ones in Murfreesboro, at the state tournament, when we have just lost our final game of the season. The pain is overwhelming, the cries uncontrollable, and to put a wonderful season into perspective at that moment is nearly impossible. To add insult to injury, certain players and coaches are asked to report to the media room. During that walk to the media room, I try to help players collect themselves, and I remind them we want to represent our program in a positive way. If you have helped players handle these situations before, they will be better able to handle them in the toughest of circumstances.

I have never been disappointed or embarrassed by my players in the media room. As painful as those interviews are, they have handled themselves with class. Watching our young ladies kindly and willingly answer question after question has made for some of my proudest moments in coaching. Many coaching victories occur off the court.

After a loss, players are also asked to talk with the newspaper and radio. We don't force players to do this, but we do encourage them and try to help them find their words. I ask them to try to be positive and to talk about getting better as a team instead of lingering on why and how we lost.

SUMMARY

- Coaches and players must treat officials with respect.
- Players should execute their pregame warm-up at game tempo to prepare them to play.
- Players need to understand how to earn a starting position—and the reasons they might lose a starting position.
- Players on the bench need to keep their heads in the game so they're ready when their opportunity to play occurs.
- Coaches set the tone for appropriate court conduct. Players take their cues from their coaches.
- When deciding on player matchups, place your better defenders on your opponent's primary offensive threats.
- When the opposition matches with your players, see if there are mismatches you can take advantage of.
- Determine what your opponent does best, then come up with a defensive game plan to take that strength away.
- Be flexible enough during a game to adjust your game plan as needed.
- There is a lot of strategy involved in how and when to substitute players.
- Always save a timeout for end-of-the-game strategies.
- Organize timeout procedures to get the most out of your time.
- Talks during timeouts, half time, and after the game need to stay positive.
- Free-throw and inbounds plays can provide coaches good opportunities to communicate with players on the court.
- Help players handle winning and losing with class and dignity.

PART VI

COACHING EVALUATION

CHAPTER 18 EVALUATING PLAYERS

If you want to achieve and maintain a high-level program, you need to be willing to evaluate your players, yourself, your assistants, and your overall program. To be useful, these evaluations need to be honest and thorough. For this to happen, everyone involved must be open minded enough to give and take criticism; everyone should understand that the evaluation process is for the good of the program. One of the toughest things to do is to evaluate those players who will eventually comprise your team.

FEEDER PROGRAMS

One of the best ways to assess the talent in your community is to get out and watch the younger players in your feeder programs. Feeder programs include your junior varsity players, freshman squad, middle school or junior high teams, and community leagues. Ideally, you have made many contacts with the players under the umbrella of your own program, your junior varsity, and freshman players.

If you are a hands-on coach, you have seen your younger players in action, both in games and in practice. These settings give you an opportunity to evaluate their skills, their coachability, their teamwork, and their work habits. You'll always want to keep in mind that young players grow and sometimes mature into different players than they were when they were younger; still, watching their development in your feeder programs can often give you an idea of the potential of these players.

Attend as many middle school or junior high games as time allows. This allows you to assess the talent pool and also shows certain players that you might be interested in having them on your team in the future. As I watch our middle school teams play and practice, I ask myself a couple of questions: Are there enough young ladies involved in the sport? Are we missing youngsters that could and should be involved? If I have concerns about either question, I address them with the middle school coaches.

Young players might also start their competitive play in a youth league or on a church team. Attending these games gives you insight into the quality of the youngest feeder programs in terms of organization, skill development, and quality of coaching and into the number of youngsters involved in basketball in your community. You might conclude that these are quality programs or feel they're in need of some changes.

TRYOUTS

The hardest part of coaching is making decisions on who will play for your team and who won't. Not all interested players are qualified to be a part of your basketball team. Besides the obvious, evaluating skills and abilities, you'll need to look into such things as a player's academic status and her behavior in school.

I don't want there to be any secrets when a player tries out for our program. I don't try to hide what our program stands for or what we represent. I don't apologize for it being a very competitive program that expects players to work hard on and off the court. In other words, I never want to place a player on the squad and then hear her say, "I didn't know it would be like this." I want all our players to know up front what "this" is all about. We always clarify what we expect from players during tryouts and what will be expected of them if they make the team.

Tryouts need to be open to all students. To ensure that all students know of the opportunity, advertise the place and time with plenty of notice. At Oak Ridge, we have the opportunity to try out our players in the spring. Our season usually concludes in March. This doesn't afford players a lot of time off before the next season's tryouts get under way. We usually hold our tryouts in early May. We do them in three parts. Any rising 10th, 11th, or 12th grader tries out in May. All rising 9th-grade tryouts are held the first two days immediately following the end of school. (Our high school basketball governing body doesn't allow 9th graders who are not in our high school's building to try out before the end of the school year.) Any new students to our high school can try out the first few days of official practice, which is in late October. Ideally, after the freshmen have tried out, our coaching staff has a good idea who will comprise each squad—varsity, junior varsity, and freshman. New students usually are few in numbers.

We begin our tryouts by letting everyone know what skills, qualities, and characteristics we're looking for in the players we'll choose to fill our squads. We'll evaluate skills, attitude, effort, coachability, and teamwork. We'll also check grades and discipline records. Based on their grades, some players might not be eligible to try out for the team. To help in our evaluation of players and in fairness to everyone, all coaches fill out a rubric on each player trying out (see figure 18.1). Tryouts usually last a couple of days. During these days, coaches are in constant communica-tion with each other, sharing thoughts and opinions. As the last day of tryouts concludes, coaches meet to make the final decisions on which players to cut and which to keep.

Filling player positions is important to consider when choosing your team. To me, the key position on our team is the point guard. Without a good point guard, your gifted post players might never touch the ball. I've asked many coaches, if they had to choose, would they rather have a great guard or a great post player? Most coaches agree they would take a guard first—unless the post player can also bring the ball up court. The point guard is valuable for both her basketball skills and leadership skills. Of course, this can make the point guard position the toughest one to fill.

Along with a point guard with basketball and leadership skills, your team will need defenders, scorers, and rebounders. One of the best movies I've seen lately is *Miracle*. In the film, players are trying out for the United States Olympic hockey team. When the coach is questioned about players he wants to keep for his team, he tells the selection committee that he doesn't want a team of the most talented players but rather of individuals who are the best team players, those players who can fill roles. I think this is something to keep in mind when you're selecting players for your basketball team.

Occasionally, players with very few skills decide to try out, and it's apparent quite early on they won't make a squad. When this occurs, I try to pull these players off to the side or catch them at the end of the first day to let them know. If one of them shows great interest in being part of the team, we might consider asking her to be a student assistant. Over the years I've learned that our program needs all the good people we can get.

Lately we've been lucky and have had to cut only one player in the past three years. Her skills were quite low, and she had never been a part of an organized team. I allowed her to be part of our summer travels and workouts to see if there would be any improvements. I wanted to give her every opportunity to get better. I shared my concerns with her and told her we were going to keep her with the team for a while and reevaluate her progress at the end of the summer. I concluded at the end of the summer that her skills were so far behind those of the

Ball Handling	
10-8 points	can handle the ball with either hand in pressure situation, keeps head up at all times
7-4 points	handles the ball with both hands but prefers strong hand, tends to look down at the ball while dribbling
3-0 points	hardly dribbles with her weak hand, constantly looks down at the ball while dribbling
Shooting	
10-8 points	has proper fundamentals when shooting the basketball AND makes a high % of her shots
7-4 points	has a few deficiencies with her technique when it comes to shooting the basketball
3-0 points	has major fundamental deficiencies that will be extremely hard to correct over time
Individual Defense	
10-8 points	really good at defending the ball, good/great foot speed and strength
7-4 points	adequate defender, has potential to be much better
3-0 points	cannot guard the ball and keep the offense out of the lane
Team Defense	
10-8 points	understands and executes help defensive principles at a high level, communicates with teammates in the majority of situations
7-4 points	has a basic knowledge of help defense and executes team defensive principles inconsistently, talks to teammates when instructed
3-0 points	main concern on defense is her man, limited/no concept of defense, communication is almost nonexistent
Individual Offense	
10-8 points	can score the ball on a consistent basis, above average offensive moves, moves well without the ball or can go 1 on 1 and score
7-4 points	scores some but is inconsistent, has a hard time scoring against someone of equal or greater athletic ability
3-0 points	a nonscore, struggles shooting the ball, has a hard time going by the defender off the dribble
Team Offense	
10-8 points	makes teammates around her better, can score but also does things to help teammates (e.g., screening, cutting, passing, knowledge of offensive principles)
7-4 points	willing to screen, pass, etc., looks to get her teammates involved, doesn't care to do other things besides score
3-0 points	does not make anyone else on the floor with her better, might only be good with the ball in her hands, limited willingness to do other things besides score
Teamwork & Effort	
10-8 points	cares about team production first and foremost, plays hard on both ends of the floor and virtually every play
7-4 points	wants to win but also wants to score a lot or she is not happy, plays hard only occasionally
3-0 points	most of the time is concerned with her performance more than her team's, limited effort
Attitude, Coachability, and Behavior (on and off floor)	
10-8 points	has an attitude that is worth catching, a joy to be around, takes instruction and attempts to correct mistakes
7-4 points	has a good attitude when she feels good, takes correction and goes forward
3-0 points	struggles controlling her attitude, has a hard time handling difficult situations, does not take coaching
Academics	
10-8 points	has an A-B average
7-4	C average
3-0	D-F average, could be ineligible

Figure 18.1 Sample rubric for tryouts.

other players that she wouldn't be able to keep pace at practices or ever contribute in games. I called her in and told her it wasn't going to work out for her to be a player on the team. But because I thought a lot of her as a person, I offered her a spot in our program as a student assistant. Unfortunately, she declined, but she left the team with no hard feelings.

I believe in giving players a second chance. Young people are inclined to make mistakes. There have been players selected for one of our teams who began initial practices in the spring and then decided for various reasons not to be a part of the team. This doesn't happen often, and when it does happen it's in the spring or during summer workouts, not during the season. Soon after their decision to leave, they sometimes change their mind and ask to rejoin the team. I handle each of these cases separately. Usually, I first speak with my coaches, and sometimes our players, before making a decision. If we're all in agreement that the player should get a second chance, I next meet with the player and her family. After this meeting, if I believe it's in the best interest of the player and the team to allow the player to return, she gets an opportunity to earn her way back onto the team. If it's not in the best interest of the team, she'll have another chance to try out the following season if she's not a senior.

In our program, all players who try out, regardless of their level in school, have the opportunity to make the varsity squad if their skills have the merit. Returning varsity players are not guaranteed their spot back or any spot on a squad. When tryouts begin, all players are given a clean slate and start from scratch. However, returning players do usually have an upper hand having been in the program for at least one year.

Some of my toughest decisions are in the placement of players on teams. Some coaches believe you should not place freshmen on the varsity squad. Others choose the 12 best players and put them on the varsity with no regard to age or grade level. Depending on your situation, you'll have to decide what works for your program and then make that decision part of your philosophy and system.

Our program has three squads, so we have seldom have a problem getting players placed on a team. But there's often much discussion about who should make which team. If a freshman can be an impact player on the varsity squad, that's where I place her. For a player to be considered an impact player, she needs to be one of the top eight. I don't want to move a freshman up to the varsity for her to sit on the bench when she could be getting valuable playing experience on the freshman squad.

Typically, my hardest decisions involve seniors with low skills. It's always tough to know what to do with a player who has been in the program but who has marginal skills and now will be at the bottom of the varsity team. Do you keep her or let her go? I think you should look at the total picture before making a decision. I have kept seniors on my team who were quite happy just to be a part of the program and accepted a small role. I have kept others on the team who became quite miserable with their small role and thus created problems for the team. When keeping a senior who is clearly a good person but a marginal player, it helps to meet with her and her parents early on to discuss her limited role. Let all parties involved know the situation from the beginning. Allow the player to either accept a small role or choose not to be a part of the team.

Fun Time of the Year

Do you know how hard it is for a player to practice at the end of the school year? They have a million other things on their mind and a hundred other places they would rather be than a hot and sweaty gym. To improve our player's attitudes during this difficult spring practice time, we let them know that this is the fun time of the year. In other words, we do few sprints, keep practices short, and run lots of five-on-five competitive drills and scrimmages. Yes, we're evaluating players and implementing our new systems during this time, but there are ways to get these done and still make our practices competitive and fun for the players. In the spring, our motto is quality of work over quantity of work, and this seems to keep players coming back.

SPRING PRACTICE

After we complete our first tryouts, we have eight days of spring practice, which usually serve as an extended evaluation time. It's during this time that we assess talent, specific skills, and position depth as we try to arrive at an offensive and defensive package that gets the most out of the newly formed squad. During spring practice, we hope leaders will emerge.

We might ask players to fill new roles or to play larger roles than they played the previous year. When seniors have graduated, we must fill in the holes. During spring practice, each new team begins to form its identity.

Spring practice time is team oriented in what we emphasize and do in our practices. We want to implement some basic offenses and defenses that we hope will complement our talent. Sometimes we completely change the look of our secondary break for the next season. Spring practice affords us the opportunity to put in this new secondary, and summer camps give us the chance to test it out. After our eight days of spring practice, players participate in three team camps, which is where we give our new offenses and defenses a test run.

SUMMER CAMPS

Summer camps provide opportunities to evaluate players and the team as a whole. In Tennessee, we're allowed 10 competitive play days in the summer. Most teams use those days in team camp settings. Team camps are organized scrimmages, and we can play several games in one day. It's now that we want to transfer what we've worked on in our spring practices to game settings. My summer game philosophy is different from my regular season game philosophy. I want all players to have a chance to play in the summer, regardless of their place on the roster. Winning and losing are secondary to evaluating players' performances on the court. Games usually provide quick answers to several questions. Do our offenses work? Are our defenses effective? Are we getting the most out of our talent? If the answer to any of these questions is no, ample time remains to make changes.

SUMMER WORKOUTS

Our summer evaluation period usually ends with our open gym sessions. In Tennessee, we have two weeks that many refer to as a dead period. During those two weeks, players and coaches may not get together for any type of workout. Outside of those two weeks, players can work out with coaches every day if they so choose. The only restriction is the 10 com-

Team Bonding

Summer camps are usually a special time for players to come together as a team. We usually host a couple of camps and also travel to a four-day overnight camp. This overnight camp is a great opportunity for players to get to know each other on and off the court. For four days and three nights, players and coaches eat and breathe basketball. Players all bunk together in a classroom, somewhat like a slumber party without the "party." Sleeping bags cover the floors of the classroom, and this is where players spend all their time when they're not playing in a game. We usually play five games a day, including varsity and junior varsity games. Playing time is not an issue—usually, trying to catch a quick nap is the issue. Card games, storytelling, and snack time fill in the gaps throughout the day. By the end of the fourth day, players have really gotten to know each other, and we're much tighter as a team, both on and off the court. These overnight camps are a great way to bring teams closer together.

petitive day rule. During the month of June, we attend team camps. During the month of July, we have "open gym" sessions for individual workouts, team scrimmages, weight workouts, and shooting sessions. Attendance during these July dates varies, as some players travel with their families on vacations, others work, and some attend AAU nationals. During the summer months, once a week players get together to scrimmage. These scrimmages are usually less structured than they are in the camps; some players can't come, so games might be four on four or three on three. The number and intensity of weight workouts, individual workouts, and shooting sessions all depend on the current needs of the team.

During the summer of 2004, we identified the need for players to participate in extra shooting sessions as well as shooting skill workouts. Throughout our spring and summer evaluations, we concluded many players shot the ball incorrectly and thus could not score in game situations. We gave players a summer calendar and challenged them all to make a minimum of 750 shots before the first day of school. We asked them to record their shooting workouts on their calendars. When they turned their calendars in, during the first week of school, we would have a team party.

To help players shoot the ball correctly and make good use of their 750 shots, we held shooting sessions throughout the summer to work on shot technique. I am a big believer that individuals improve their skills during the off-season. Because most players want to score, they have eagerly been in the gym shooting and working on their shot technique. Many players embrace the challenge and make well over their 750 shot minimum.

Summer workouts also allow a coaching staff to evaluate a player's workout routine, her work ethic, and her commitment to the sport. Basketball is not just an in-season sport, practiced and played from October through March. If they want to stay at the top of their game, good players commit to working out for a good portion of the off-season. You can learn a lot about a player by what she does and doesn't do during the off-season.

The benefits of off-season practice will shine through during the regular season.

FALL MEETINGS

The off-season is a great time to sit down with players individually, evaluate their summer progress, define roles for the upcoming season, and help players set personal goals. Players will have had the opportunity to practice in the spring and attend team camp games and open gym sessions in the summer. They should have had ample opportunity to show their skills, improve their skills, and begin defining their role on the team.

At this time, we want to be very honest with our players as we discuss their summer progress together. Have they improved? Did they work hard? Are they headed in the right direction? We give them plenty of feedback as we answer these questions and seek their input. Next, we ask each player what role they want to play for our team and discuss if that role is realistic. If it is, we plan a course of action together to help them achieve that role. If the role they hope to play is not realistic, we work together to come up with a role she can hope to fill. Finally, I want our players to set individual improvement goals they'll work on during the fall. I want our players to always believe they can get better—because they can—and with improvement they can enhance their role for the team. Setting individual goals is a good way to accomplish this.

During these meetings, I also want players to share any concerns they have. These concerns might regard the summer or the beginning of the school year. Perhaps I have evaluated a player and my assessment of her is quite different from her own assessment of herself. This meeting is the time to share our thoughts and work through our differences before the season starts.

EVALUATING PRACTICES

Practices are so valuable that I want to make sure we accomplish as much as we can in each one. I value the input of my assistants before and after practice. Prior to practices, as a staff we've already discussed the practice outline and goals for the week. After practice, I try to take a few minutes to meet with my staff to solicit feedback. I want to make sure I hear their voices and that all suggestions concerning practice are considered. Maybe we're introducing information too quickly, and my assistants see what I don't see, that players are confused. Or perhaps we've discussed implementing a new defense, and my assistants don't think, based on recent practices, that we're skilled enough in the right positions to be effective in that defense. By just taking a few minutes of my staff's time, I can evaluate practices, change things if needed, and, ideally, get the most out of our players during practice time.

I also like to solicit feedback from players from time to time. I remember last season we were going through some tough days in January when practices seemed to be a chore for both coaches and players. When I met with my captains, they asked if our drills could be more competitive because players were getting a little bored and losing their edge. I took their advice, and the next few practices were some of our best. Their feedback proved to be quite valuable.

Student assistants can also be helpful in evaluating practices. Decide what it is you want to monitor or keep track of during practice, and let them help you. Maybe you want to chart shooting, turnovers, or post feeds. Maybe you'll have a controlled scrimmage, and student assistants can keep regular game stats. Find ways to get your assistants plugged into your practices.

Videotaping practices is another good tool for evaluation purposes. The videotape doesn't lie. It's one of the best teaching tools coaches have at their disposal. I have sat down with many a player and watched game tape and practice tape to help correct mistakes and to highlight good play. Videotaping practices provides a couple of things. First of all, if you don't video every day, players turn the intensity up a notch when the camera gets turned on. They don't want to be caught on film giving less than 100 percent. Second, you can see things on video that you might have missed during practice. Finally, videotaping is a great way to provide players with feedback. If they're frustrated about their shot, for example, they can watch the tape and see themselves in practice, and maybe they can see something in their shot they can correct.

Sometimes you can tell a player something over and over again, but until she sees herself doing it, she either doesn't get it or doesn't really believe she's doing what she's doing. One year I had a player go into quite a shoot-ing slump. After each game, I edited her game shots, and we sat down to analyze the problem. The video showed a player who took very quick and often off-balanced shots. The player thought her problem was all in her form. With this new knowledge, she began making better shot selections and shooting on balance. Her scoring improved with each game after that.

Watching videotape is also a great way to analyze team aspects of the game. It's easy to see what your execution looks like on both ends of the floor. When we watch tape together as a team, we'll ask players to chart offensive and defensive possession and rate our execution. For many players, this is a great way to learn.

EVALUATING GAMES

To make sure all areas of the game are covered and can be evaluated at some time, divide up responsibilities among your staff. As the head coach, decide what you need to be responsible for and divide up the rest.

All coaches try to make player contacts and subjective pregame evaluations before each game. Players report to our games one hour early. During that time, my assistant coaches and I try to make a contact with each player to get a feel for her pregame demeanor. I also try to do the little things necessary to be organized for the start of a game. For example, I fill out the official game book, putting in the names and number of all players. My assistant double-checks the book before the start of each game.

One of my assistants is in charge of the student assistants, particularly the girls who keep the statistics. She makes sure the stats are downloaded for all coaches at halftime and at the end of the game. During the game, she also keeps a chart of timeouts and fouls for both teams. As the game begins, she sits next to me, and we discuss what we see on the court. We're constantly observing and commenting on strategy, player substitution, and other aspects of the game. My second assistant keeps an offensive and defensive possession chart. If a team breaks our press three times in a row, he lets us know. If we have not scored in transition, he keeps us informed. This chart provides great feedback during the game and helps us make necessary adjustments.

When a timeout is being awarded, the first thing I do is talk with my staff. We discuss our strategy for the timeout and what we want our play to be when we return to the court. During a timeout, there's little time for an assistant to talk with a player, but she might be able to catch her ear on the way into or out of the huddle. During the timeout, players hear only one voice, and that's usually mine. They don't need several coaches telling them different things at the same time.

As the head coach, I constantly try to see the big picture and encourage my assistants to see smaller pictures. Sometimes each assistant is assigned one part of the game to zero in on. In most games, I want my assistant to focus on our opponent. With the help of two assistants, student assistants, stats, and videotaping, we have several avenues for evaluating our games.

At the end of the game, in the locker room, all assistants are given time to share their feelings and thoughts with the team. These talks are usually brief, and they usually focus on the positive. My assistants put so much of themselves into the team—I want to make sure they have an opportunity to voice their feedback after a game.

POSTGAME EVALUATION

After games, we meet briefly as a staff to discuss the game. We look over stats and offer suggestions for improvement. Then I usually take the videotape home, watch the game film, and write down additional observations. If we agreed in our postgame discussions that our press hurt us more than helped us, I will watch the film and break down our press to see how and where it was we got beat. The possession chart tells us that we did in fact get beat, but the film usually gives us additional insights on why and how.

The next morning I e-mail my video notes to my assistants. They e-mail me back their thoughts and opinions. Then we will meet before practice to devise our plan to fix our press. When we meet with the players in practice, we share our thoughts, describe what the stats and video told us, and outline our plans to improve

our areas of weakness. We want to fix the trouble spots quickly and move forward.

SUMMARY

- Your program begins with your feeder schools. Let them know you care about them and their team.
- Make your tryouts open to all players in your school.
- When player's try out for your team, have a set criteria you can evaluate them on, such as a rubric.
- If you need to cut a player, talk with her beforehand.
- Evaluate players by position as well as by talent.
- Spring practice can be a fun and exciting time for players at the end of the school year.
- Summer team camps let coaches evaluate individual players as well as team Xs and Os.
- Players who take advantage of summer workouts can significantly improve their individual skills.
- Player meetings in the fall give coaches a chance to provide players with their summer workout progress, set goals for the future, and define their roles.
- Meet with your assistants to evaluate practices.
- Use student assistants to chart needed information during practices.
- Videotape practices for additional feedback.
- Assign duties and responsibilities to your assistants and student assistants during games.
- Meet with your assistants immediately after games to solicit their feedback.
- Use the first practice after a game to share with players game insights that coaches, stats, and video provide.
- Correct game mistakes in the next day's practice.

CHAPTER 19 EVALUATING YOUR PROGRAM

As each season draws to a close, there is still work to be done. This is a good time to reflect on your past season, evaluate your overall program, and make decisions about changes for the following year. Time spent on this process now is time saved the next year. How long program evaluation takes varies from a couple of days to a couple of weeks, depending on how successful your season was and how many staff members and players are returning the next season.

POSTSEASON EVALUATION

Regardless of the kind of season you have just completed, it is important to sit down and thoroughly evaluate your program. How did you do with what you had? In what direction is your program heading? Evaluation helps you discover what needs to be changed and what should be left alone.

The 2004 season concluded abruptly for our team. We lost a game we believed we should have won. We had been playing so well until that point, so the loss was heartbreaking. It took me a long time to watch the tape of that game, but when I did, I charted every possession. I wanted to evaluate every aspect of that game to find out exactly what went wrong, how it went wrong, and what could be done so it would never happen again. I couldn't change the way the season ended, but I desperately wanted to learn from the loss and find ways to fix those areas that could be fixed. The same goes for my entire basketball program. At evaluation time, we're always asking, What works well? What needs fixing? We don't want to take any aspect of the program for granted. We evaluate the total program. We reinforce what works and change what doesn't.

Meeting With Your Assistant Coaches

At the end of your season, ask for input from your assistant coaches. They can often provide insight gained during the season that can benefit the program and help it move in the direction it needs to go. They have been there, day in and day out, just as you have, but their perspective is often different. They have not called the shots; they have just offered their ideas. Now, when you meet with them, they get a chance to either reiterate those ideas or offer fresh suggestions. Plus, because they often have a different relationship with the players than you have, they can sometimes give you information about players you can't get elsewhere.

I've found the best way to get feedback from my assistant coaches is face to face. I'm fortunate to have an excellent relationship with my assistants, and they know how much their views are appreciated. We all agree that the most important thing is the program. I want to be open to any idea that benefits the program and the players. Encourage your assistants to be completely honest in their season evaluation. It's important to let them know you value their thoughts, opinions, and ideas. You need their feedback for any immediate changes they believe are necessary for the future. You might prefer a written evaluation rather than a face-to-face conversation, depending on the relationship you have with your assistants. Whatever method that will get you the most honest and complete information is the best way to go.

Besides seeking my assistant coaches' feedback, I also want to evaluate their performances for the past season. To do this, we sit down together and discuss their areas of strengths and areas that need improvement. Again, this evaluation can also be done in writing, though you should meet with coaches individually after they have seen their evaluations so you can discuss them. As our program continues to grow, I want my assistants' roles to grow. My assistant coaches' areas of improvement often involve additional involvement in those growing areas. I am fortunate that my assistant coaches continue to be students of the game and are eager to learn and expand their knowledge. This helps us grow as a staff and allows us to make changes as needed.

If your assistant coaches' contributions have not been what you had expected or wanted, this needs to also be addressed. Be specific about what they did or did not do that causes your concerns. A coach should have the opportunity to make changes if at all possible. Perhaps meeting with your assistant early in the season and addressing problems then may make a difference in the end.

Meeting With the Athletic Director

I meet with my athletic director twice during the year to discuss the direction of the basketball program. We meet once in the fall, just before the season starts, and again at the end of the season.

In the fall meeting, we discuss realistic goals for the team, roles for assistant coaches, and anything else the athletic director needs to be aware of in the program. No administrator likes to be caught off guard. If there are concerns, they need to be addressed as early as possible.

In the postseason conference I share my views concerning how the season went, what went well and what didn't, and what I see as the direction of the program. My athletic director offers his views of the season and shares any concerns about the past season or the future of the program. This is also an excellent time to voice any concerns I have regarding administrative support.

I have an excellent relationship with my athletic director, so he's very familiar with the program, players, coaches, and parents. He is visible at games and practices and regularly converses with players during the school day. This gives him good insight into the personnel on our team and staff and the way we run our program. I value his opinions and respect his evaluation of the basketball program and of me. I know his goals are the same as mine: to have a first-class program.

Benefiting From Seniors

Your senior basketball players can offer valuable feedback on both the past season and their entire four years of involvement in your program. Ask seniors to share not only what they liked and felt was beneficial but also what they didn't like and what changes they would like to see in the program. This can be done face to face or in writing. Some players are great verbal communicators and are quite comfortable talking in person. Others might find one-on-one interaction intimidating and not open up as freely as they would in writing. The input you get might not be what you want to hear, but it might be beneficial to the program. Whether the information is good or bad, soliciting feedback from your seniors is a great way to evaluate your program postseason. It also shows these players that you value their thoughts and ideas.

Holding the Postseason Player Conference

To get a complete evaluation of your program, you also need feedback from your returning players. After the season ends and players and coaches have had a few days for reflection, hold player conferences. Meet with each player one on one to evaluate her season performance honestly and to discuss her future plans.

To get player conferences started on a positive note, I begin each meeting by thanking the player for her contributions to the team. I usually discuss the specific positive contributions she has made to the team. I want each player to know she had something positive to give the team and that her contributions didn't go unnoticed. Next, I ask the player to share concerns she had about the season. I ask her to be brutally honest. Many times players discuss their roles on the team and speak frankly about expectations that weren't met.

We conclude our meeting by discussing the future: what areas of the game they need to improve on and a plan for that improvement. We again discuss their role and what, if any, changes need to occur. Often, after senior players have graduated and moved on, a returning player might need to enhance her role for the upcoming season. Some players simply want more responsibility for the team's success, so their roles might need to be enhanced. Players also share their spring and summer plans, which for many include summer camps, exposure camps, and AAU plans. I provide them with the team's summer plans, which include summer practices, team camps, and open gym opportunities.

For players eager to get started on the next season, postseason conferences can be a catalyst to jump-start them into action. For other players, the meetings provide relief. They have finally been able to unload an issue they've carried much of the season. I always express to all players the importance of communication. I can't change what I don't know. I can't fix what I don't know is broken. Their honest communication to me is as important as mine is to them.

SUMMARY

- When your season concludes, evaluate all phases of your program honestly.
- Be receptive to what your assistant coaches have to say.
- Meet with your athletic director to get his or her view on the direction of your program.
- Remain open minded as you meet with the many people in your program.
- Talk to your graduating seniors; they have four years of insight to give you.
- Give returning players a chance to express their concerns and ideas about the past season.
- Provide returning players with a plan for individual and team improvement.
- Be genuine in your efforts to improve the program.

INDEX

Note: The italicized *f* following page numbers refers to figures.

ABOUT THE AUTHOR

Jill Prudden is the head girls' basketball coach and assistant athletic director at Oak Ridge (Tennessee) High School and a physical education teacher at Robertsville Middle School. Over the course of her coaching career, she has won more than 700 games and earned 3 state titles, 5 state runner-up finishes, 18 regional championships, and 22 district titles.

Under Prudden's guidance, Oak Ridge has appeared in *USA Today*'s final national rankings several times. She has coached 45 players who have received college scholarships, including Olympian and professional player Jennifer Azzi. USA Basketball and the Women's Basketball Coaches Association (WBCA) have selected Prudden for various coaching duties, including court coach for the 2001 USA Basketball Women's Junior National Team Trials and coach for the 1997 WBCA all-star game. She also served as the USA basketball coach at the 1998 World Youth Games.

A three-time Tennessee Coach of the Year and seven-time East Tennessee Coach of the Year, Prudden is a member of the WBCA, the USA Basketball Youth and Cadet Committee, and the McDonald's High School All-American Selection Committee. She was inducted into the Oak Ridge Sports Hall of Fame in 1997 and the Knoxville Sports Hall of Fame in 2002. In 1998 Prudden received the Sports Hall of Fame TSSAA Distinguished Service Award.

Prudden resides in Knoxville, Tennessee, where she enjoys jogging and golfing and is involved with compassion ministries.

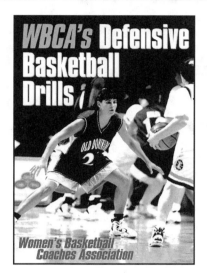
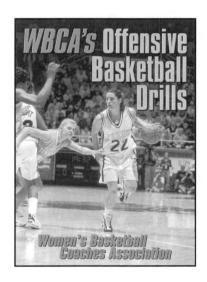